Four More Wars!!!

MIKE LUCKOVICH

ECW Press

To Margo
The Love of My Life

Published by ECW PRESS
2120 Queen Street East, Suite 200, Toronto, Ontario, Canada M4E 1E2

LIBRARY AND ARCHIVES OF CANADA CATALOGUING IN PUBLICATION
Luckovich, Mike, 1960–
Four more wars! / Mike Luckovich.
ISBN 1-55022-737-8
1. Editorial cartoons—United States. 2. American wit and humor,
Pictorial. 3. United States—Politics and government—2001 —Caricatures
and cartoons. I. Title.
NC1429.L82A4 2006   973.93102'07   C2006-904111-3

Cover and Text Design: Tania Craan
Production: Mary Bowness
Printing: Webcom

Second Printing

DISTRIBUTION
CANADA: Jaguar Book Group, 100 Armstrong Avenue, Georgetown, ON, L7G 5S4
UNITED STATES: Independent Publishers Group, 814 North Franklin Street, Chicago, Illinois 60610

ECW PRESS
ecwpress.com

TABLE OF CONTENTS

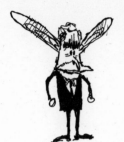

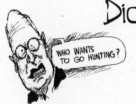

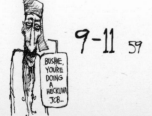

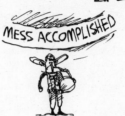

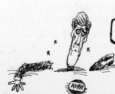

The
Republicans 157

Clinton 209

Supreme
Court 189

Serious Stuff 227

Religion 177

Introduction

Officer Humvee's Probing Billy Club
Or, How I Met Mike Luckovich
By Dave Barry

NEW YORK — This is turning out to be way more exciting than the Democratic convention. At the Democratic convention, the only dramatic tension came from wondering, when you went to a party, whether Ben Affleck would be there, or Ben Affleck plus a Baldwin brother.

But here in New York, a *lot* of stuff is happening. Maybe too much stuff.

This is what I was thinking when I was having my right kidney probed by a billy club, at the other end of which was a New York City police officer the size of a Humvee.

This happened in Herald Square at rush hour. On hand for the festivities were hundreds of slogan-shouting protesters, hundreds of police, hundreds of media people, the occasional Republican delegate with the facial expression of a gerbil realizing it has just been set down inside a python cage, and 3.6 million New York City residents who just want to get on the subway and go home.

I was standing with a clot of media people observing this scene when a bunch of protesters started moving towards an area where the police didn't want them to be. Unfortunately, this put my clot directly between the protesters and the police, and suddenly, a dozen officers, including Officer Humvee, came charging at us shouting, *"Move, move, move."*

Except I couldn't move, because I was already pressed up against a dense wad of protesters and camera guys. I was trapped, a slice of luncheon meat in a mob sandwich. I wanted to shout: "I'm not a protester!

I'm a professional journalist, here for the free food and liquor!" But all I could get out was, quote, "Oog," which is the sound you make when you think you may be experiencing a kidney puncture.

Fortunately, just then, the protesters lunged off in a different direction, and I escaped. I took refuge in the doorway of a Burger King with Mike Luckovich, who is a cartoonist. (In dangerous situations, you always want to be with a cartoonist, because if something bad happens, he can draw a funny picture of it.)

Mike and I witnessed a dramatic confrontation: a lone, courageous police officer faced an entire sidewalk full of commuters and told them he could not let them through to their subway station. Now if this had happened in, say, Des Moines, the crowd would have peacefully dispersed, because a) Iowans are low-key, and b) Des Moines has no subway.

But these were New Yorkers, and every single one of them felt the need to loudly criticize, in the strongest possible terms, the police, the protesters, the city of New York, the Bush administration, and humanity in general. Finding the police officer unresponsive, some of them began voicing their complaints to Mike and me, huddled in the Burger King doorway.

They apparently believed we had some authority, because we both had credentials around our necks. Mine was a press credential; Mike's was the "Do Not Disturb" sign from his hotel. Cartoonists.

President Carter's Foreword Writing Formula
By Mike Luckovich

Mike Luckovich's cartoons cut through political spin with humor and provide warning bells that put the powerful on notice.

Sincerely,
President Jimmy Carter

I asked President Carter's assistant if the president would write something to open my book. She said he would and asked me to send *exactly* what I wanted written.

I felt silly doing that. I didn't want to write some glowing thing for him to sign his name to, but she insisted. Apparently he gets many requests like this and it saves time if he doesn't have to think too hard about what to write and he makes everyone happy since he's transcribing what they've written.

I couldn't bring myself to do that. Instead I sent this:

When I wake up in the morning, the first thing I look at is _____ (a. Roslyn, b. the alarm clock, c. Mike's cartoon). What _____ (a. Roslyn, b. the alarm clock, c. Mike's cartoon) says cuts through the spin and gets to the truth. _____ (a. Roslyn, b. the alarm clock, c. Mike's cartoon) is a warning bell that puts the powerful on notice. Thank goodness for _____ (a. Roslyn, b. the alarm clock, c. Mike's cartoon).

Sincerely,
_____ (a. President Carter, b. President Jimmy Carter, c. Jimmy)

As you can see, he took my multiple choice thing and created a sentence. Knowing how he prefers to operate, this will be the foreword for my next book:

Pimps and ho's, Mike Luckovich is a straight-up mo-fo, so buy his phat book or I'll show your insides style by puttin' one of my gators up yo ass.

Foshizzle,
President Jimmy Carter

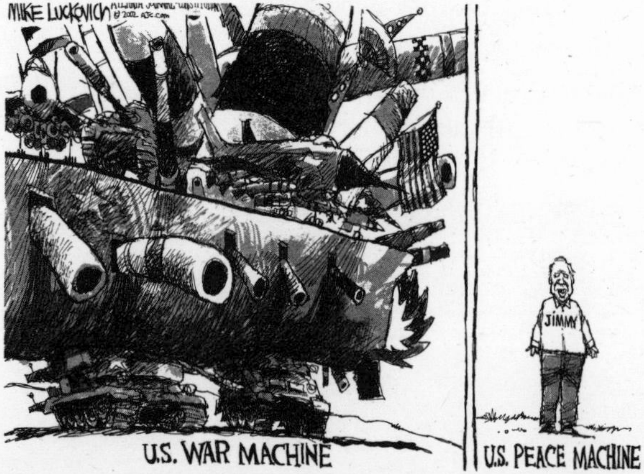
MIKE LUCKOVICH
JIMMY
U.S. WAR MACHINE
U.S. PEACE MACHINE

Bush

Bush is a walking disaster. In virtually every aspect, America is in worse shape because of his actions. From his handling of Iraq, to the tax cuts, to ignoring global warming, Katrina, the war on science, illegal wiretapping, torture, Harriet Miers. . . . The list is endless.

Two groups have overwhelmingly benefited by having Bush in office. Rich people and cartoonists.

What drives me nuts is no matter how much Bush screws up and lies about it, over thirty percent of Americans still support him. I'm sure that if he were to take a crap on his Oval Office desk, that same thirty percent would salute it. Not only that, right-wing media types like Rush and Sean Hannity would start calling it "the Pyramid of Freedom."

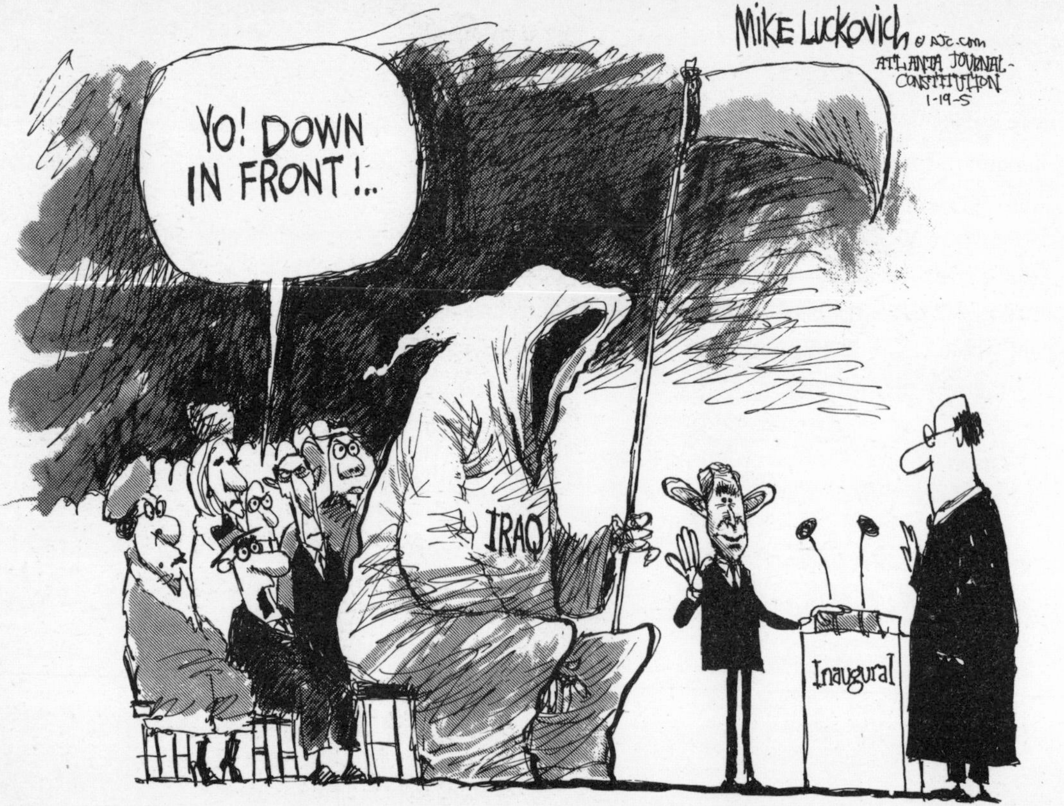
MIKE LUCKOVICH © AJC.com
ATLANTA JOURNAL-CONSTITUTION
1-19-5
YO! DOWN IN FRONT!..
IRAQ
Inaugural

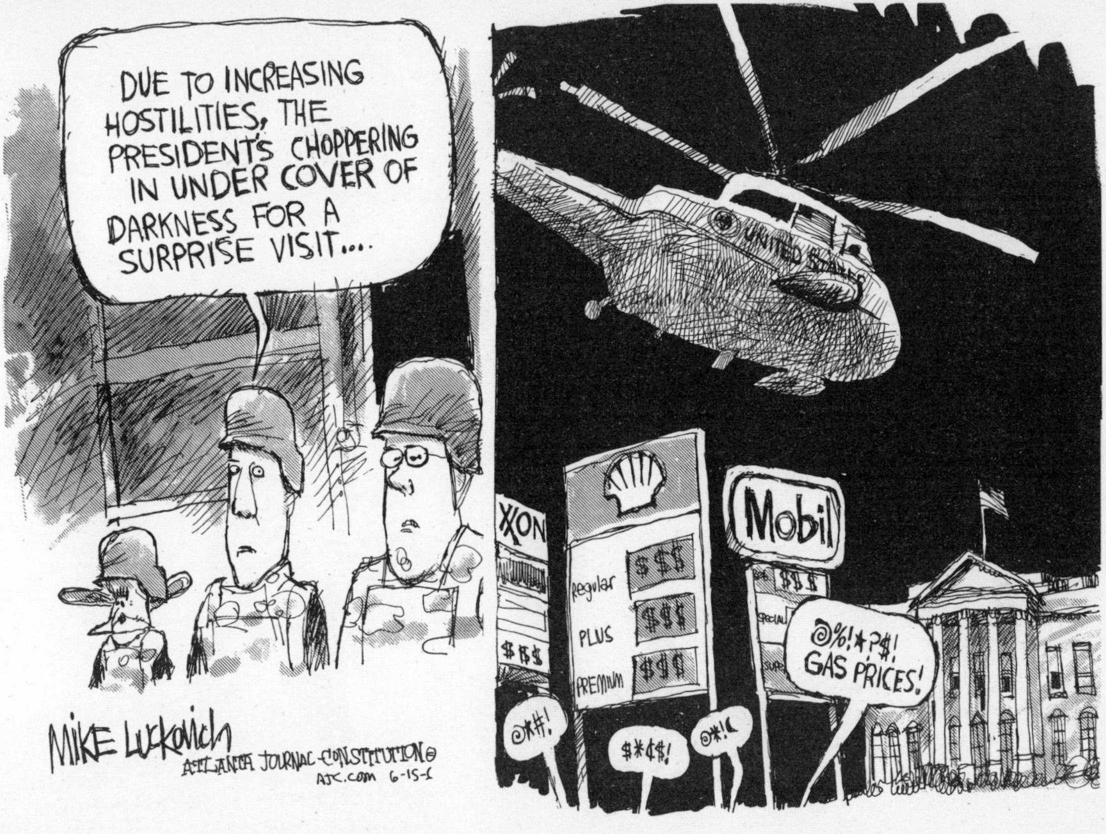
DUE TO INCREASING HOSTILITIES, THE PRESIDENT'S CHOPPERING IN UNDER COVER OF DARKNESS FOR A SURPRISE VISIT....
UNITED STATES
XXON
$$$
Regular
PLUS
PREMIUM
Mobil
@%!*?$! GAS PRICES!
@*#!
$*¢$!
@*!(
MIKE LUCKOVICH
ATLANTA JOURNAL-CONSTITUTION
AJC.com 6-15-1

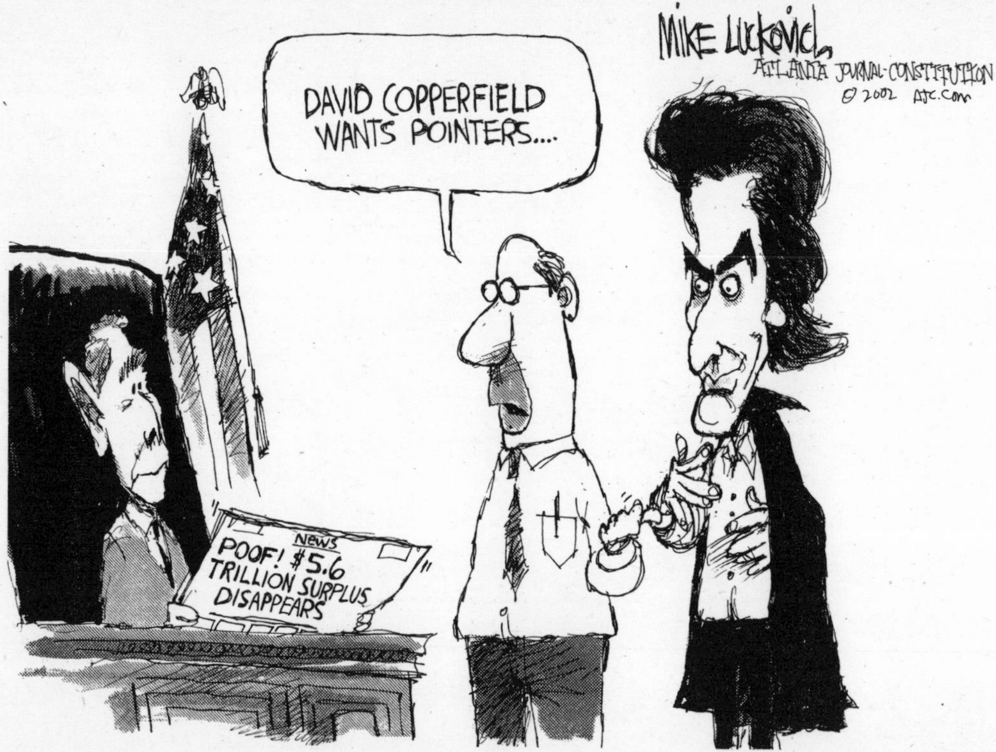
MIKE LUCKOVICH
ATLANTA JOURNAL-CONSTITUTION
©2002 AJC.com
DAVID COPPERFIELD WANTS POINTERS....
NEWS
POOF! $5.6 TRILLION SURPLUS DISAPPEARS

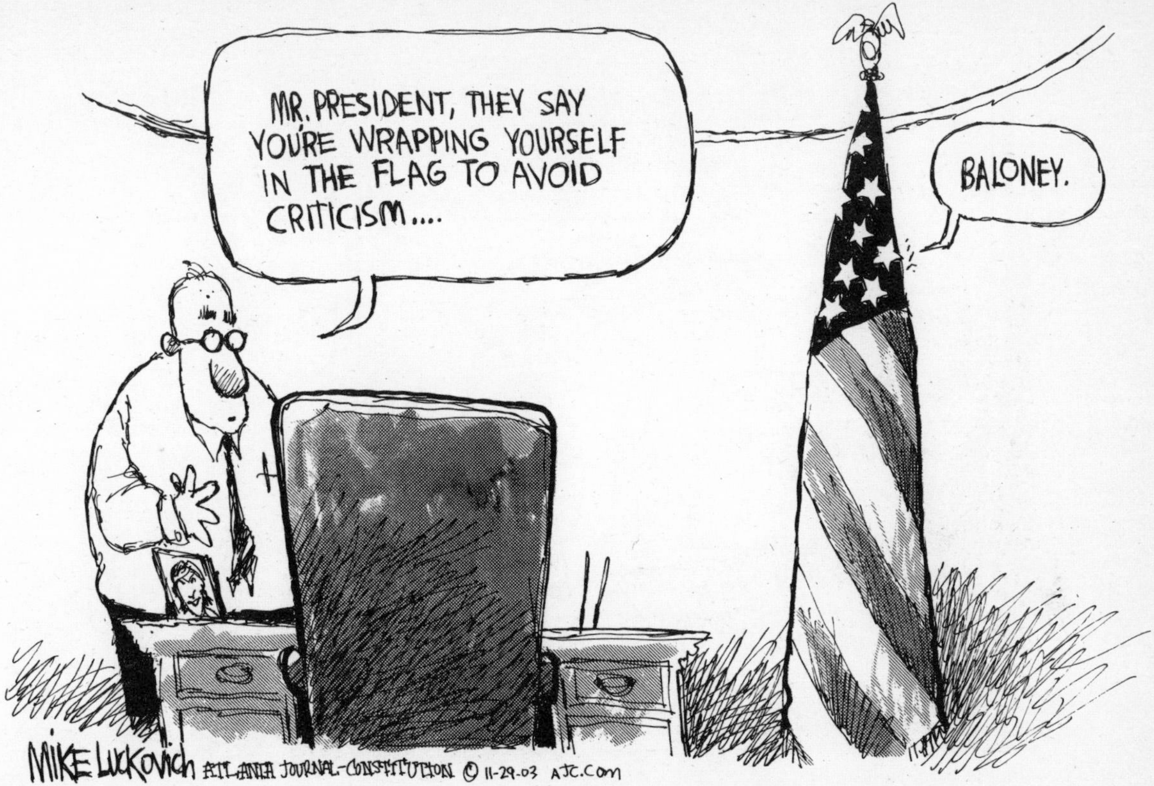
MR. PRESIDENT, THEY SAY YOU'RE WRAPPING YOURSELF IN THE FLAG TO AVOID CRITICISM....
BALONEY.
MIKE LUCKOVICH ATLANTA JOURNAL-CONSTITUTION © 11-29-03 AJC.COM

YOU OUTED AN AGENT, CASTING A CLOUD OVER THE WHITE HOUSE.... KARL ROVE, YOU'RE NOT FIRED!...
I MISS TRUMP....
W
MIKE LUCKOVICH ATLANTA JOURNAL-CONSTITUTION & AJC.com 7-2005

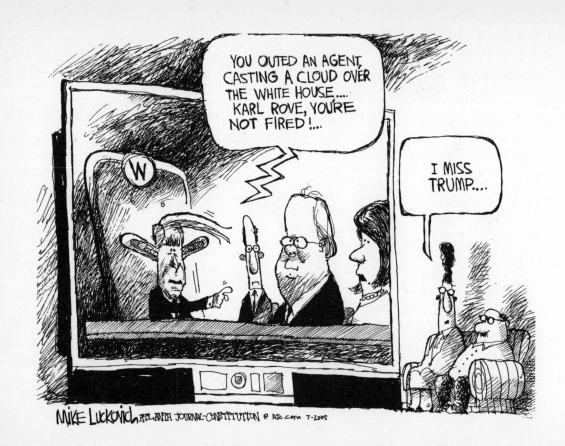

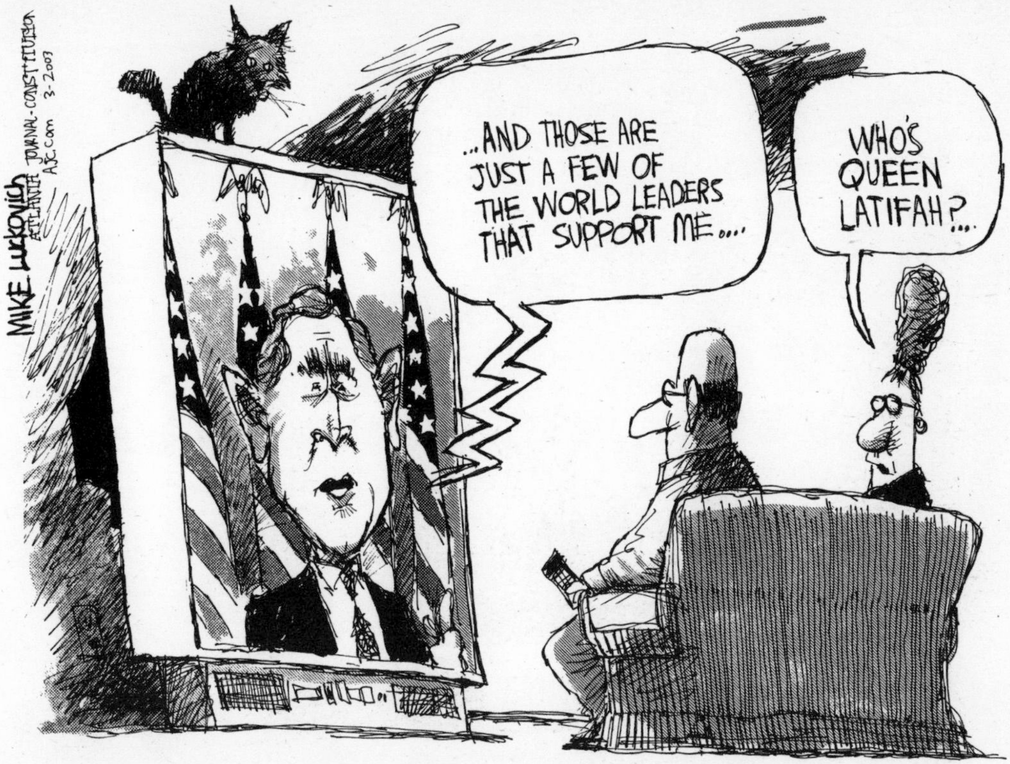
MIKE LUCKOVICH ATLANTA JOURNAL-CONSTITUTION AJC.com 3-2003
...AND THOSE ARE JUST A FEW OF THE WORLD LEADERS THAT SUPPORT ME....
WHO'S QUEEN LATIFAH?...

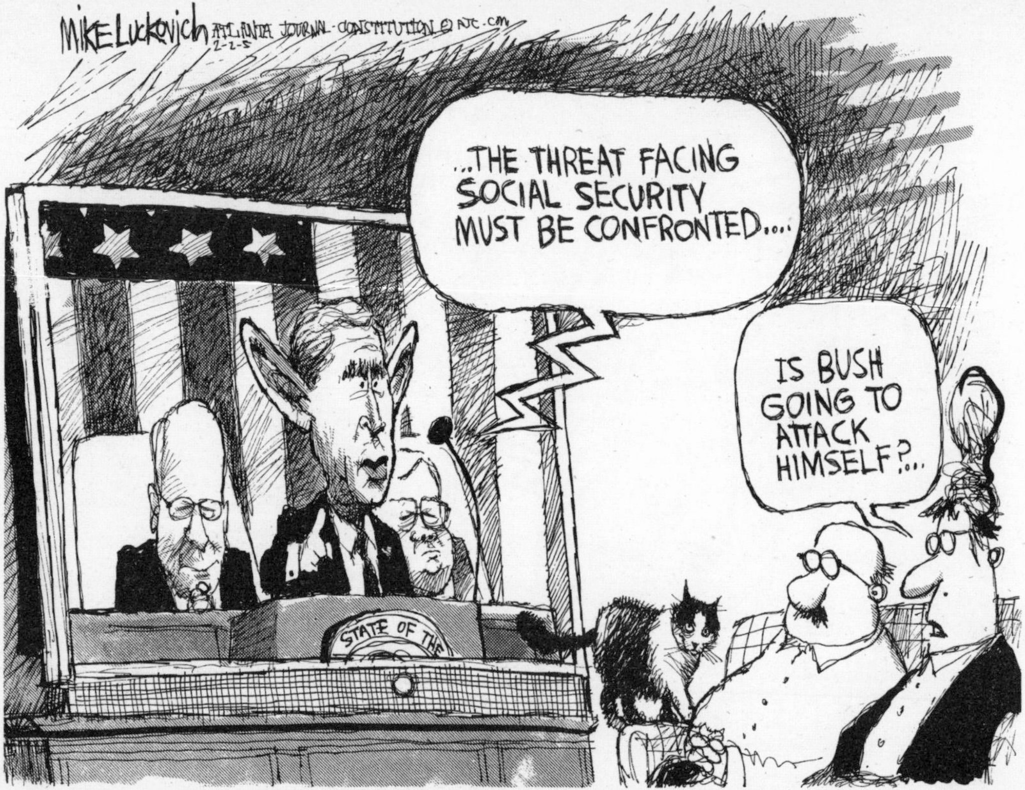
MIKE LUCKOVICH ATLANTA JOURNAL-CONSTITUTION © AJC.COM
2-2-5
...THE THREAT FACING SOCIAL SECURITY MUST BE CONFRONTED....
IS BUSH GOING TO ATTACK HIMSELF?...
STATE OF THE

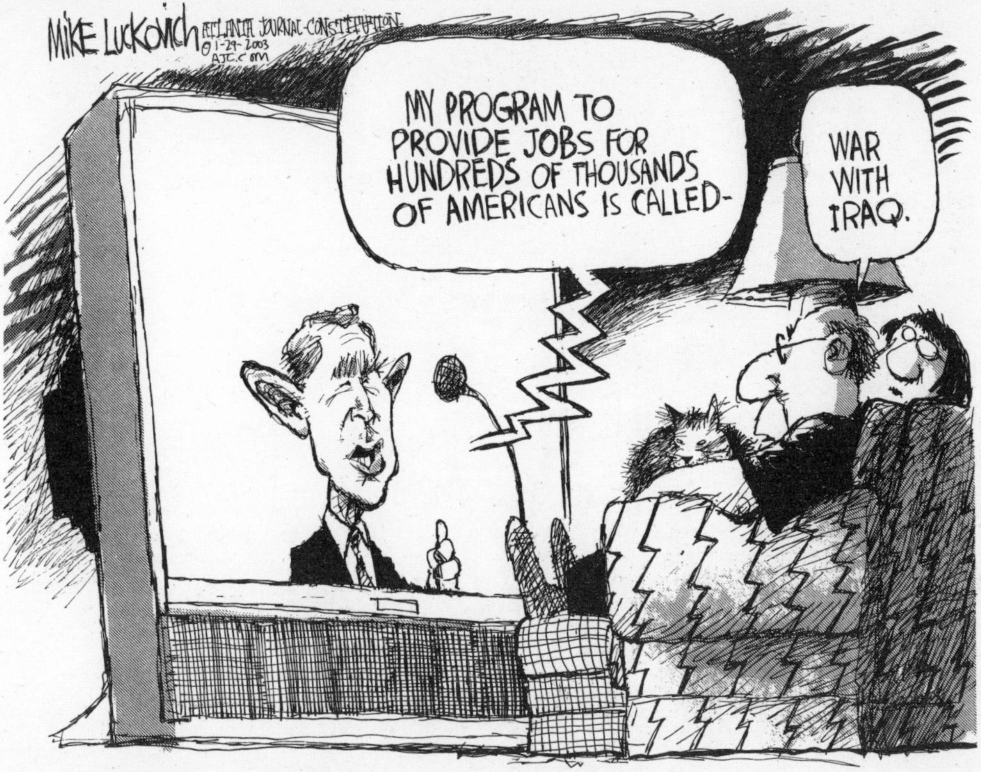
MIKE LUCKOVICH ATLANTA JOURNAL-CONSTITUTION ©1-29-2003 AJC.com
MY PROGRAM TO PROVIDE JOBS FOR HUNDREDS OF THOUSANDS OF AMERICANS IS CALLED-
WAR WITH IRAQ.

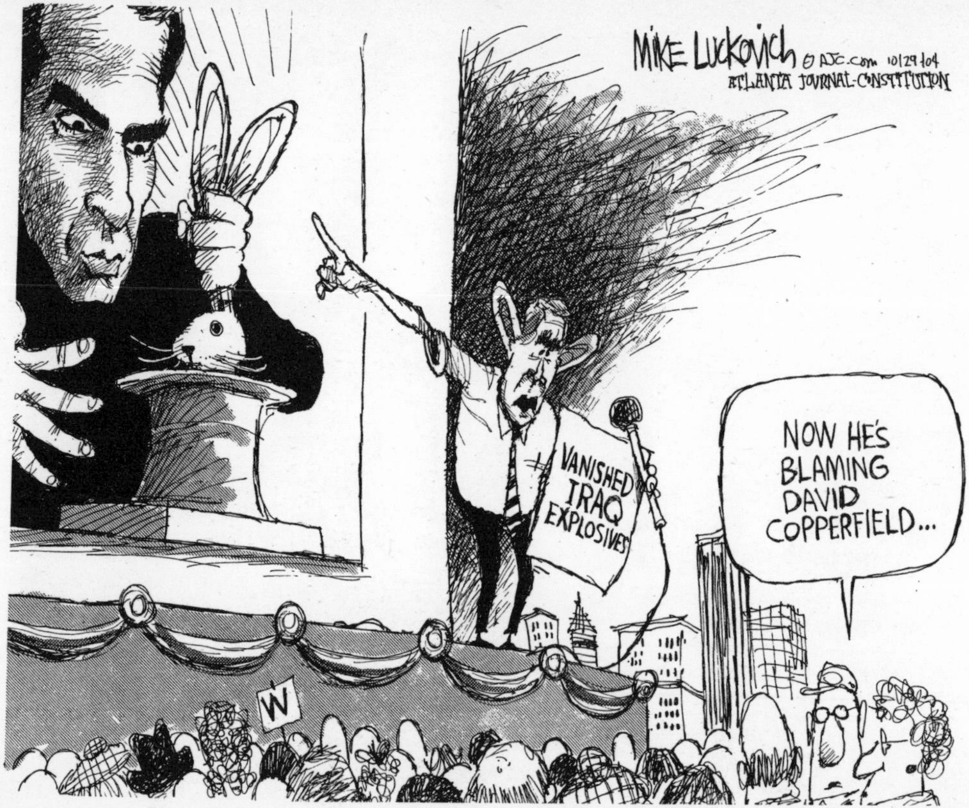
MIKE LUCKOVICH © AJC.com 10/29/04
ATLANTA JOURNAL-CONSTITUTION
VANISHED IRAQ EXPLOSIVES
NOW HE'S BLAMING DAVID COPPERFIELD...
W

LUCKOVICH ATLANTA JOURNAL-CONSTITUTION
AJC.com
GAS IS HIGH. THE DEFICIT'S EXPLODING. U.S. COMMANDERS IN IRAQ ARE GLUM. AND THE REST OF THE WORLD HATES US....
@★!#(*!★ NEWSWEEK!

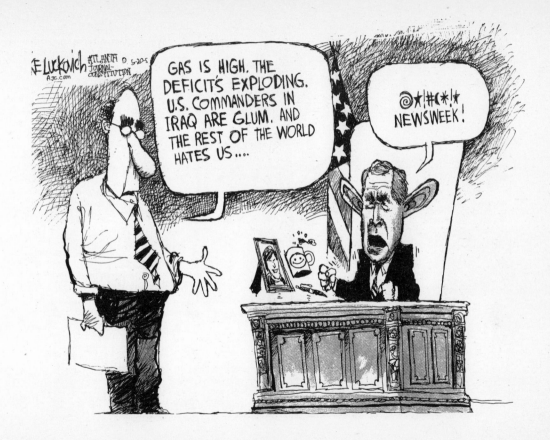

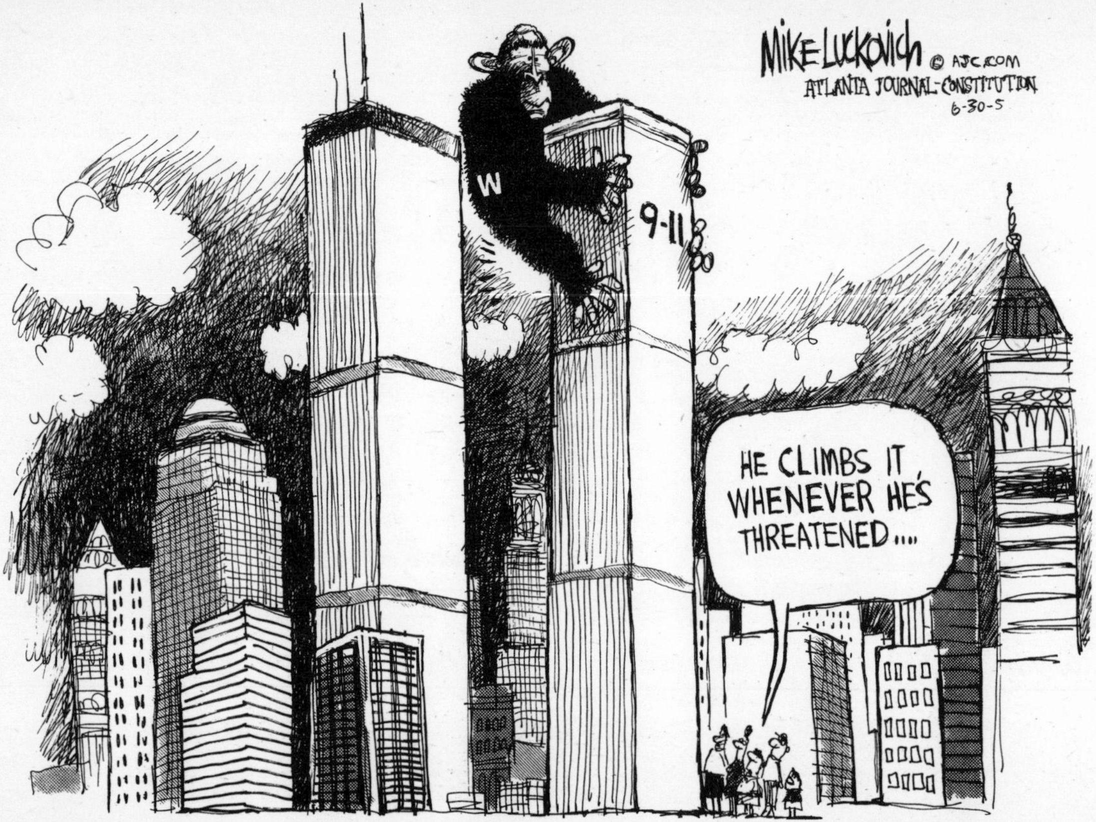
MIKE LUCKOVICH © AJC.COM
ATLANTA JOURNAL-CONSTITUTION
6-30-5
W
9-11
HE CLIMBS IT WHENEVER HE'S THREATENED....

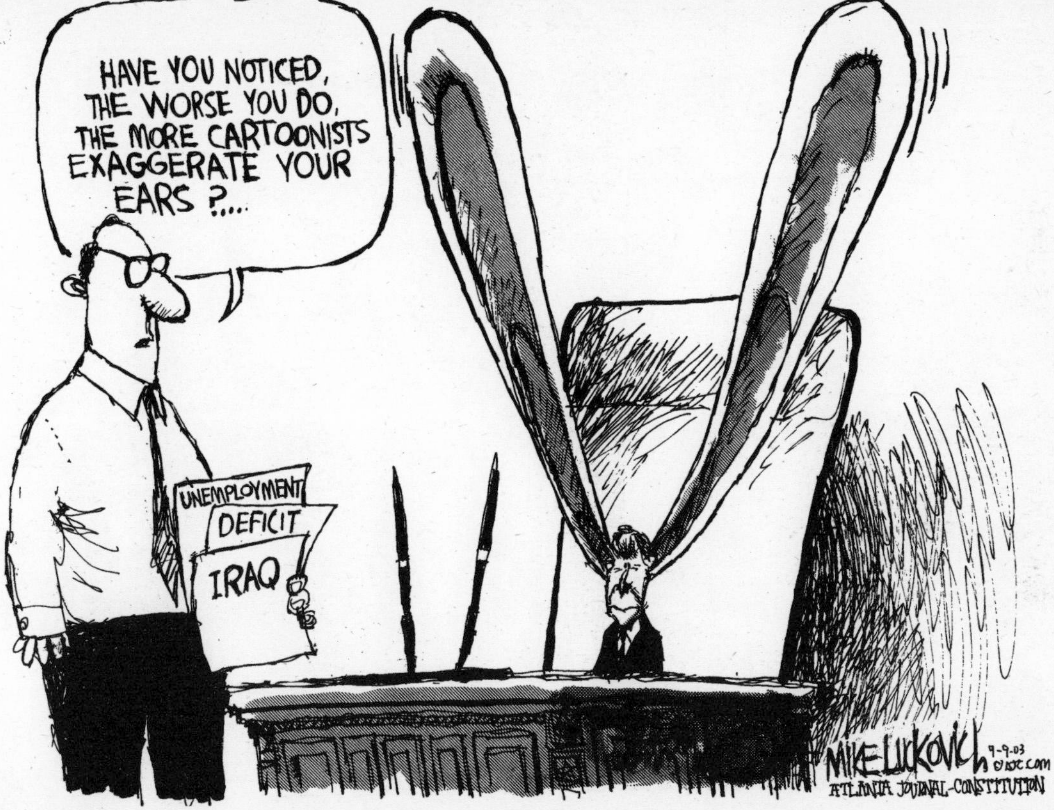
HAVE YOU NOTICED, THE WORSE YOU DO, THE MORE CARTOONISTS EXAGGERATE YOUR EARS ?....
UNEMPLOYMENT
DEFICIT
IRAQ
MIKE LUCKOVICH
9-9-03
©AJC.com
ATLANTA JOURNAL-CONSTITUTION

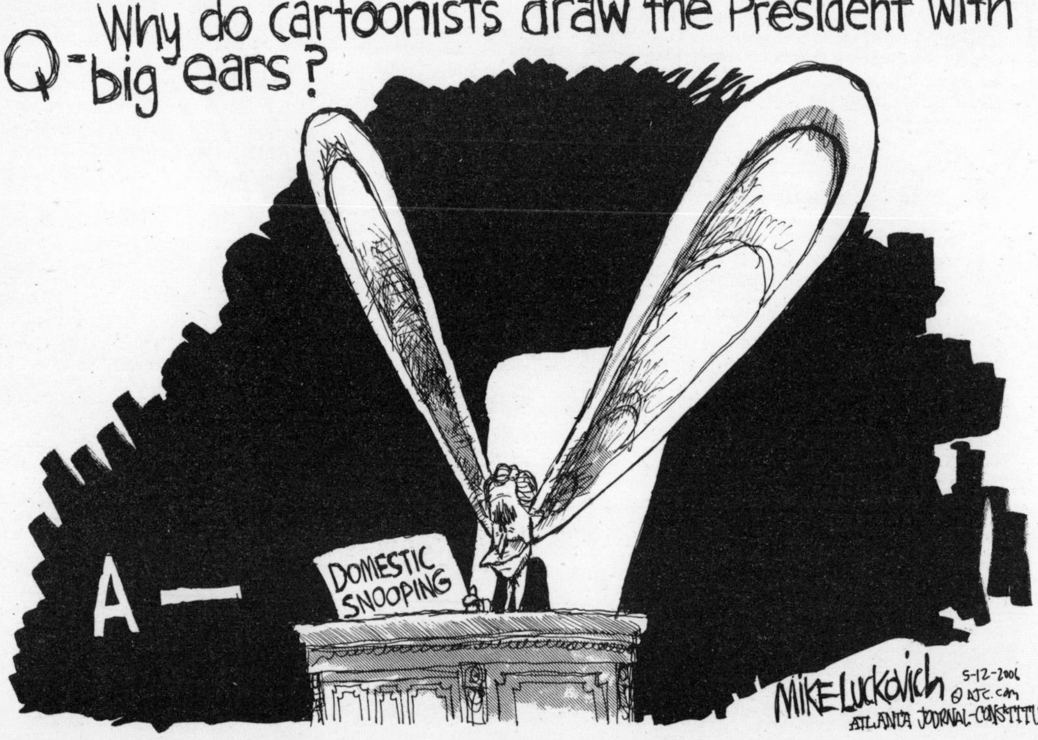
Q-Why do cartoonists draw the President with big ears?
A-
DOMESTIC SNOOPING
MIKE LUCKOVICH
5-12-2006
©AJC.com
ATLANTA JOURNAL-CONSTITUTION

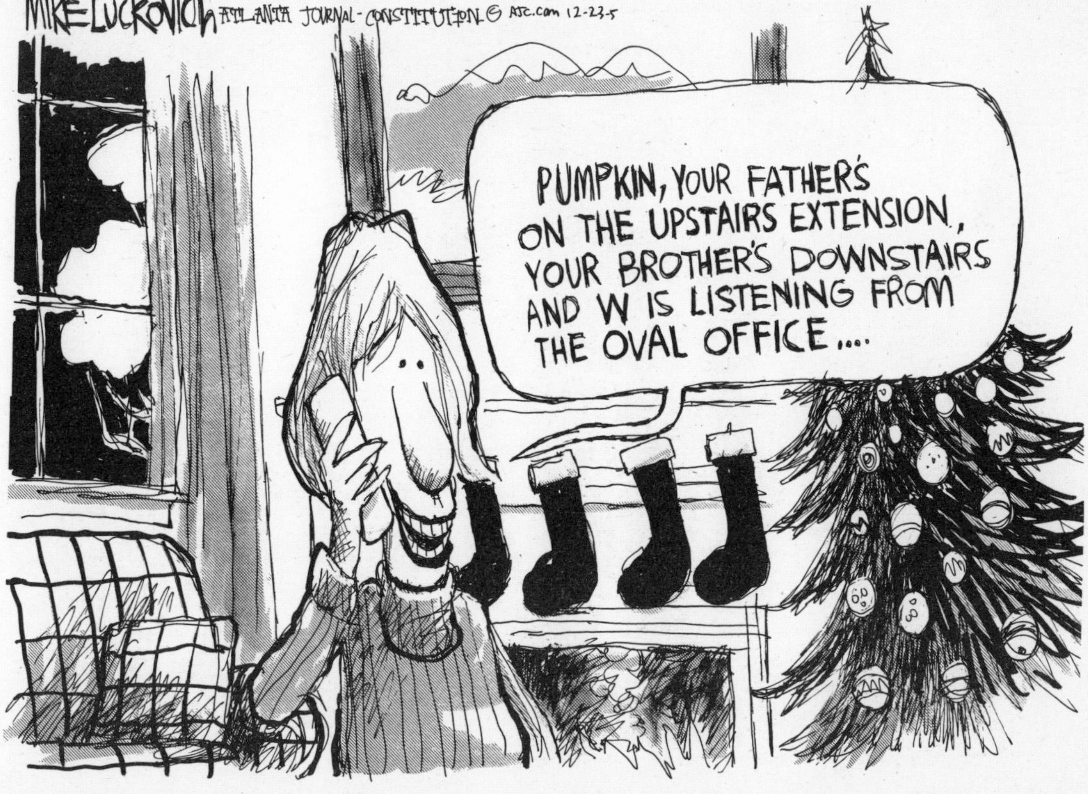
MIKE LUCKOVICH ATLANTA JOURNAL-CONSTITUTION © AJC.com 12-23-5
PUMPKIN, YOUR FATHER'S ON THE UPSTAIRS EXTENSION, YOUR BROTHER'S DOWNSTAIRS AND W IS LISTENING FROM THE OVAL OFFICE....

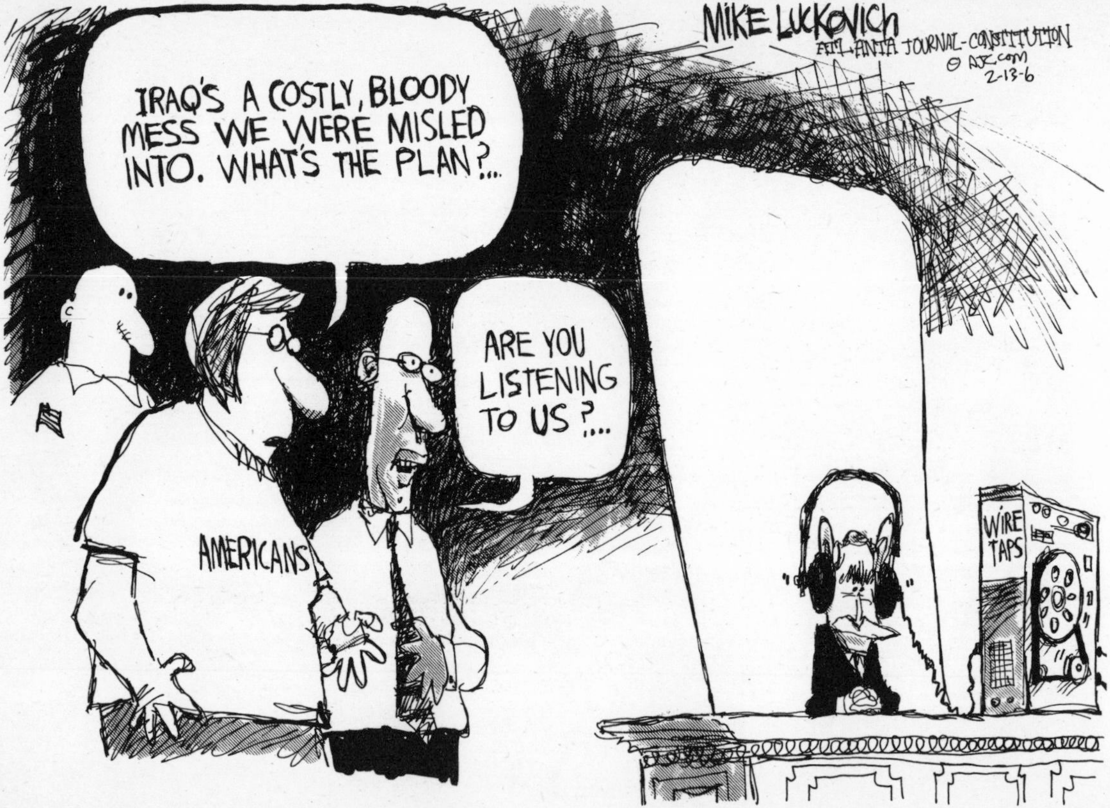
IRAQ'S A COSTLY, BLOODY MESS WE WERE MISLED INTO. WHAT'S THE PLAN?...
ARE YOU LISTENING TO US?...
AMERICANS
WIRE TAPS
MIKE LUCKOVICH
ATLANTA JOURNAL-CONSTITUTION
© AJC.com
2-13-6

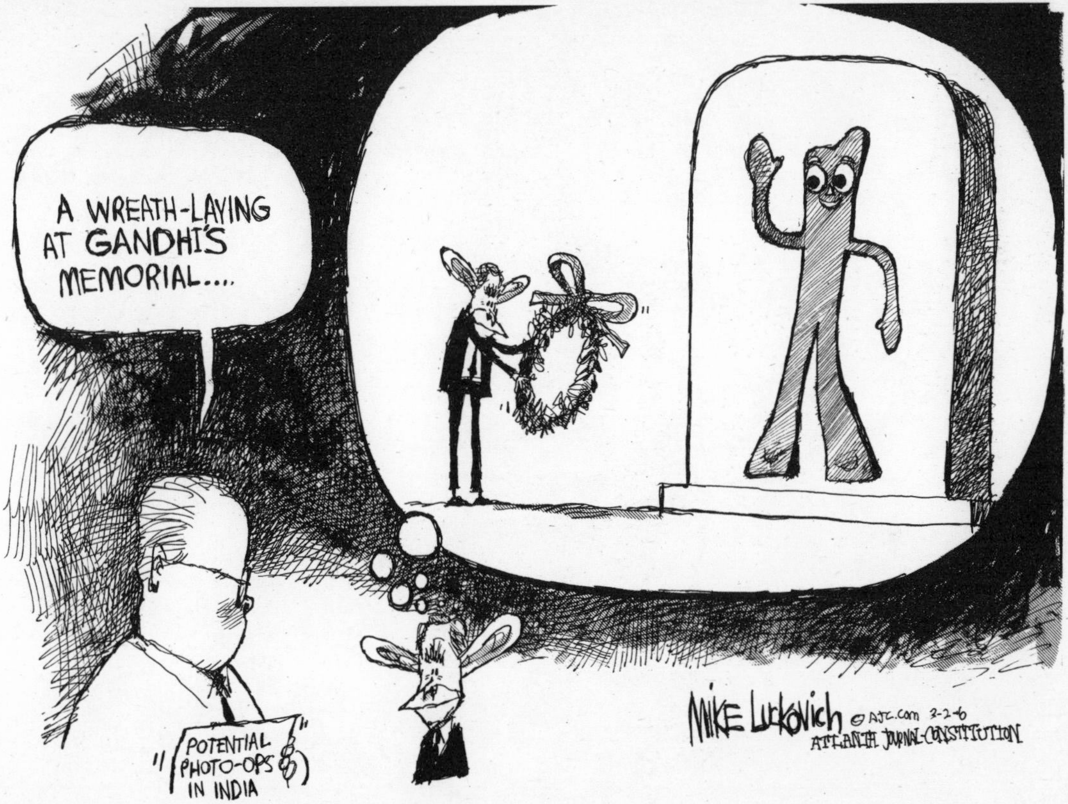
A WREATH-LAYING AT GANDHI'S MEMORIAL....
POTENTIAL PHOTO-OPS IN INDIA
MIKE LUCKOVICH ©AJC.com 3-2-06
ATLANTA JOURNAL-CONSTITUTION

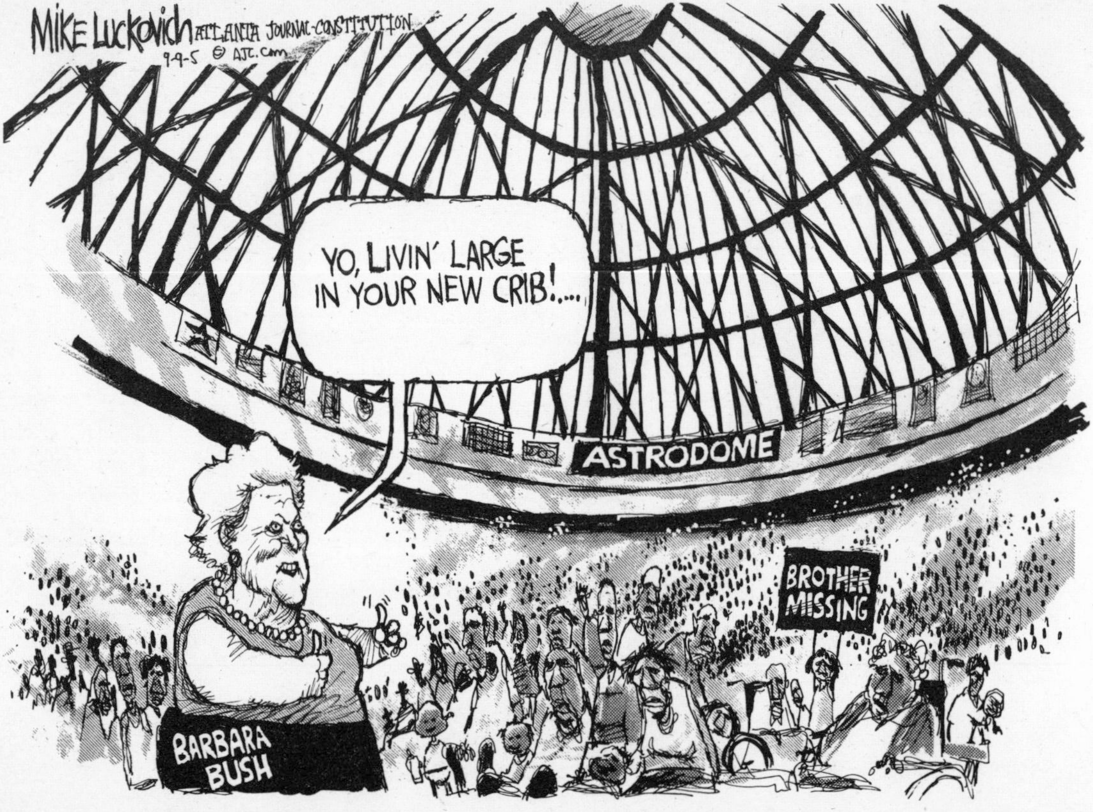
MIKE LUCKOVICH ATLANTA JOURNAL-CONSTITUTION
9-9-5 © AJC.com
YO, LIVIN' LARGE IN YOUR NEW CRIB!....
ASTRODOME
BROTHER MISSING
BARBARA BUSH

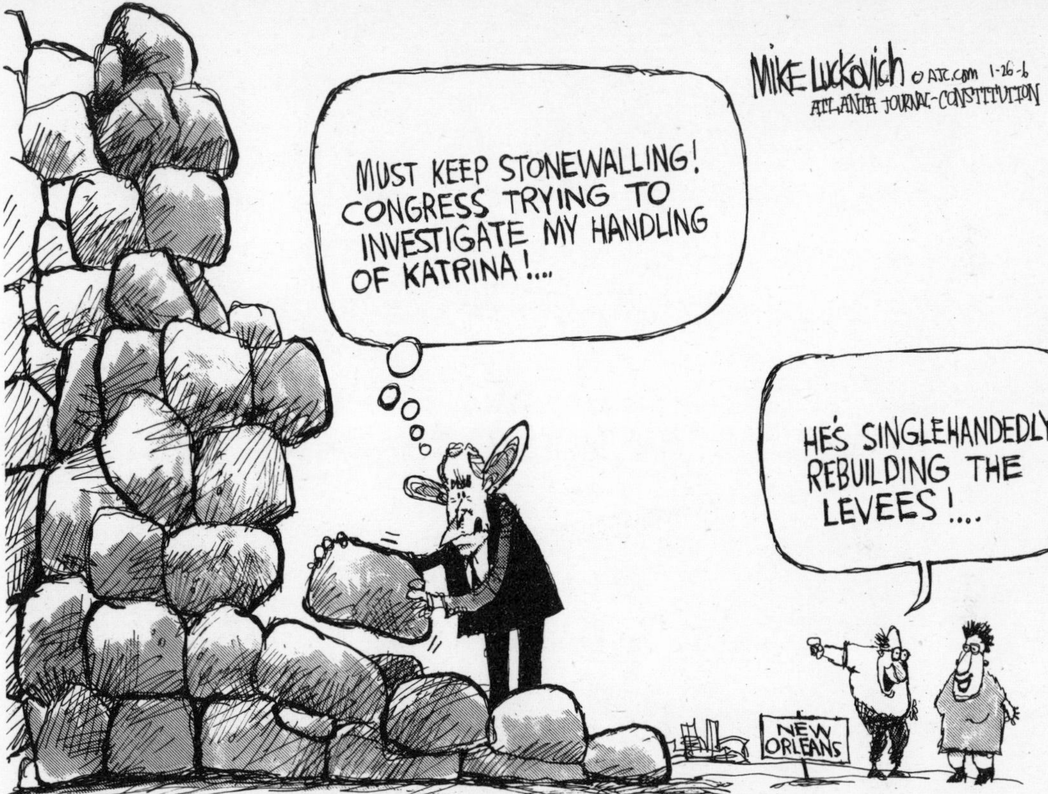
MIKE LUCKOVICH © AJC.com 1-26-6
ATLANTA JOURNAL-CONSTITUTION
MUST KEEP STONEWALLING! CONGRESS TRYING TO INVESTIGATE MY HANDLING OF KATRINA!...
HE'S SINGLEHANDEDLY REBUILDING THE LEVEES!...
NEW ORLEANS

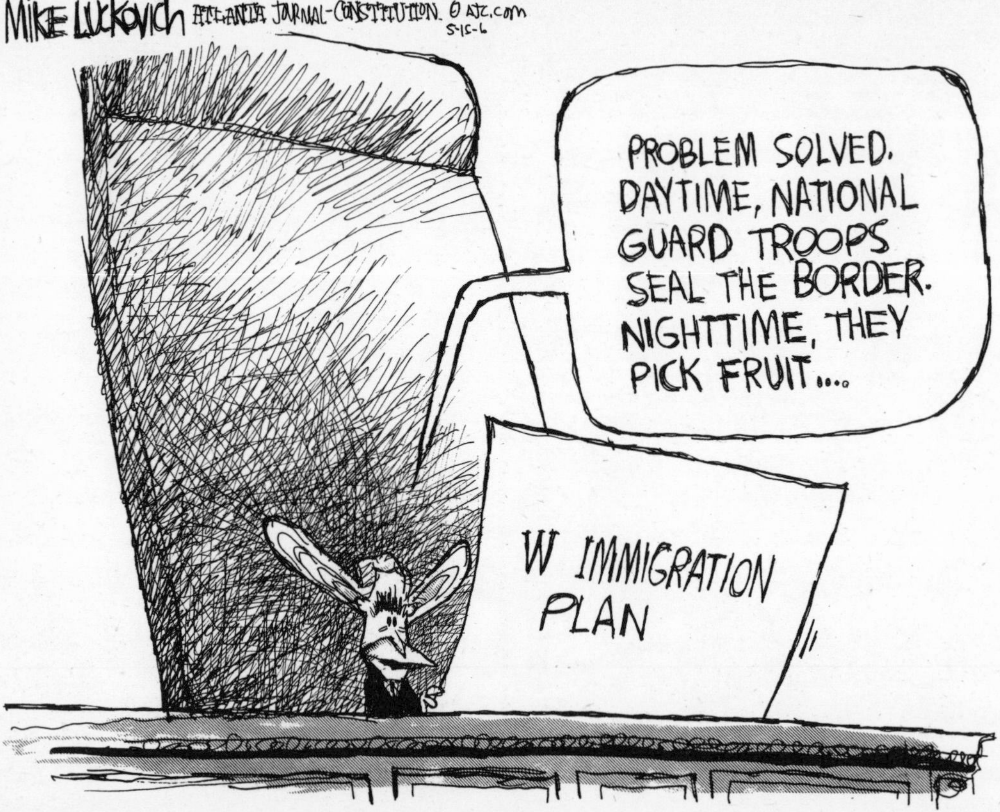
MIKE LUCKOVICH ATLANTA JOURNAL-CONSTITUTION ©AJC.com
5-15-6
PROBLEM SOLVED. DAYTIME, NATIONAL GUARD TROOPS SEAL THE BORDER. NIGHTTIME, THEY PICK FRUIT....
W IMMIGRATION PLAN

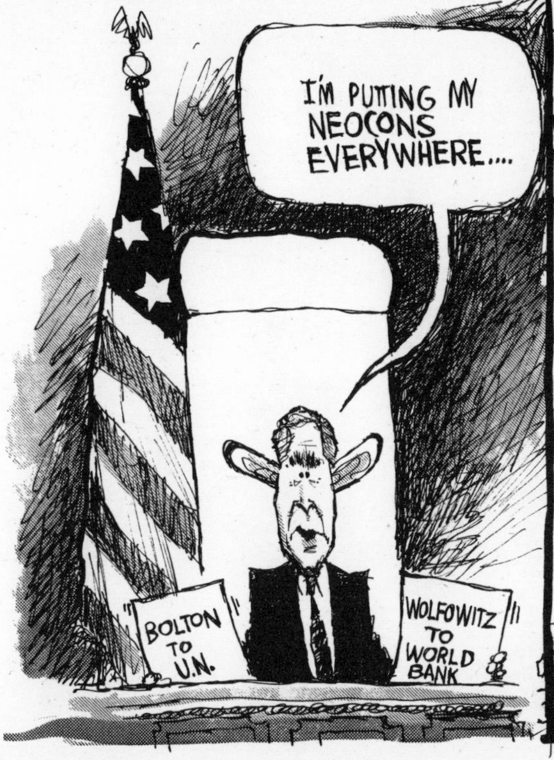
I'M PUTTING MY NEOCONS EVERYWHERE....
"BOLTON TO U.N."
"WOLFOWITZ TO WORLD BANK"

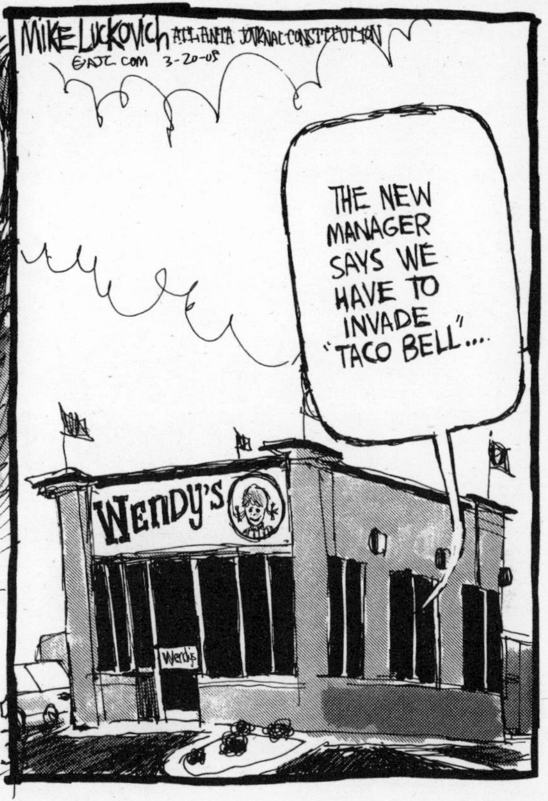
MIKE LUCKOVICH ATLANTA JOURNAL-CONSTITUTION
©AJC.COM 3-20-05
THE NEW MANAGER SAYS WE HAVE TO INVADE "TACO BELL"....
Wendy's
Wendy's

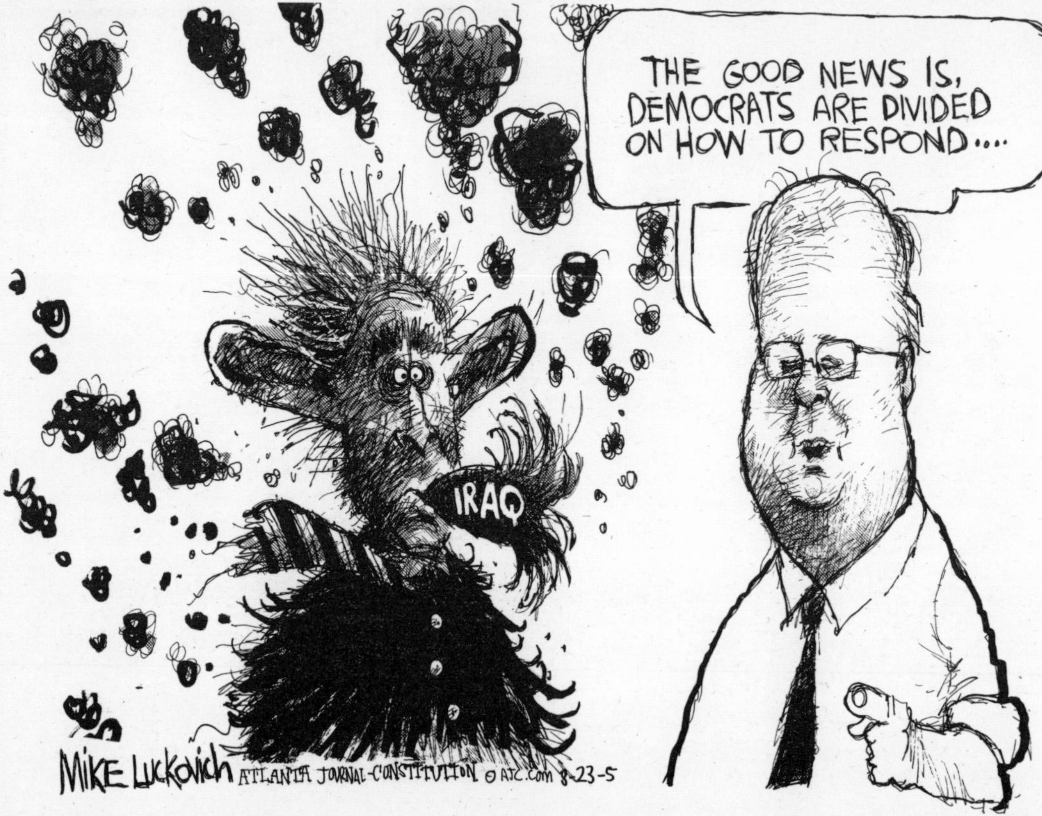
THE GOOD NEWS IS, DEMOCRATS ARE DIVIDED ON HOW TO RESPOND....
IRAQ
MIKE LUCKOVICH ATLANTA JOURNAL-CONSTITUTION © AJC.com 8-23-5

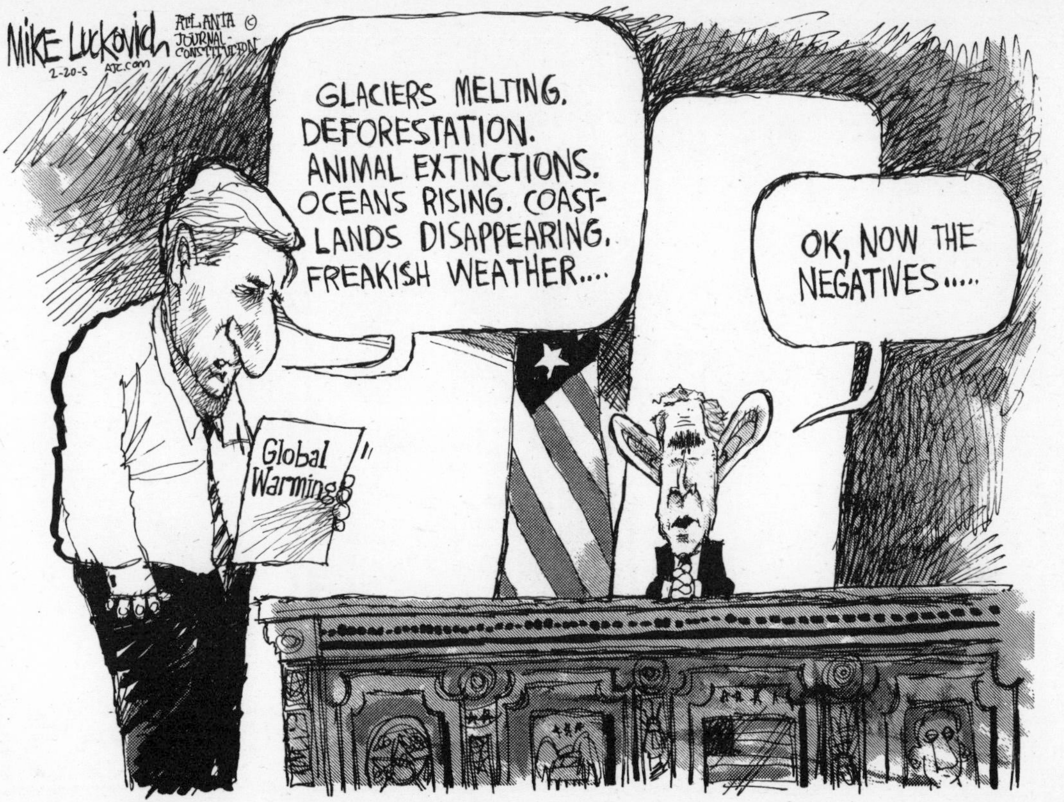
MIKE LUCKOVICH
ATLANTA JOURNAL-CONSTITUTION ©
2-20-5 AJC.com
GLACIERS MELTING. DEFORESTATION. ANIMAL EXTINCTIONS. OCEANS RISING. COAST-LANDS DISAPPEARING. FREAKISH WEATHER....
Global Warming
OK, NOW THE NEGATIVES.....

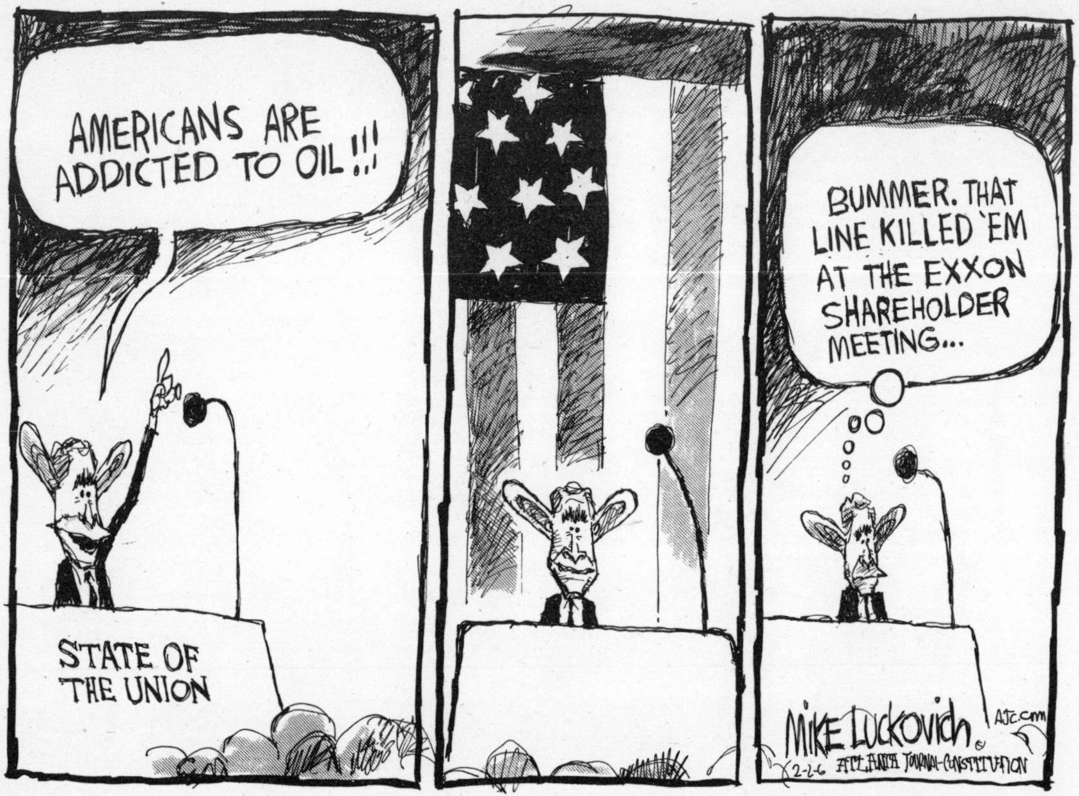
AMERICANS ARE ADDICTED TO OIL!!!
STATE OF THE UNION
BUMMER. THAT LINE KILLED 'EM AT THE EXXON SHAREHOLDER MEETING...
MIKE LUCKOVICH
AJC.com
2-2-6 ATLANTA JOURNAL-CONSTITUTION

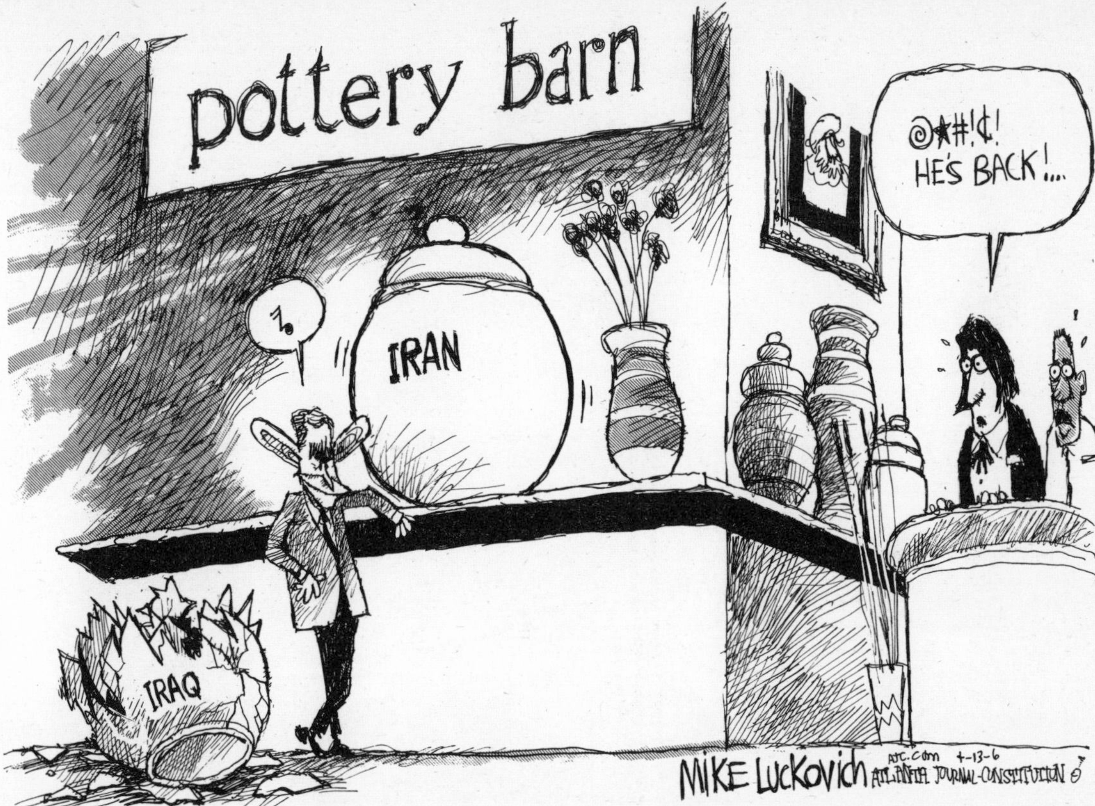
pottery barn
Z
IRAN
IRAQ
@★#!¢!
HE'S BACK!...
MIKE LUCKOVICH ajc.com 4-13-6
ATLANTA JOURNAL-CONSTITUTION

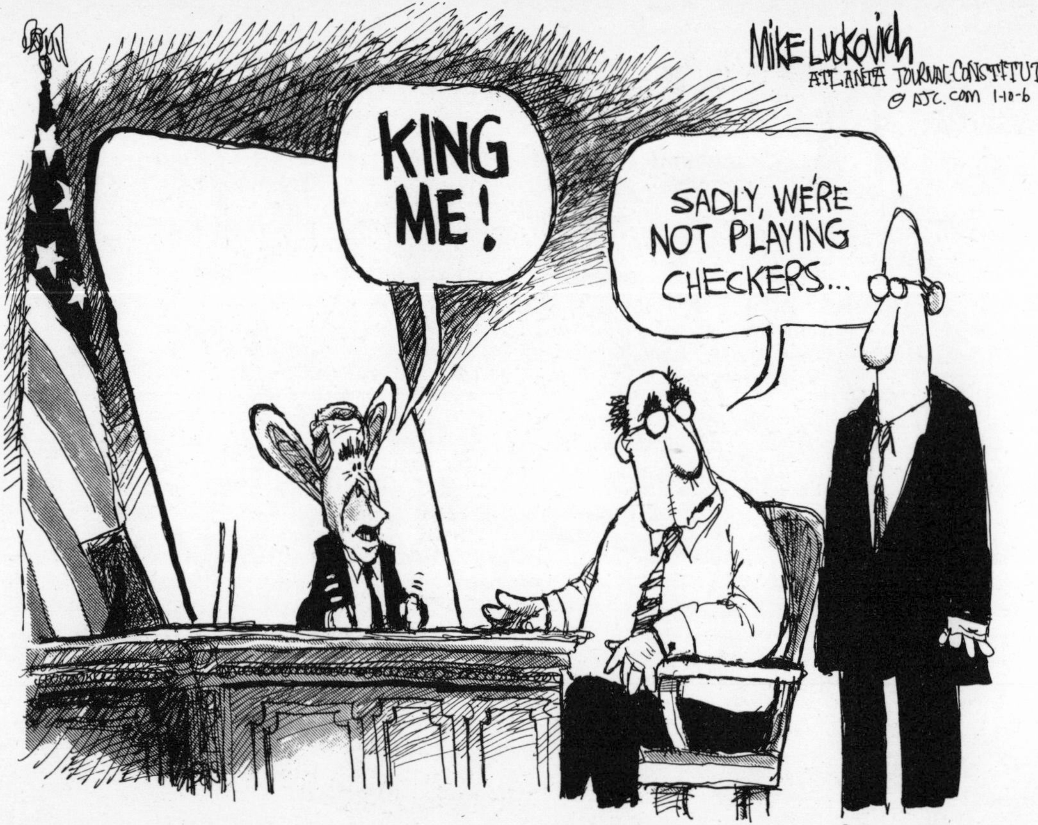
MIKE LUCKOVICH
ATLANTA JOURNAL-CONSTITUTION
© AJC.com 1-10-6
KING ME!
SADLY, WE'RE NOT PLAYING CHECKERS...

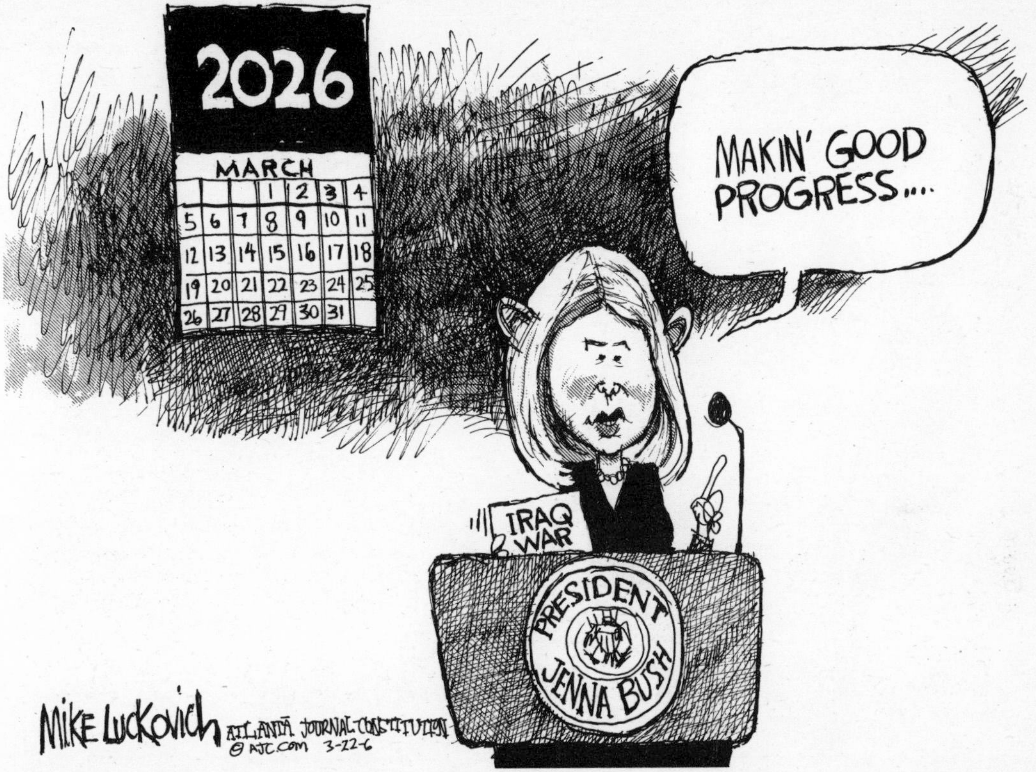
2026
MARCH
1 2 3 4
5 6 7 8 9 10 11
12 13 14 15 16 17 18
19 20 21 22 23 24 25
26 27 28 29 30 31
MAKIN' GOOD PROGRESS....
IRAQ WAR
PRESIDENT JENNA BUSH
MIKE LUCKOVICH
ATLANTA JOURNAL-CONSTITUTION
© AJC.COM 3-22-6

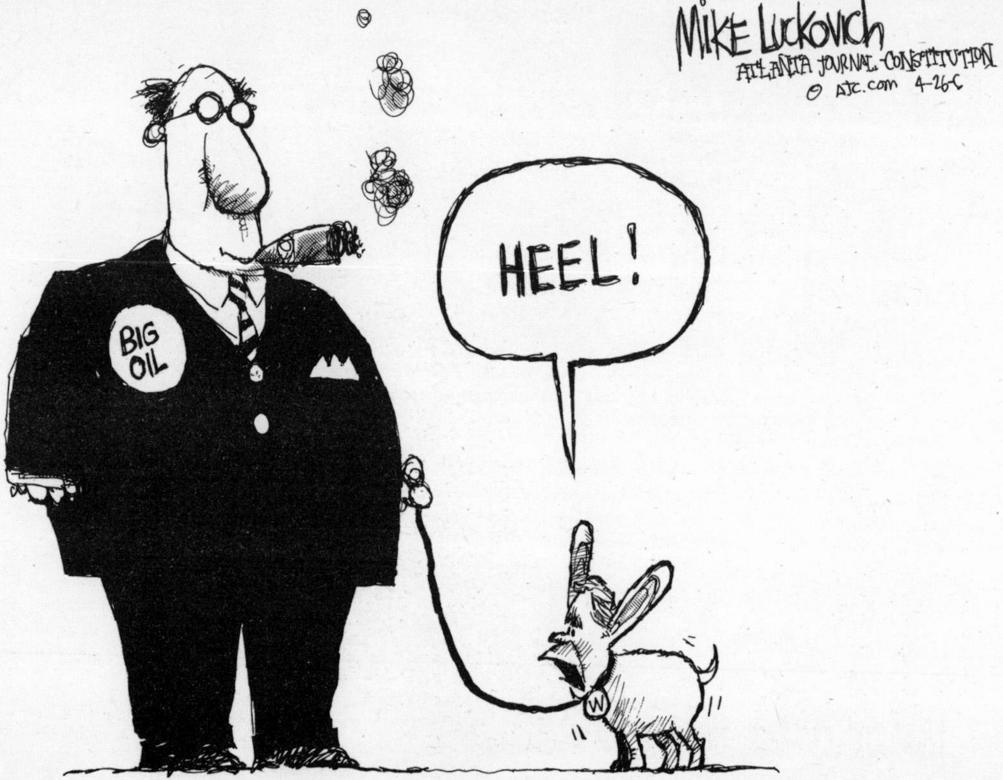
Mike Luckovich
ATLANTA JOURNAL-CONSTITUTION
© AJC.com 4-26-C
BIG OIL
HEEL!
W

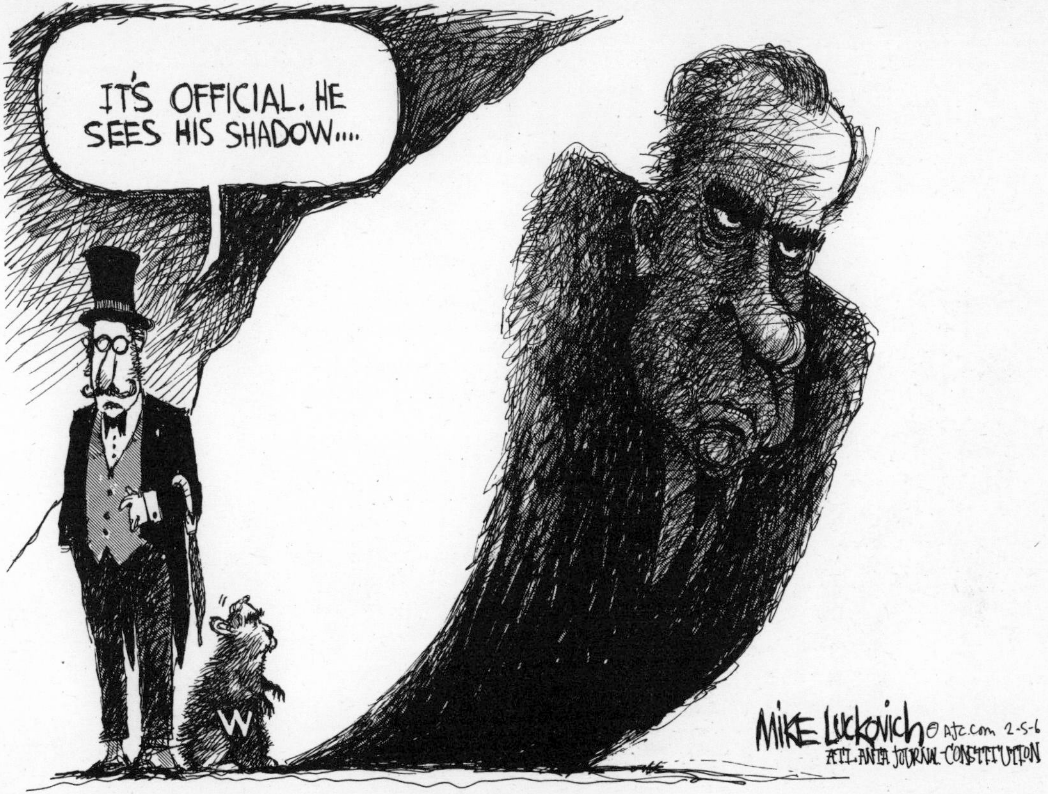
IT'S OFFICIAL. HE SEES HIS SHADOW....
W
MIKE LUCKOVICH © AJC.com 2-5-6
ATLANTA JOURNAL-CONSTITUTION

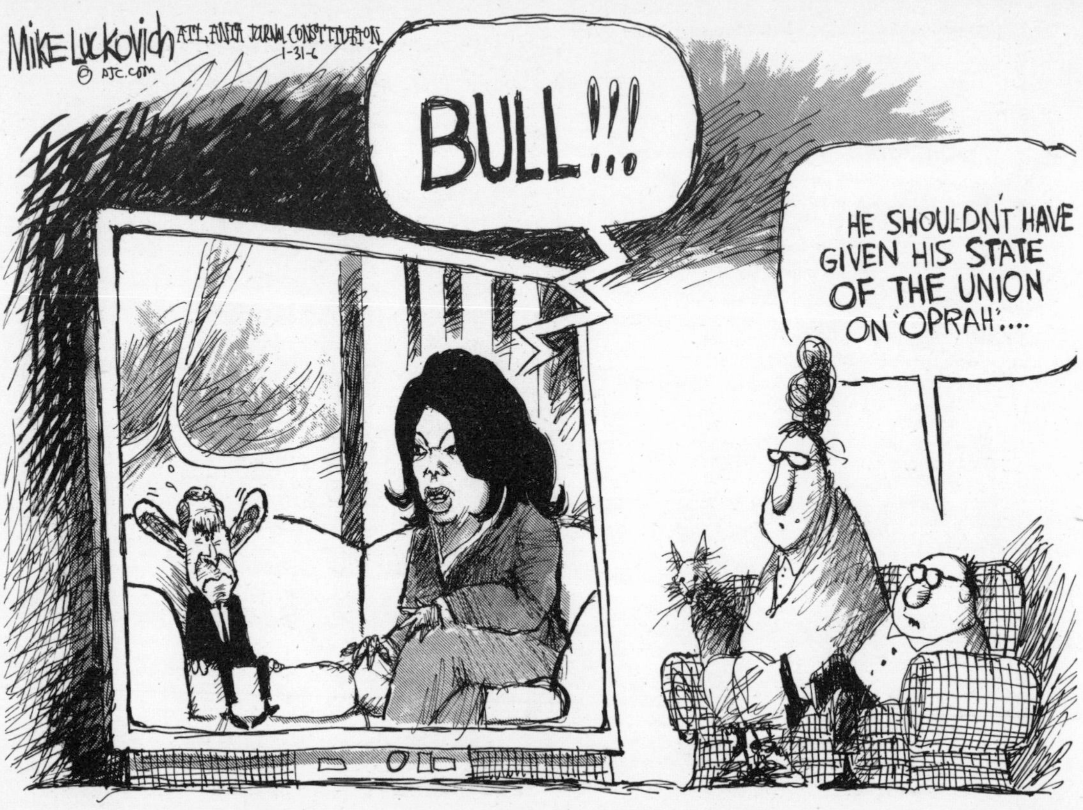
MIKE LUCKOVICH ATLANTA JOURNAL-CONSTITUTION
1-31-6
© AJC.com
BULL!!!
HE SHOULDN'T HAVE GIVEN HIS STATE OF THE UNION ON "OPRAH"....

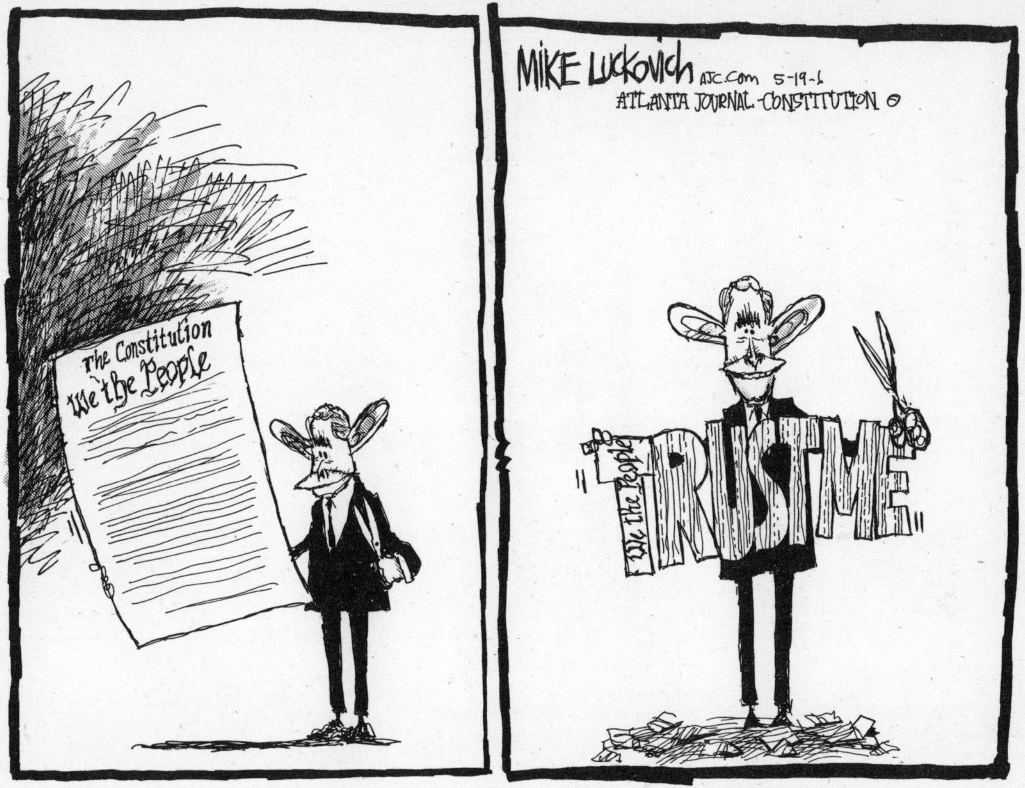
The Constitution
We the People
MIKE LUCKOVICH AJC.COM 5-19-6
ATLANTA JOURNAL-CONSTITUTION ©
We the People
"TRUST ME"

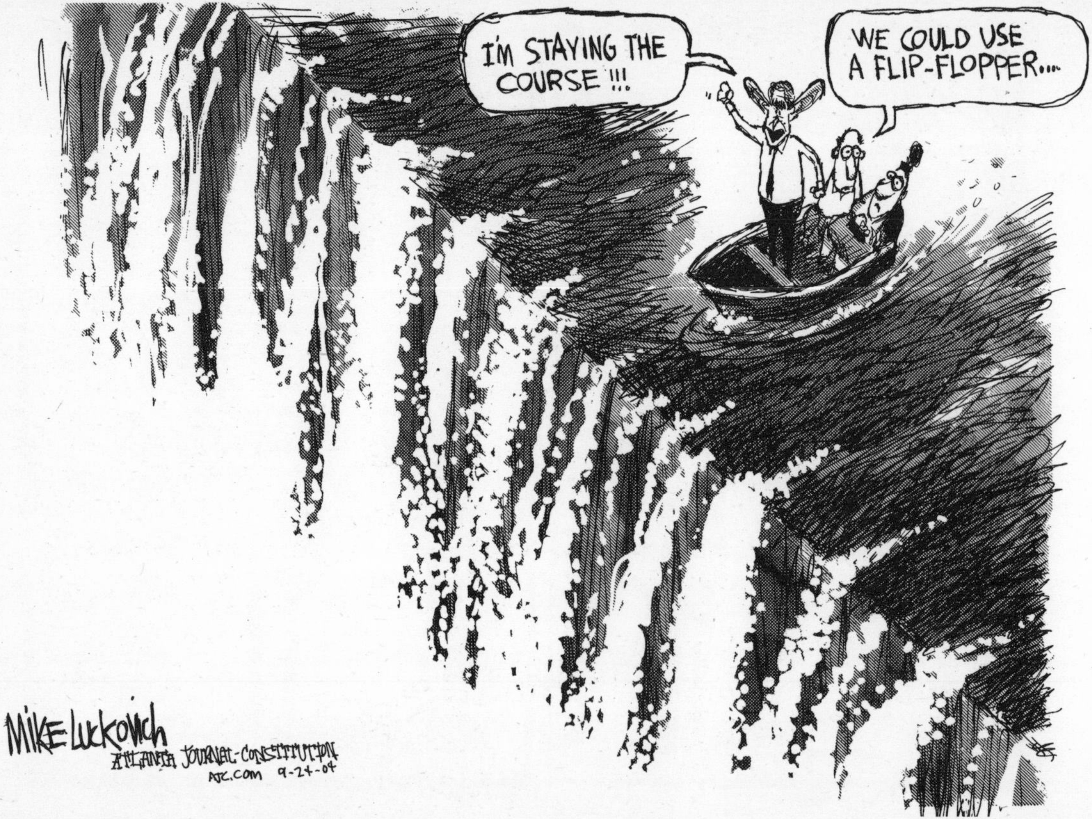
I'M STAYING THE COURSE !!!
WE COULD USE A FLIP-FLOPPER....
MIKE LUCKOVICH
ATLANTA JOURNAL-CONSTITUTION
AJC.COM 9-24-04

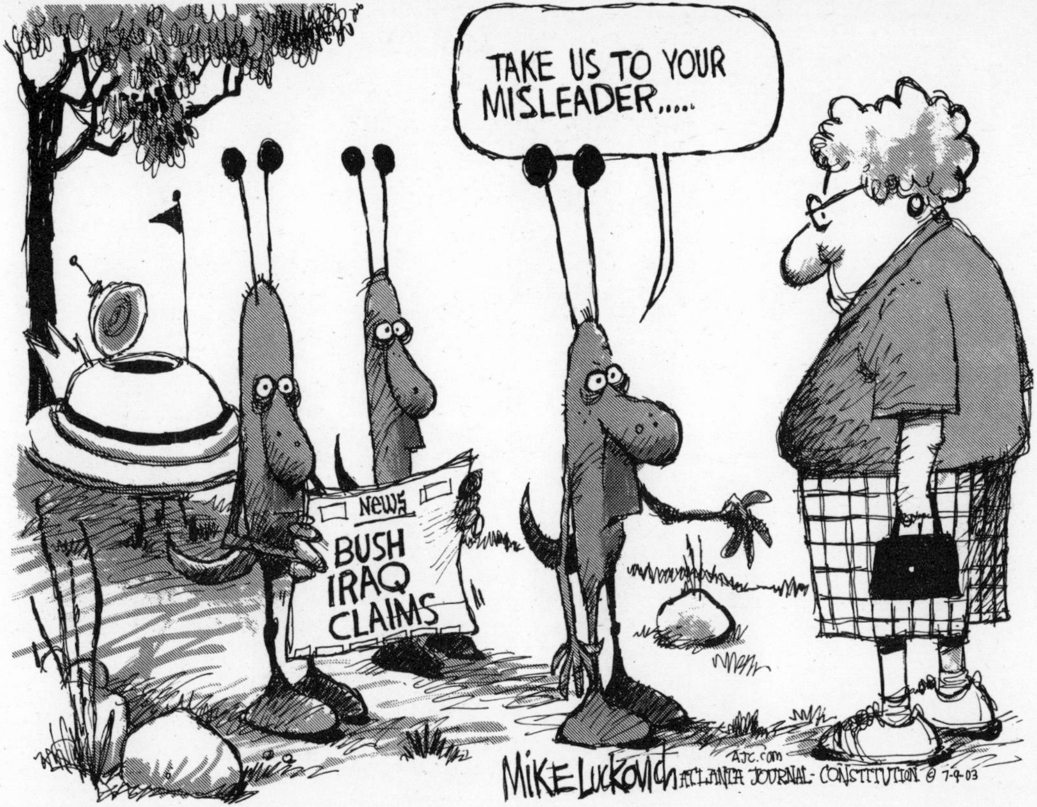
TAKE US TO YOUR MISLEADER.....
NEWS
BUSH IRAQ CLAIMS
MIKE LUCKOVICH
AJC.com
ATLANTA JOURNAL-CONSTITUTION © 7-9-03

I PREDICT 2.6 MILLION NEW JOBS BY THE END OF THIS YEAR....
Later-
THE STATEMENT STANDS MINUS THE WORD "MILLION"....
SPOKESMAN
MIKE LUCKOVICH
© AJC.com 2-19-04
ATLANTA JOURNAL-CONSTITUTION

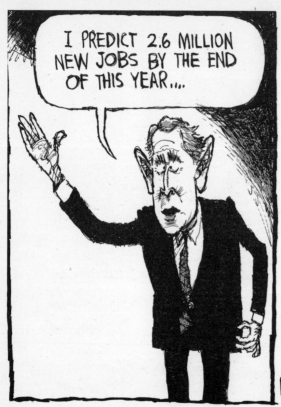

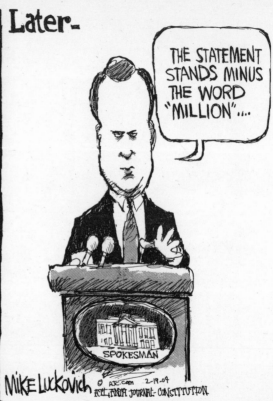

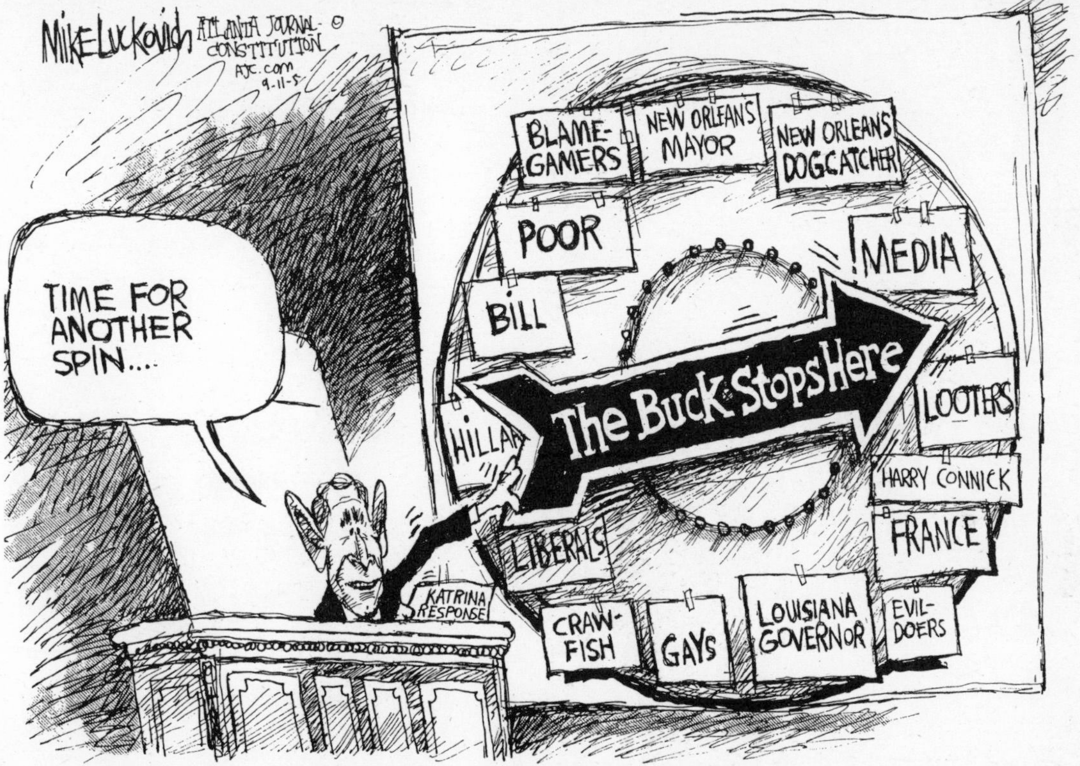
Mike Luckovich Atlanta Journal-Constitution © ajc.com 9-11-5
TIME FOR ANOTHER SPIN....
BLAME-GAMERS
NEW ORLEANS MAYOR
NEW ORLEANS DOGCATCHER
POOR
MEDIA
BILL
The Buck Stops Here
LOOTERS
HARRY CONNICK
FRANCE
LIBERALS
KATRINA RESPONSE
CRAW-FISH
GAYS
LOUISIANA GOVERNOR
EVIL-DOERS

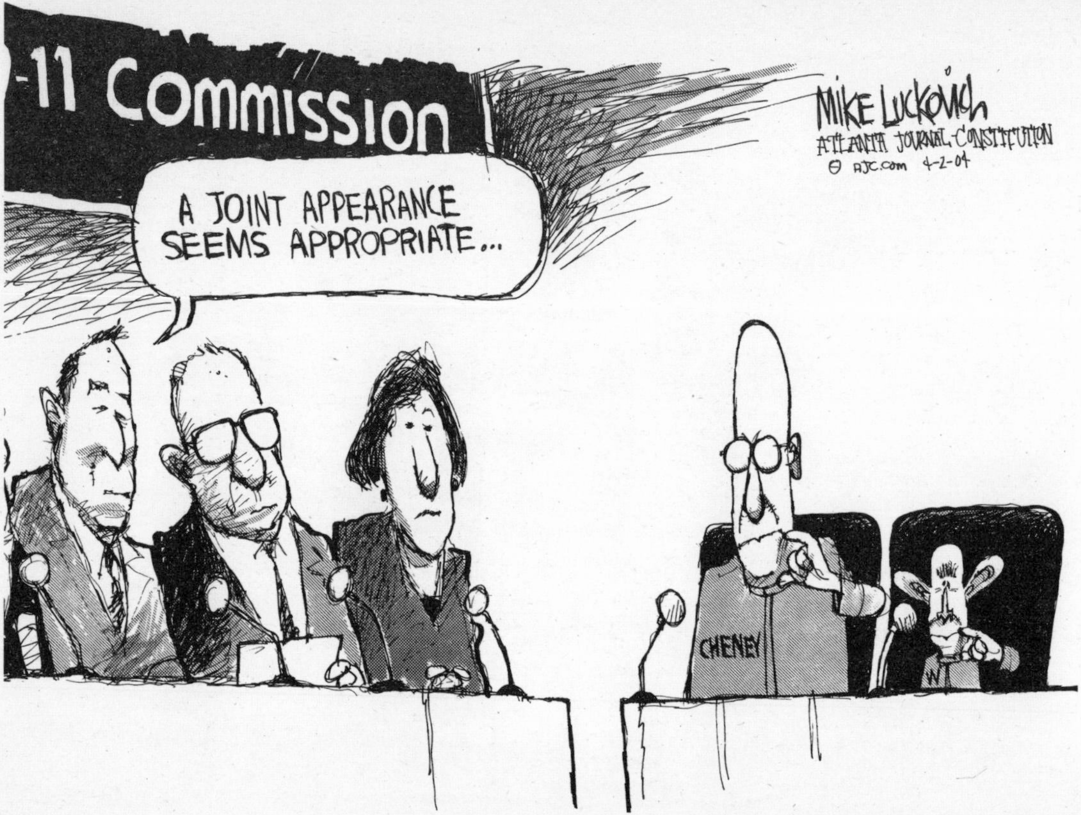
-11 Commission
A JOINT APPEARANCE SEEMS APPROPRIATE...
MIKE LUCKOVICH
ATLANTA JOURNAL-CONSTITUTION
© AJC.com 4-2-04
CHENEY
W

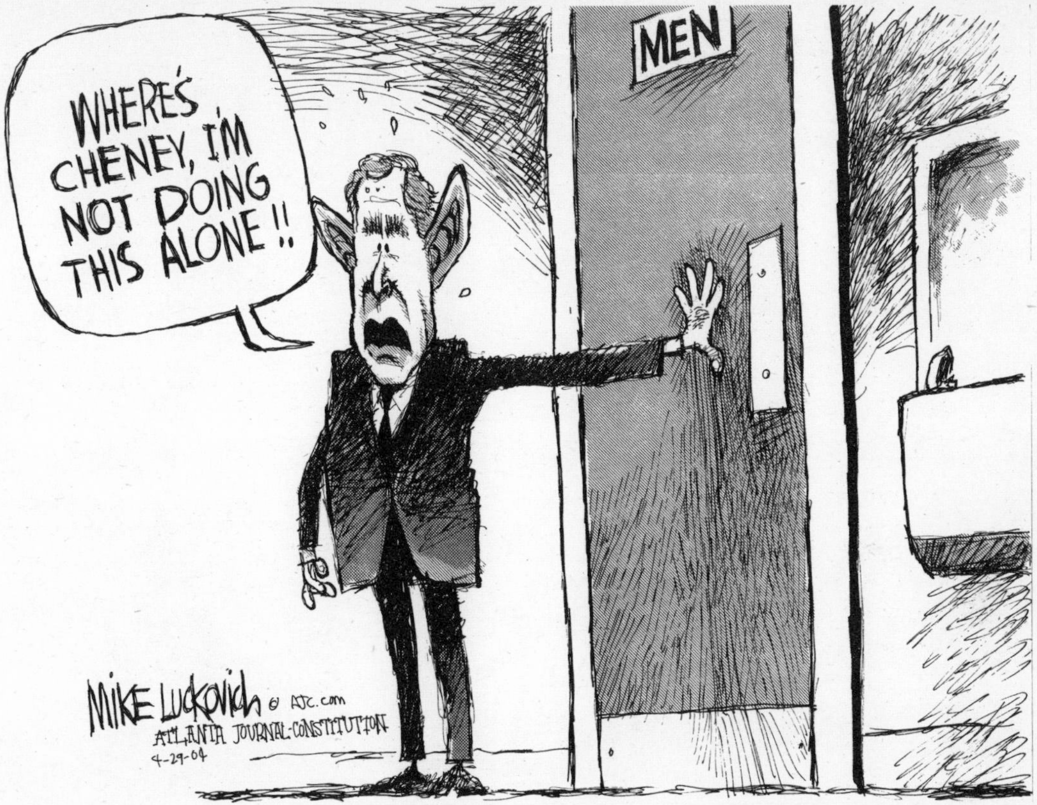
WHERE'S CHENEY, I'M NOT DOING THIS ALONE !!
MEN
MIKE LUCKOVICH © AJC.com
ATLANTA JOURNAL-CONSTITUTION
4-29-04

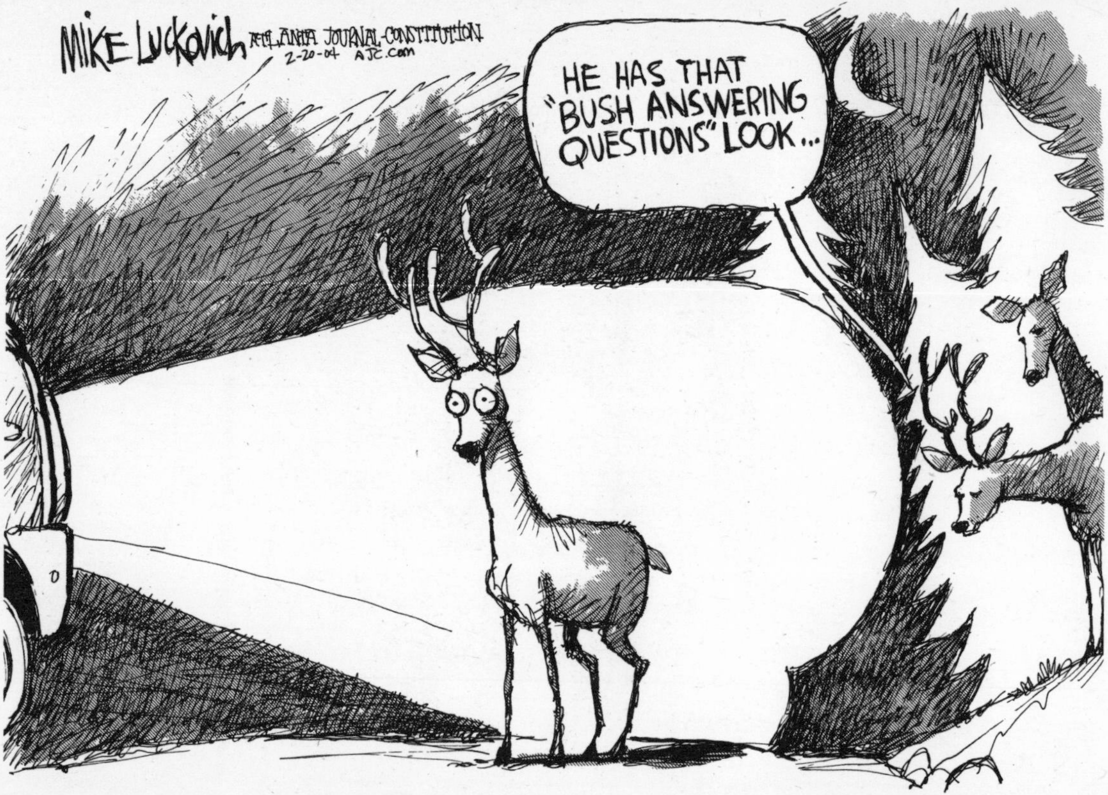
MIKE LUCKOVICH ATLANTA JOURNAL-CONSTITUTION
2-20-04 AJC.com
HE HAS THAT "BUSH ANSWERING QUESTIONS" LOOK...

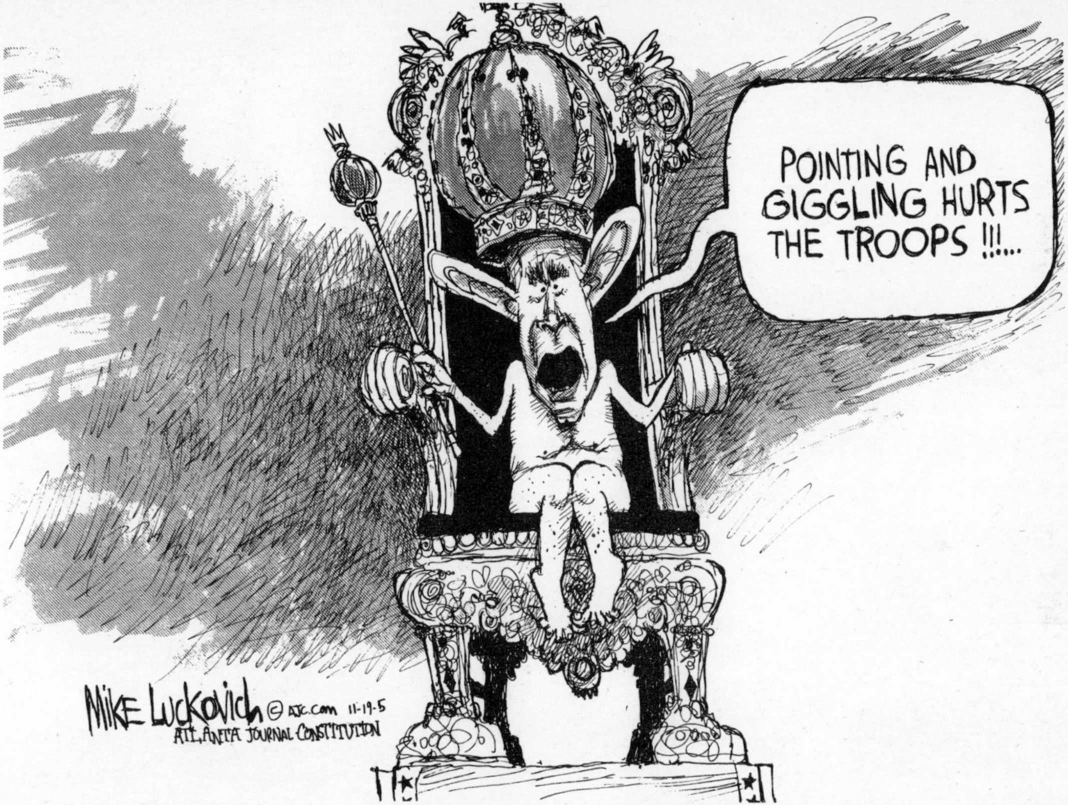
POINTING AND GIGGLING HURTS THE TROOPS !!!...
MIKE LUCKOVICH © AJC.com 11-19-5
ATLANTA JOURNAL-CONSTITUTION

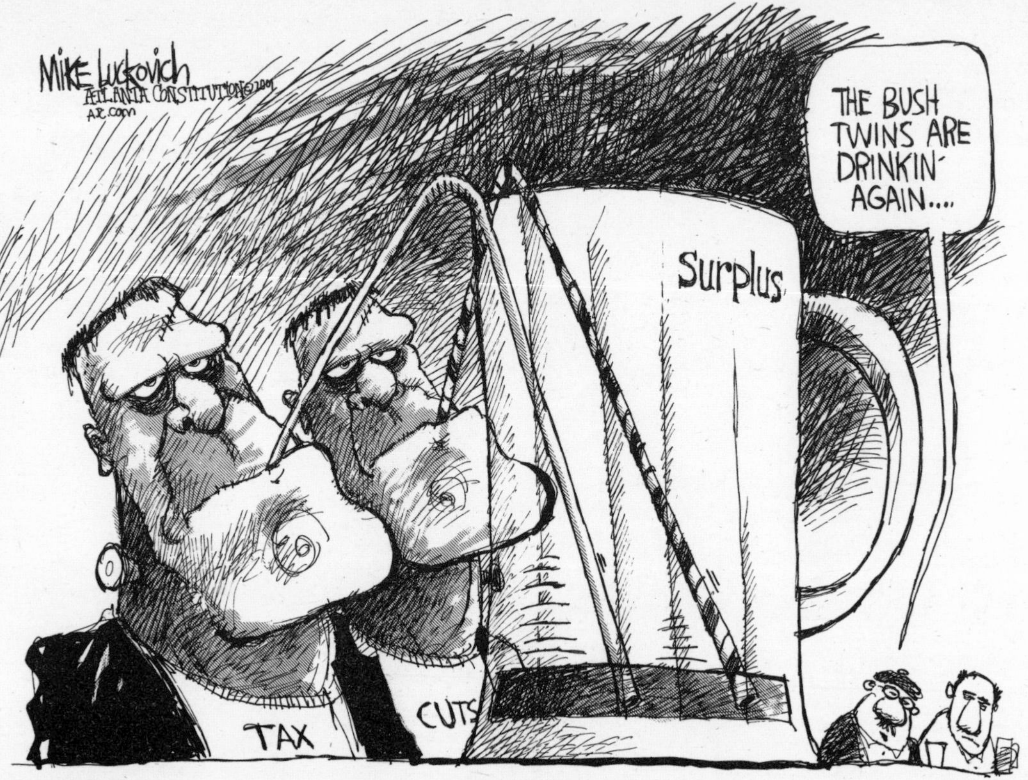
MIKE LUCKOVICH
ATLANTA CONSTITUTION ©2001
AJC.com
THE BUSH TWINS ARE DRINKIN' AGAIN....
Surplus
TAX
CUTS

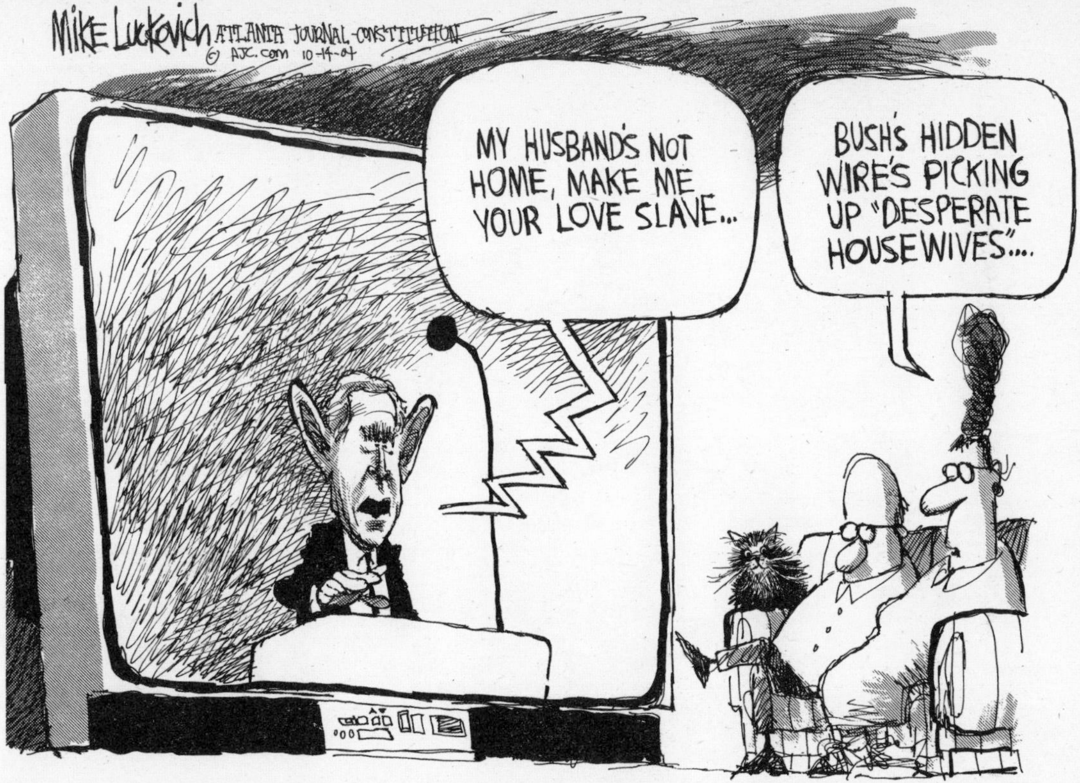
MIKE LUCKOVICH ATLANTA JOURNAL-CONSTITUTION
© AJC.COM 10-14-04
MY HUSBAND'S NOT HOME, MAKE ME YOUR LOVE SLAVE...
BUSH'S HIDDEN WIRE'S PICKING UP "DESPERATE HOUSEWIVES"....

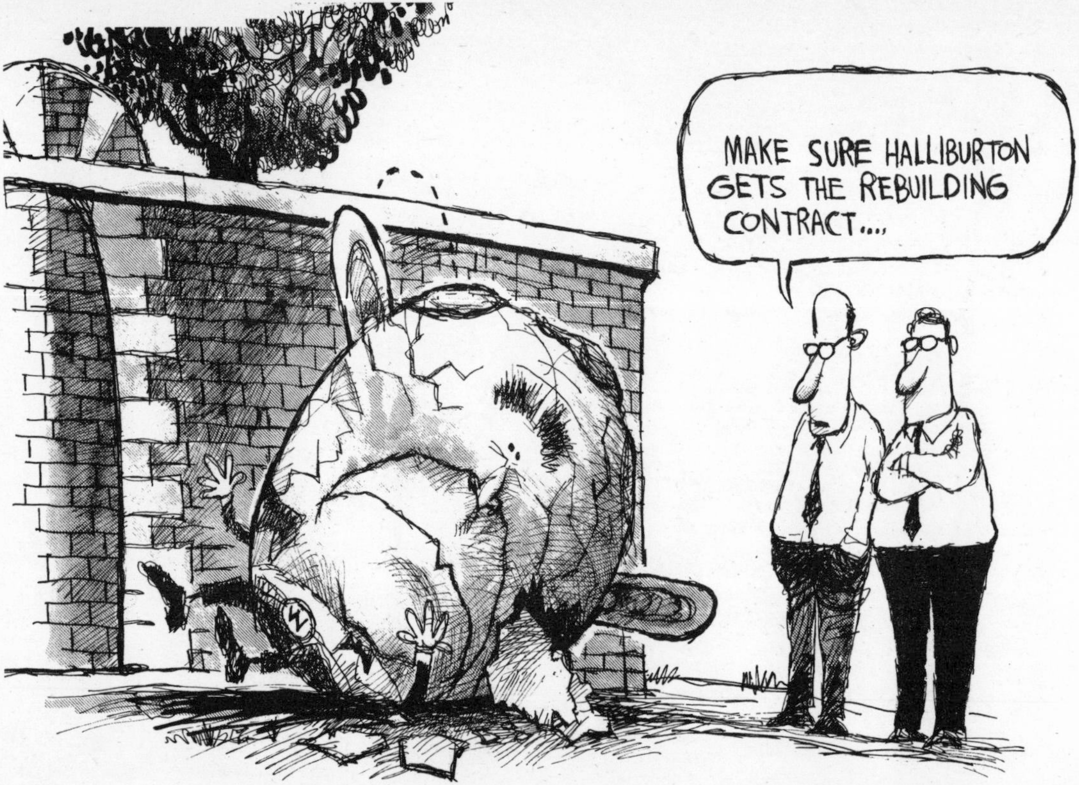
MAKE SURE HALLIBURTON GETS THE REBUILDING CONTRACT....

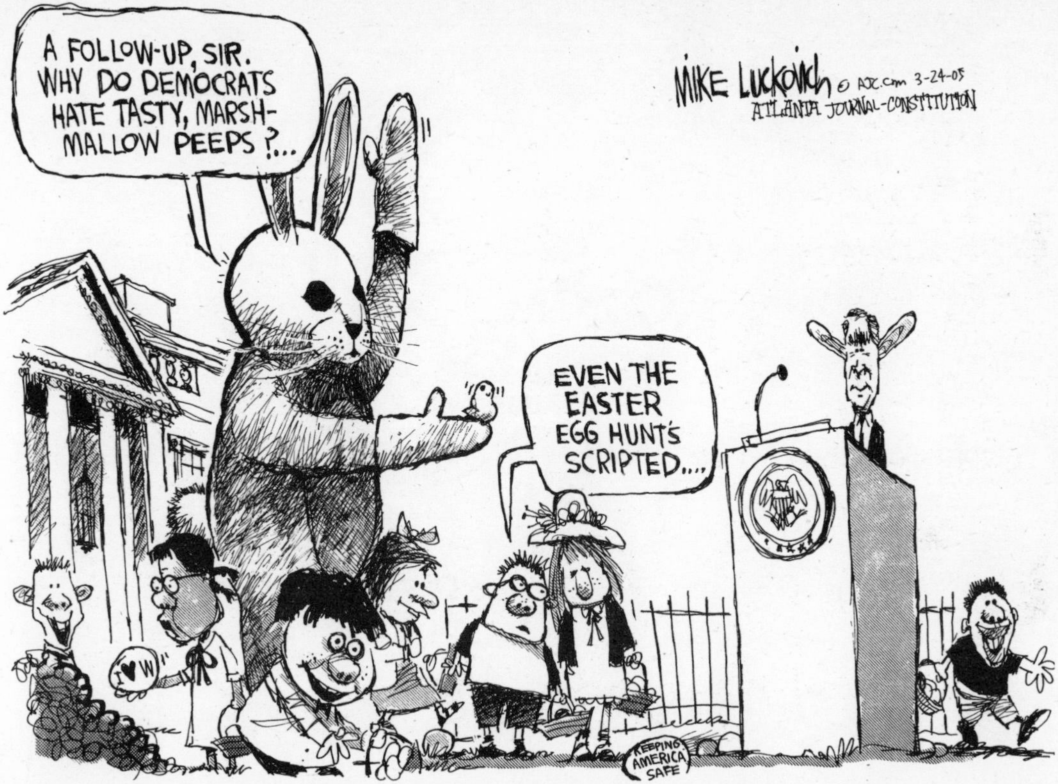
A FOLLOW-UP, SIR. WHY DO DEMOCRATS HATE TASTY, MARSH-MALLOW PEEPS?...
EVEN THE EASTER EGG HUNT'S SCRIPTED....
KEEPING AMERICA SAFE
I ♥ W
MIKE LUCKOVICH © AJC.Com 3-24-05
ATLANTA JOURNAL-CONSTITUTION

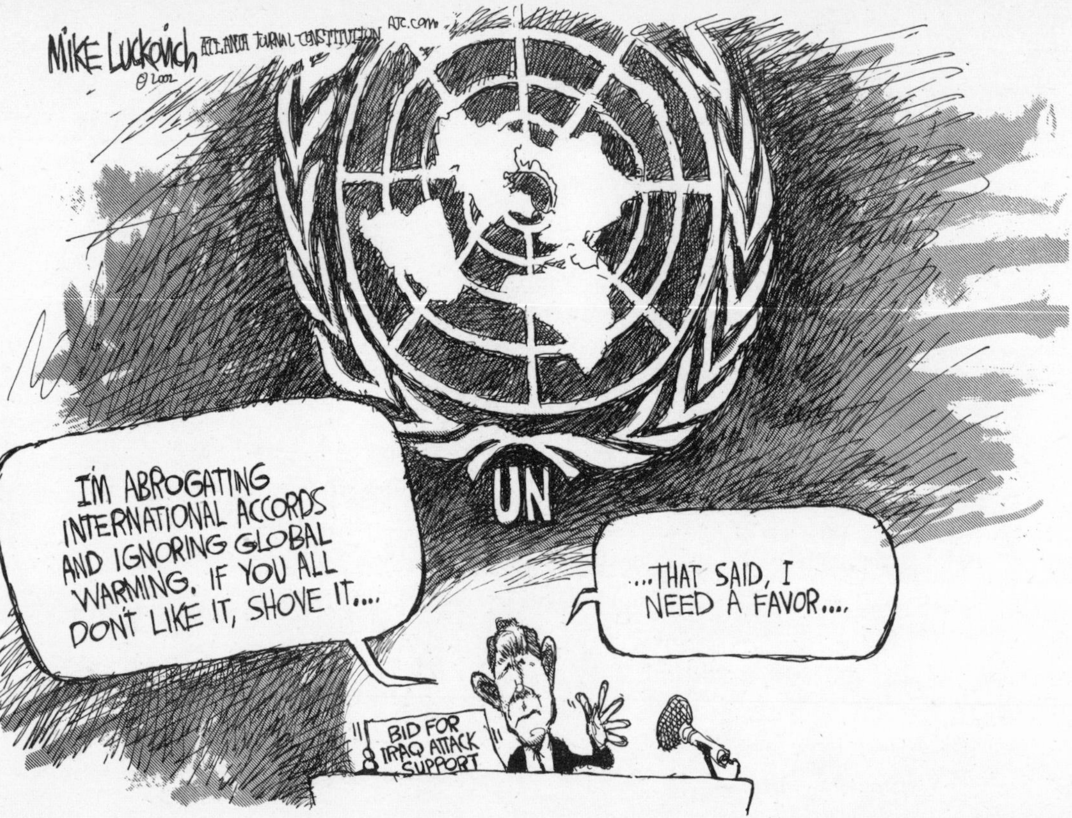
MIKE LUCKOVICH ATLANTA JOURNAL CONSTITUTION AJC.COM
©2002
UN
I'M ABROGATING INTERNATIONAL ACCORDS AND IGNORING GLOBAL WARMING. IF YOU ALL DON'T LIKE IT, SHOVE IT....
...THAT SAID, I NEED A FAVOR....
BID FOR IRAQ ATTACK SUPPORT

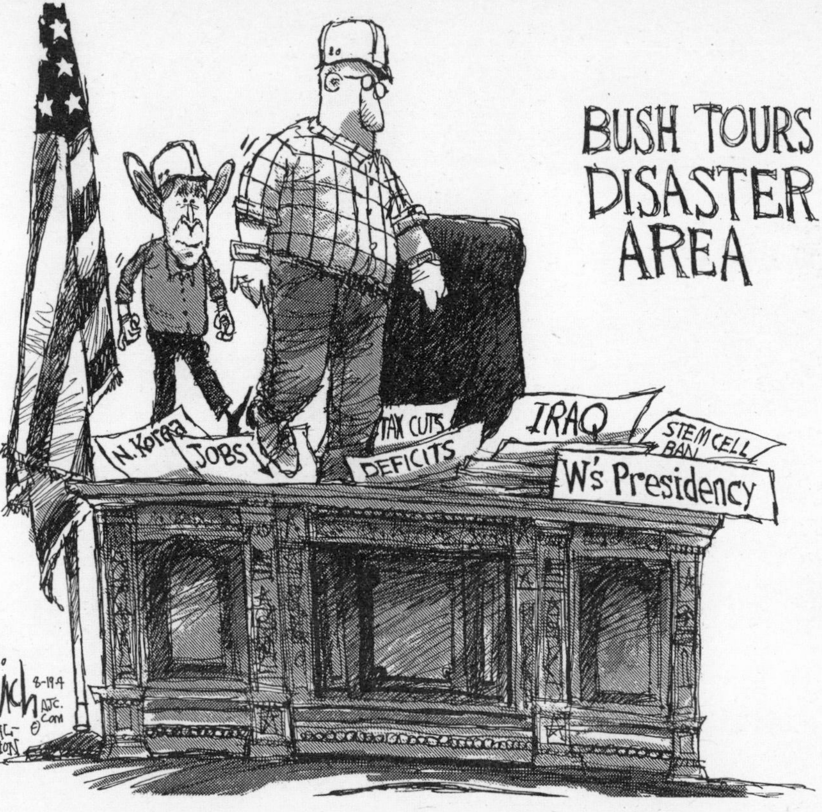
BUSH TOURS DISASTER AREA
N. Korea
JOBS
TAX CUTS
DEFICITS
IRAQ
STEM CELL BAN
W's Presidency
MIKE LUCKOVICH
ATLANTA JOURNAL-CONSTITUTION

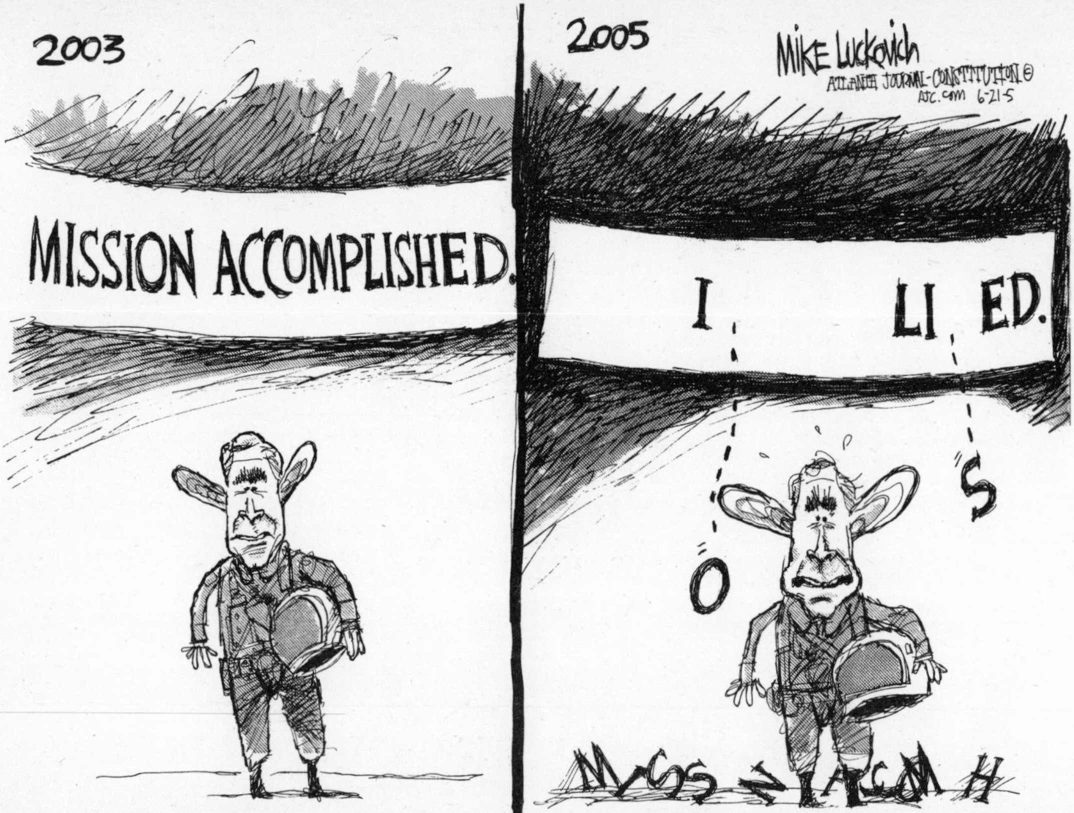
2003
MISSION ACCOMPLISHED.
2005
MIKE LUCKOVICH
ATLANTA JOURNAL-CONSTITUTION ©
AJC.com 6-21-5
I LI ED.
O
S

Dick Cheney

I love Cheney's certainty. He seems so completely confident and informed, there is no reason to doubt him, except that everything he says is completely wrong. There were no weapons of mass destruction. No links between Saddam and Osama. We weren't greeted as liberators and the insurgency isn't in its last throes. And after shooting his hunting buddy in the face, he claimed he'd bagged the world's largest quail.

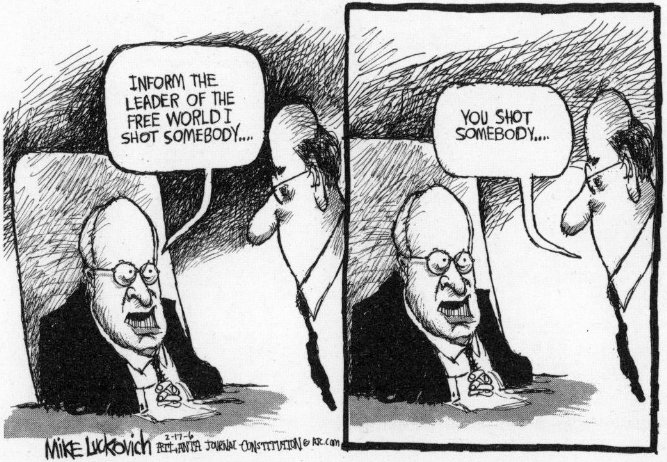
INFORM THE LEADER OF THE FREE WORLD I SHOT SOMEBODY....
YOU SHOT SOMEBODY....
MIKE LUCKOVICH
2-17-6
ATLANTA JOURNAL-CONSTITUTION

SORRY FOR SENDING YOUR KID TO FIGHT A FRAUDULENT WAR IN IRAQ
MIKE LUCKOVICH © ajc.com ATLANTA JOURNAL-CONSTITUTION 2-16-6
AND FOR OUR PATHETIC RESPONSE AS YOUR CITY, NEW ORLEANS, DROWNED
AND FOR ILLEGALLY TAPPING YOUR PHONE
...OH, AND FOR SHOOTING YOU....

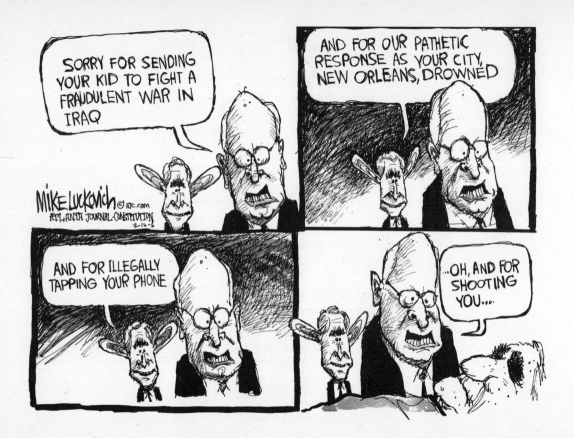

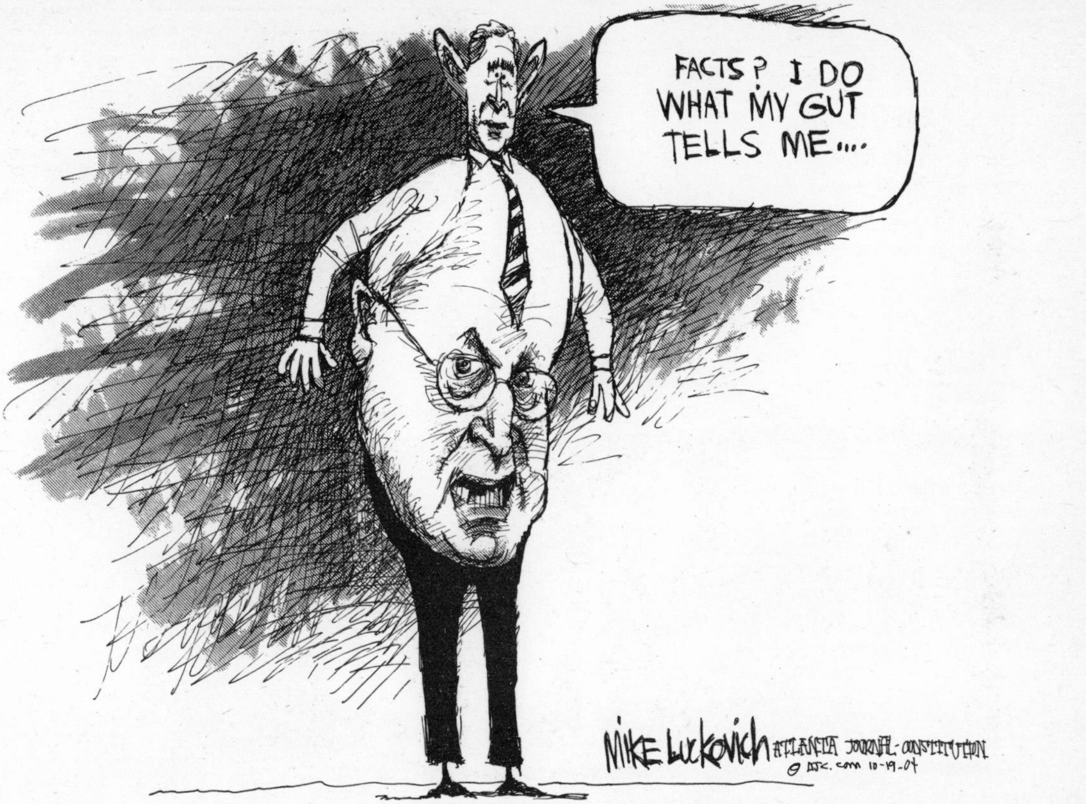
FACTS? I DO WHAT MY GUT TELLS ME....
MIKE LUCKOVICH ATLANTA JOURNAL-CONSTITUTION
© AJC.com 10-19-04

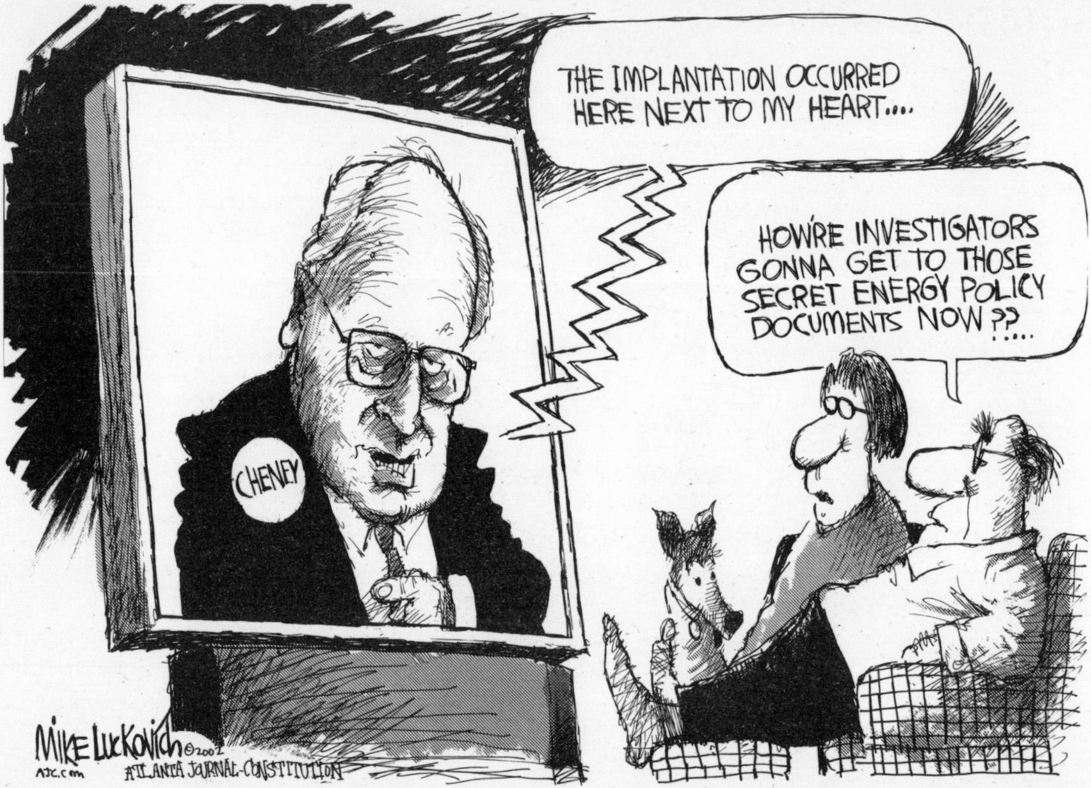
THE IMPLANTATION OCCURRED HERE NEXT TO MY HEART....
HOW'RE INVESTIGATORS GONNA GET TO THOSE SECRET ENERGY POLICY DOCUMENTS NOW??....
CHENEY
MIKE LUCKOVICH ©2001
AJC.com
ATLANTA JOURNAL-CONSTITUTION

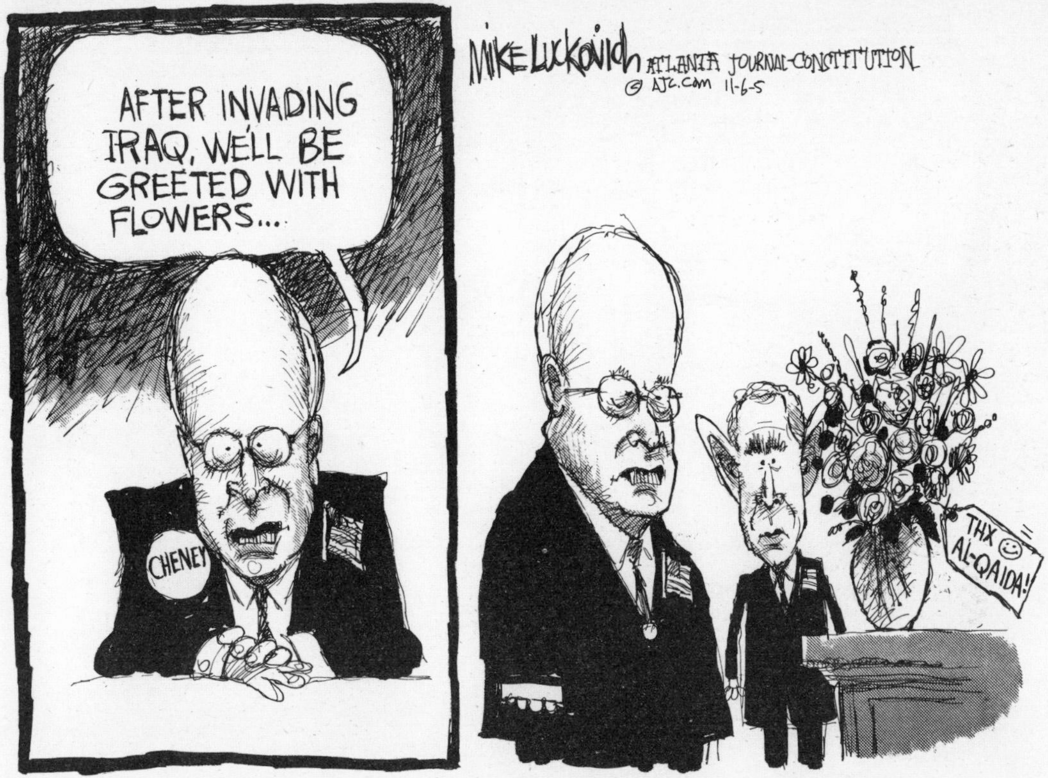
AFTER INVADING IRAQ, WE'LL BE GREETED WITH FLOWERS...
CHENEY
MIKE LUCKOVICH ATLANTA JOURNAL-CONSTITUTION
© AJC.com 11-6-5
THX ☺ AL-QAIDA!

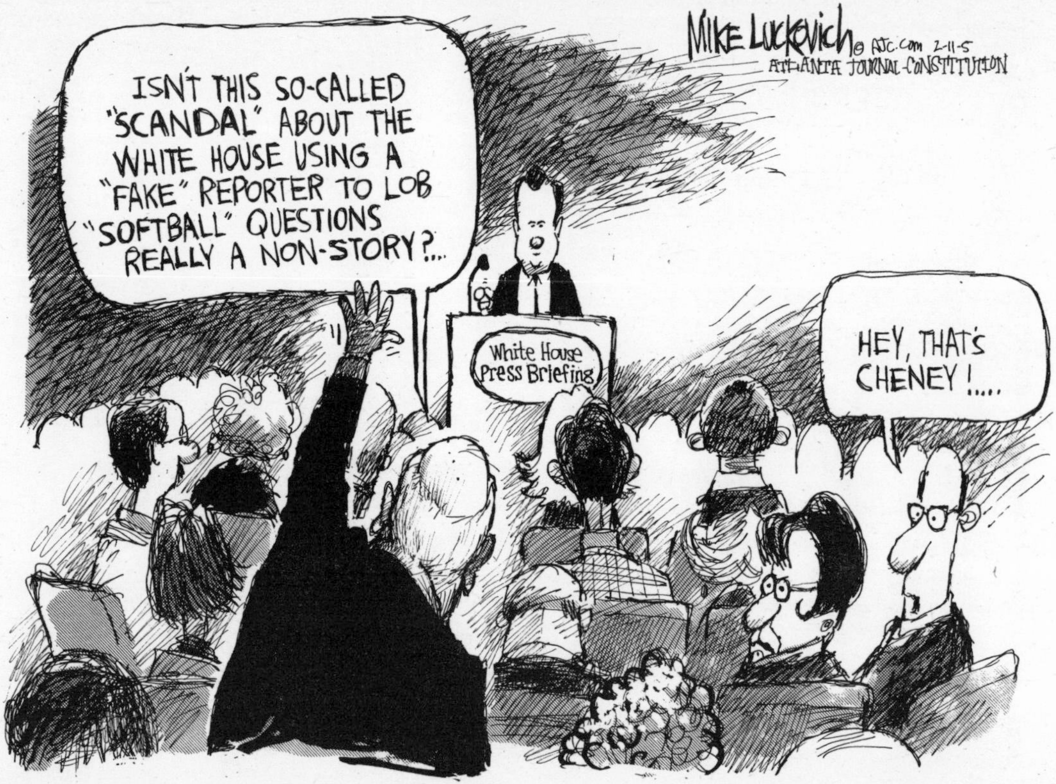
MIKE LUCKOVICH © AJC.com 2-11-5
ATLANTA JOURNAL-CONSTITUTION
ISN'T THIS SO-CALLED "SCANDAL" ABOUT THE WHITE HOUSE USING A "FAKE" REPORTER TO LOB "SOFTBALL" QUESTIONS REALLY A NON-STORY?...
White House Press Briefing
HEY, THAT'S CHENEY!....

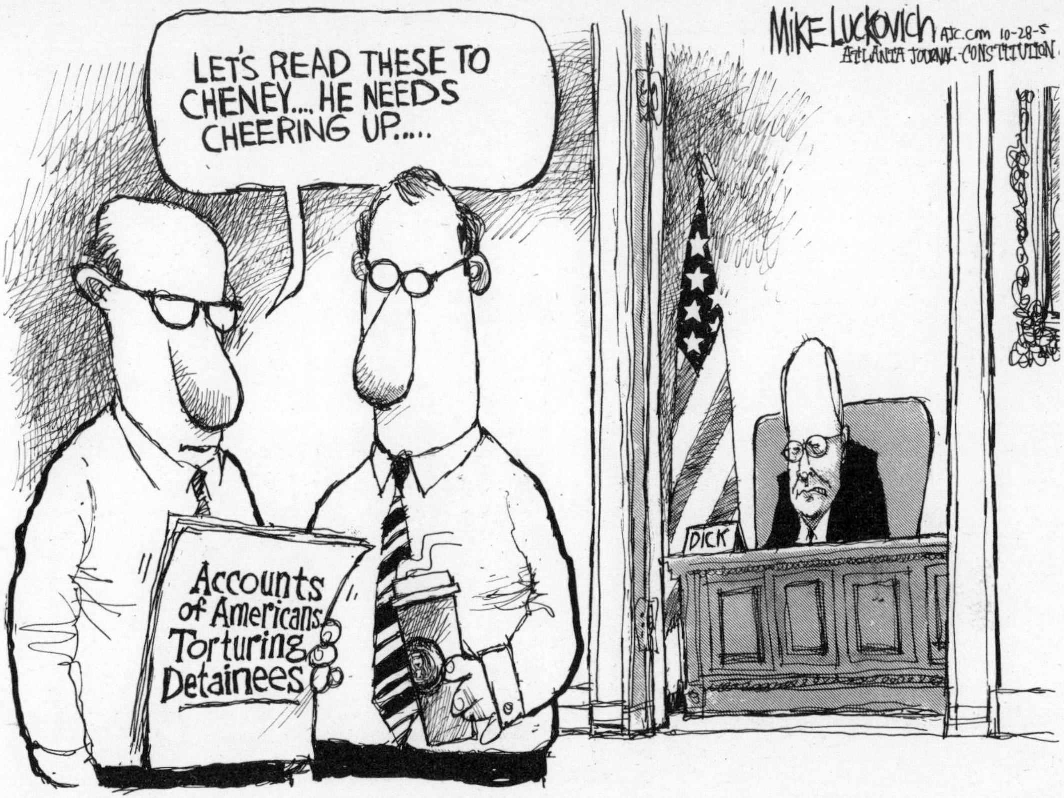
LET'S READ THESE TO CHENEY.... HE NEEDS CHEERING UP.....
MIKE LUCKOVICH AJC.com 10-28-5
ATLANTA JOURNAL-CONSTITUTION
DICK
Accounts of Americans Torturing Detainees

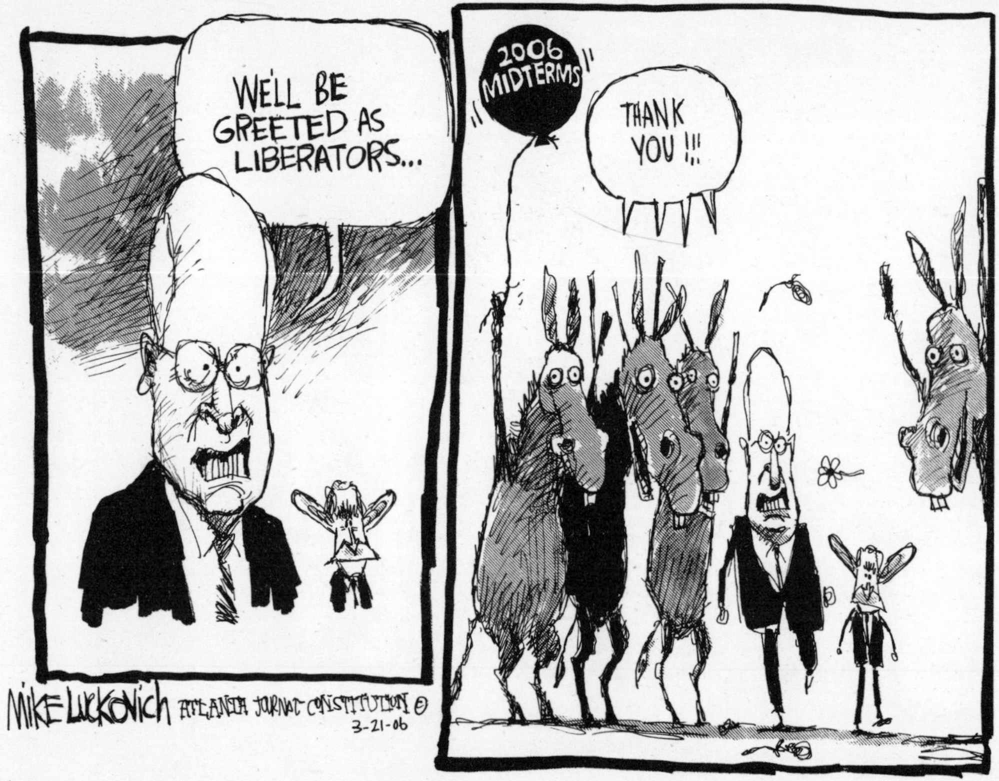
WE'LL BE GREETED AS LIBERATORS...
2006 MIDTERMS
THANK YOU !!!
MIKE LUCKOVICH ATLANTA JOURNAL CONSTITUTION ©
3-21-06

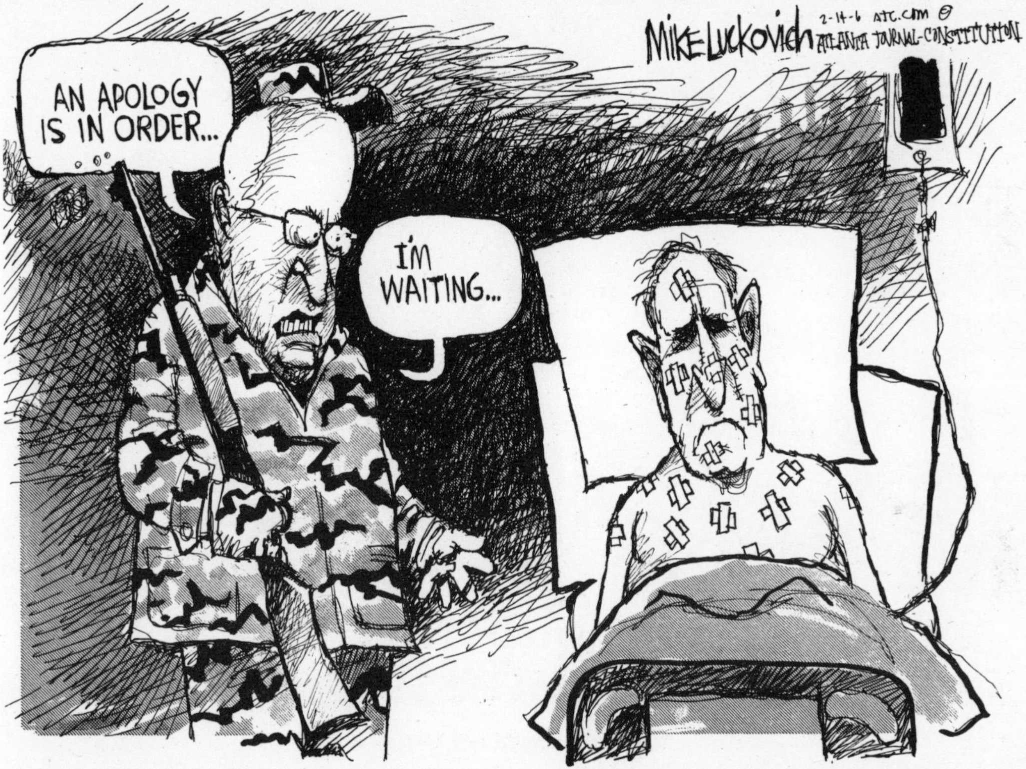
MIKE LUCKOVICH 2-14-6 AJC.com © ATLANTA JOURNAL-CONSTITUTION
AN APOLOGY IS IN ORDER...
I'M WAITING...

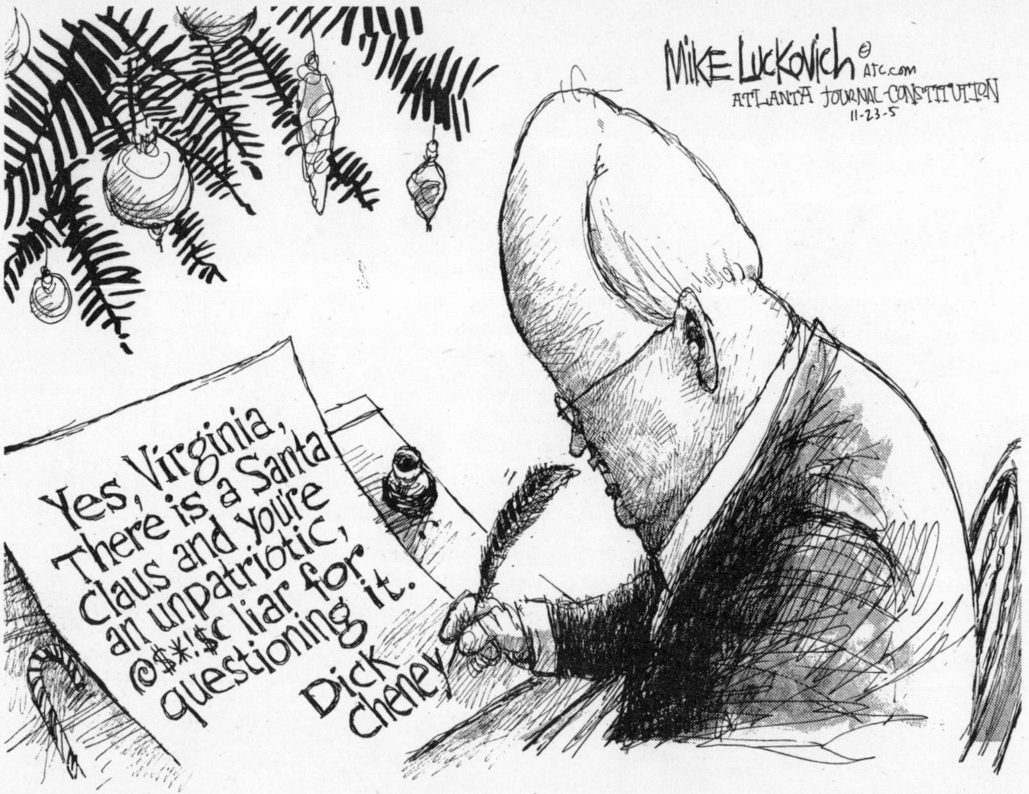
MIKE LUCKOVICH © AJC.com
ATLANTA JOURNAL-CONSTITUTION
11-23-5
Yes, Virginia, There is a Santa Claus and you're an unpatriotic, @$*!$c liar for questioning it.
Dick Cheney

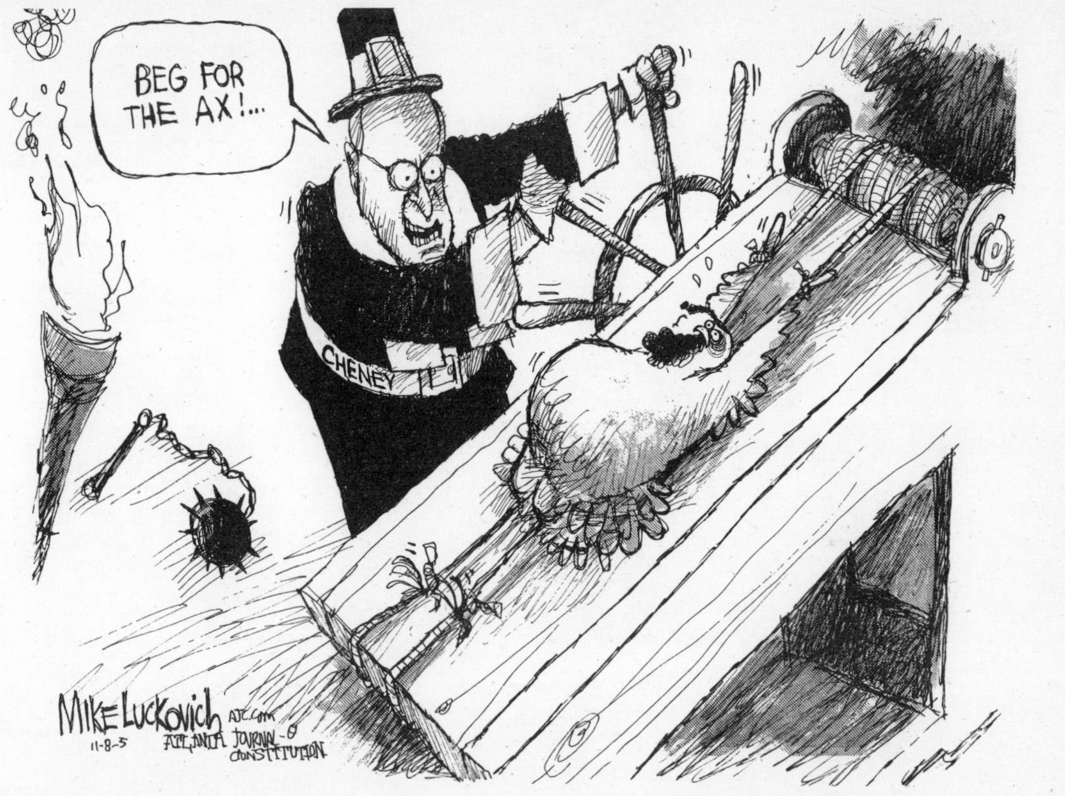
BEG FOR THE AX!...
CHENEY
MIKE LUCKOVICH AJC.com
11-8-5 ATLANTA JOURNAL-CONSTITUTION

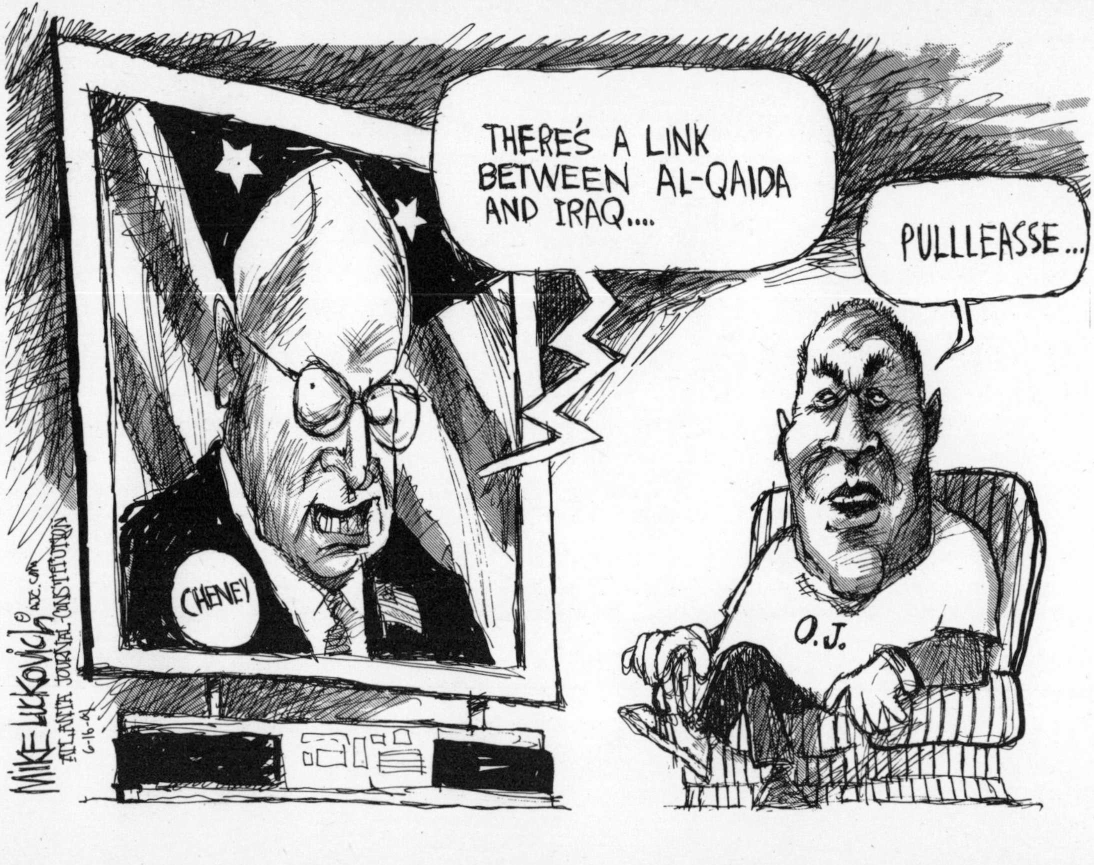
THERE'S A LINK BETWEEN AL-QAIDA AND IRAQ....
PULLLEASSE...
CHENEY
O.J.
MIKE LUCKOVICH © AJC.COM ATLANTA JOURNAL-CONSTITUTION 6-16-04

9-11

I try making points in my cartoons using humor. However, humor isn't appropriate when commenting on a tragedy. Especially one as horrific as 9-11. After watching the terrible events unfold on TV at home and then driving to my newspaper, I knew it was going to be a drawing challenge.

I spent all day trying to come up with an idea that reflected the shock, sorrow, and sadness we were all feeling. Finally, as it was getting close to my deadline, I thought of something and began drawing. A while later, my editor came by to see what I'd come up with. When he saw it, I could feel myself blushing from embarrassment, because I hated the cartoon. Here, the most important event I'd ever drawn a cartoon about and I failed. After arriving home, I showed my wife the cartoon. She liked it. The next day it ran in my newspaper and readers began calling and e-mailing saying the cartoon had moved them, which completely surprised me.

I ended up drawing the twin towers being hit by the second plane reflected in Lady Liberty's tear-filled eyes.

Within a day or two, my paper — in conjunction with Kroger supermarkets, which have a large presence in the Atlanta area — had printed full-color posters of the cartoon and were selling them at Kroger, which raised $250,000 for the 9-11 fund.

With an editorial cartoon, you have to make your statement using a single image. The reason I didn't initially like the cartoon was with so many different emotions going through me about what had happened, no single image would've satisfied me.

The next day, 9-12, was another challenge. I'd commented on the overall tragedy, so I narrowed my focus to various aspects of what we knew had occurred. I kept returning to those firefighters and police who had gone running up into those burning buildings to save lives.

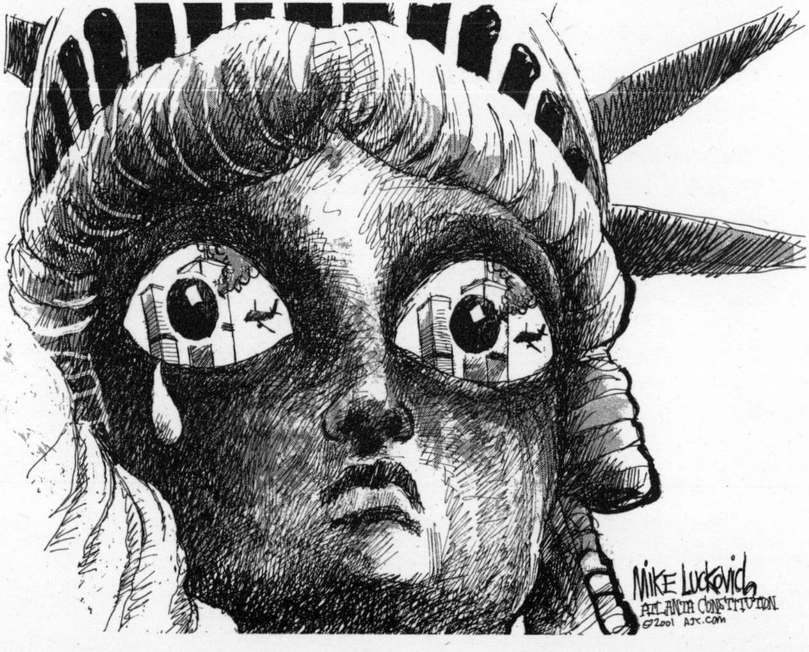
MIKE LUCKOVICH
ATLANTA CONSTITUTION
©2001 AJC.COM

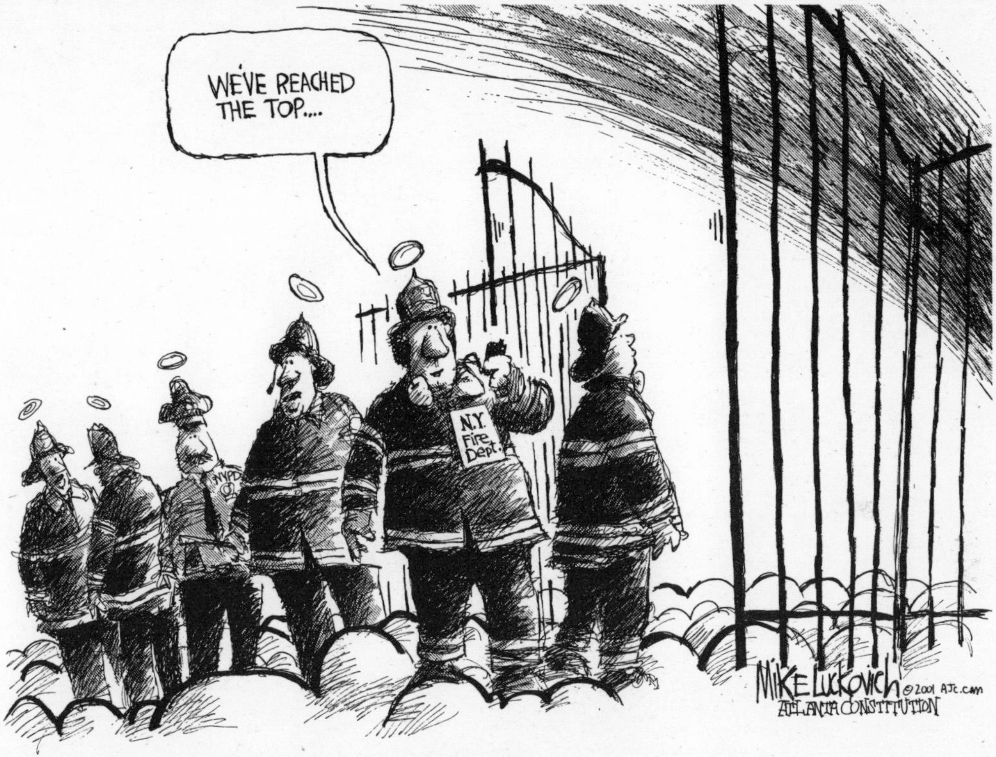
WE'VE REACHED THE TOP....
N.Y. Fire Dept.
NYPD
MIKE LUCKOVICH ©2001 AJC.com
ATLANTA CONSTITUTION

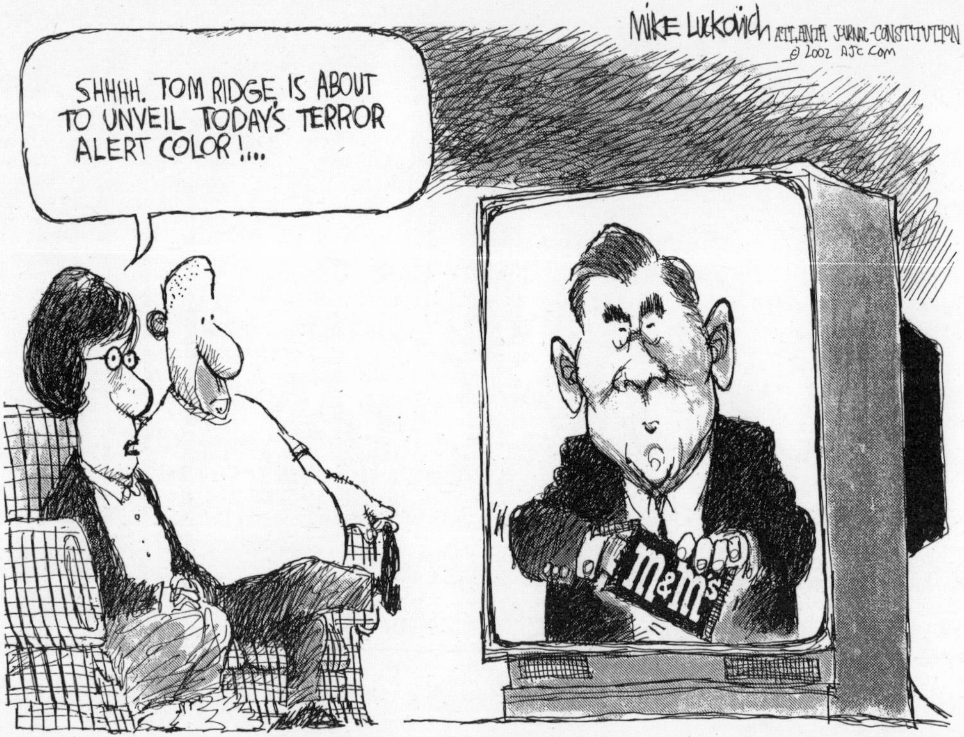
MIKE LUCKOVICH ATLANTA JOURNAL-CONSTITUTION
© 2002 AJC.com
SHHHH. TOM RIDGE IS ABOUT TO UNVEIL TODAY'S TERROR ALERT COLOR!...
M&M's

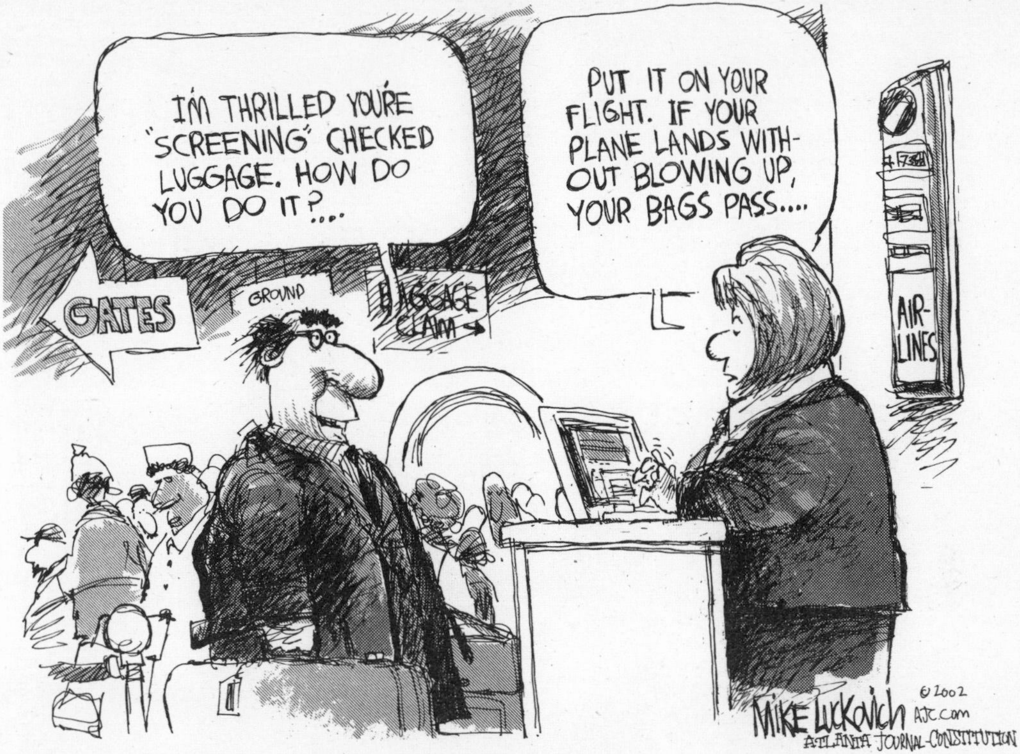
I'M THRILLED YOU'RE "SCREENING" CHECKED LUGGAGE. HOW DO YOU DO IT?....
PUT IT ON YOUR FLIGHT. IF YOUR PLANE LANDS WITHOUT BLOWING UP, YOUR BAGS PASS....
GATES
GROUND
BAGGAGE CLAIM
AIR-LINES
©2002
MIKE LUCKOVICH
AJC.com
ATLANTA JOURNAL-CONSTITUTION

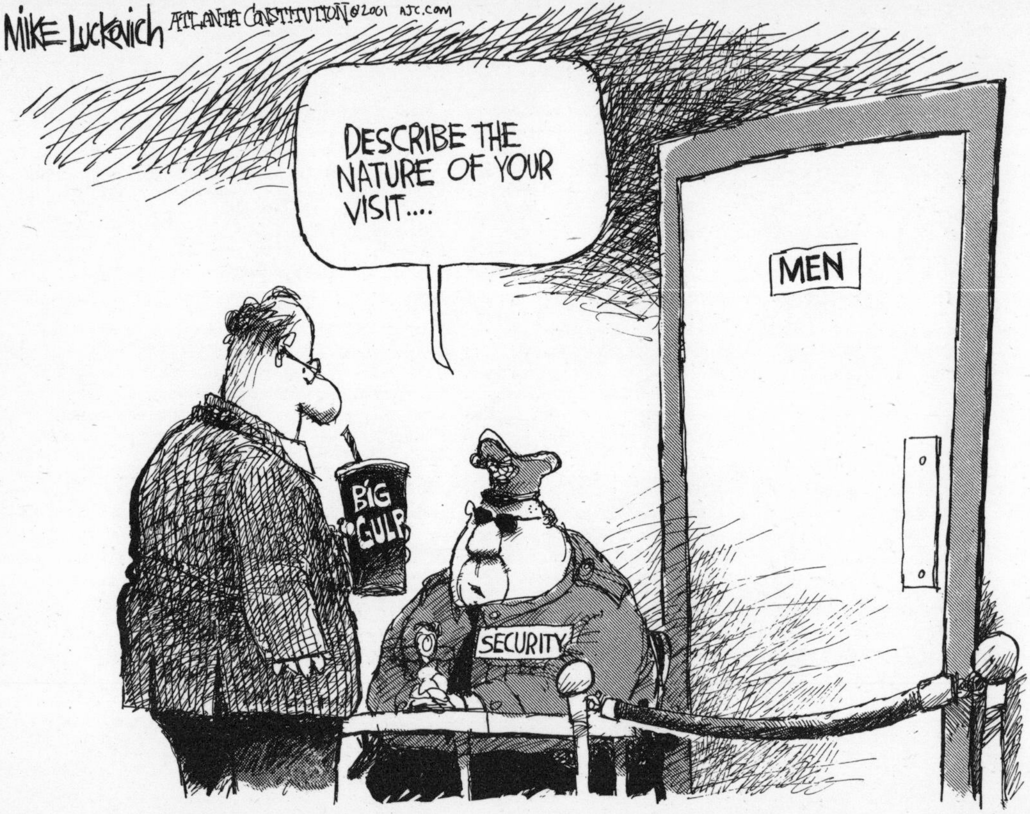
MIKE LUCKOVICH ATLANTA CONSTITUTION ©2001 AJC.COM
DESCRIBE THE NATURE OF YOUR VISIT....
MEN
BIG GULP
SECURITY

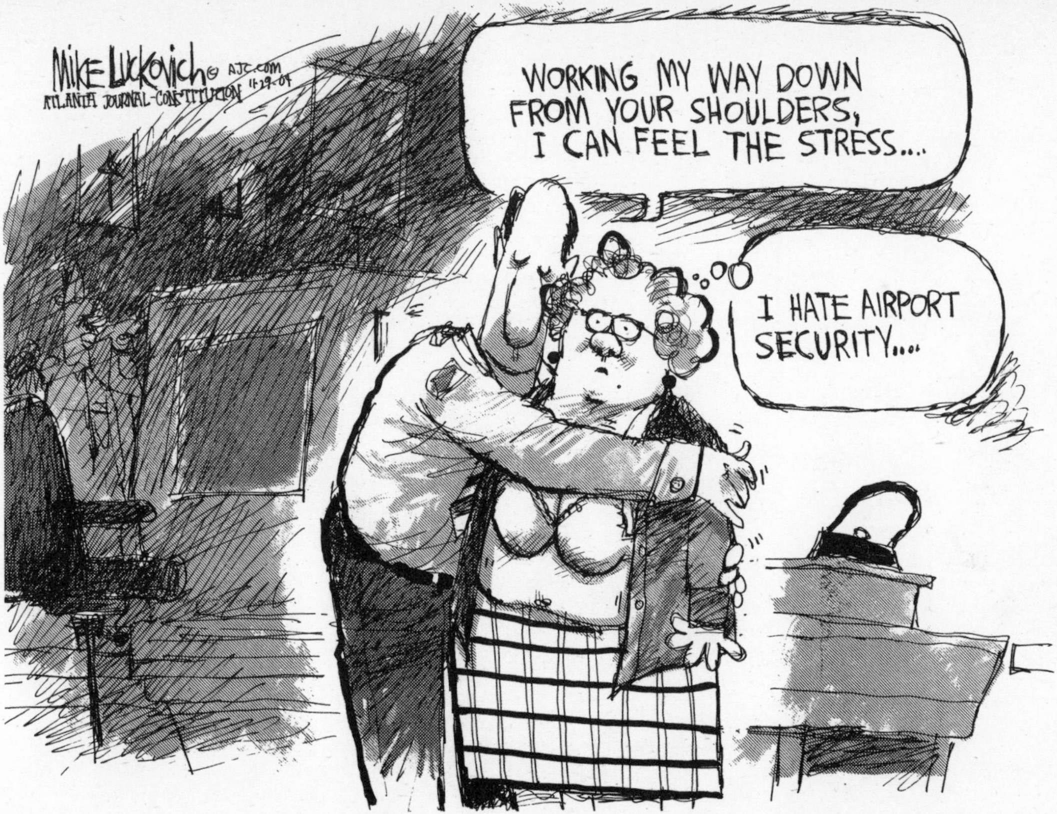
MIKE LUCKOVICH © AJC.COM 11-29-04
ATLANTA JOURNAL-CONSTITUTION
WORKING MY WAY DOWN FROM YOUR SHOULDERS, I CAN FEEL THE STRESS....
I HATE AIRPORT SECURITY....

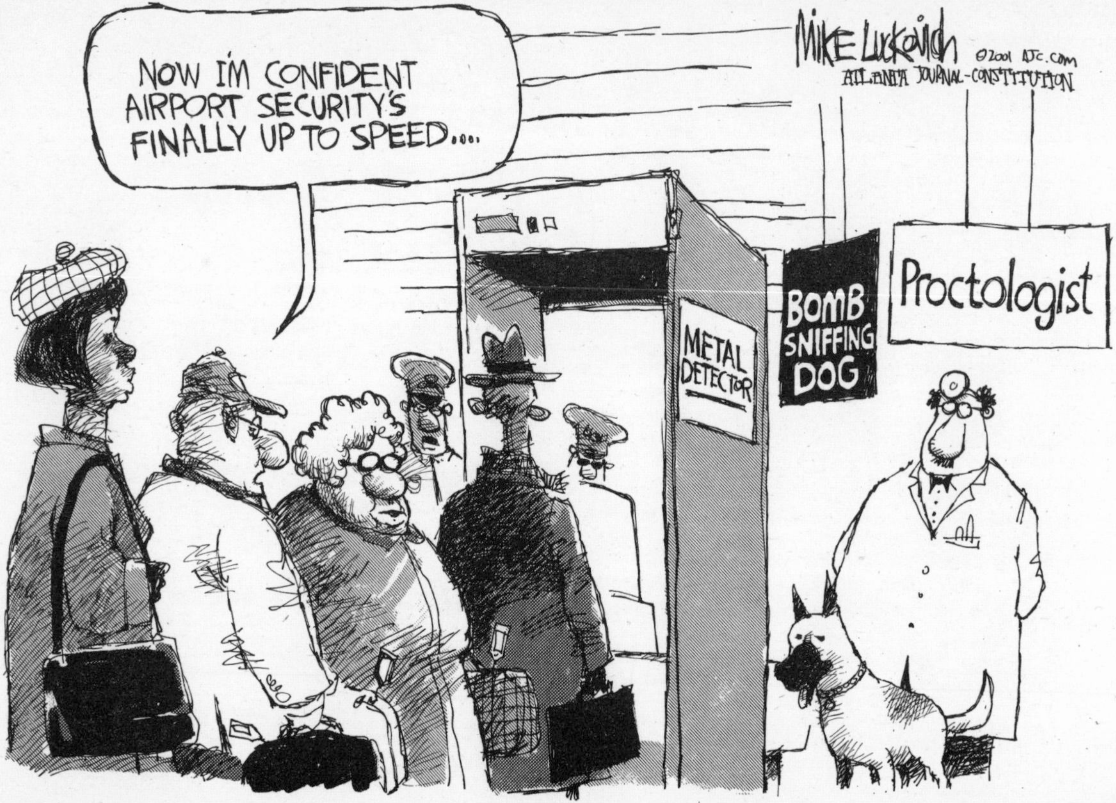
NOW I'M CONFIDENT AIRPORT SECURITY'S FINALLY UP TO SPEED....
MIKE LUCKOVICH ©2001 AJC.COM
ATLANTA JOURNAL-CONSTITUTION
METAL DETECTOR
BOMB SNIFFING DOG
Proctologist

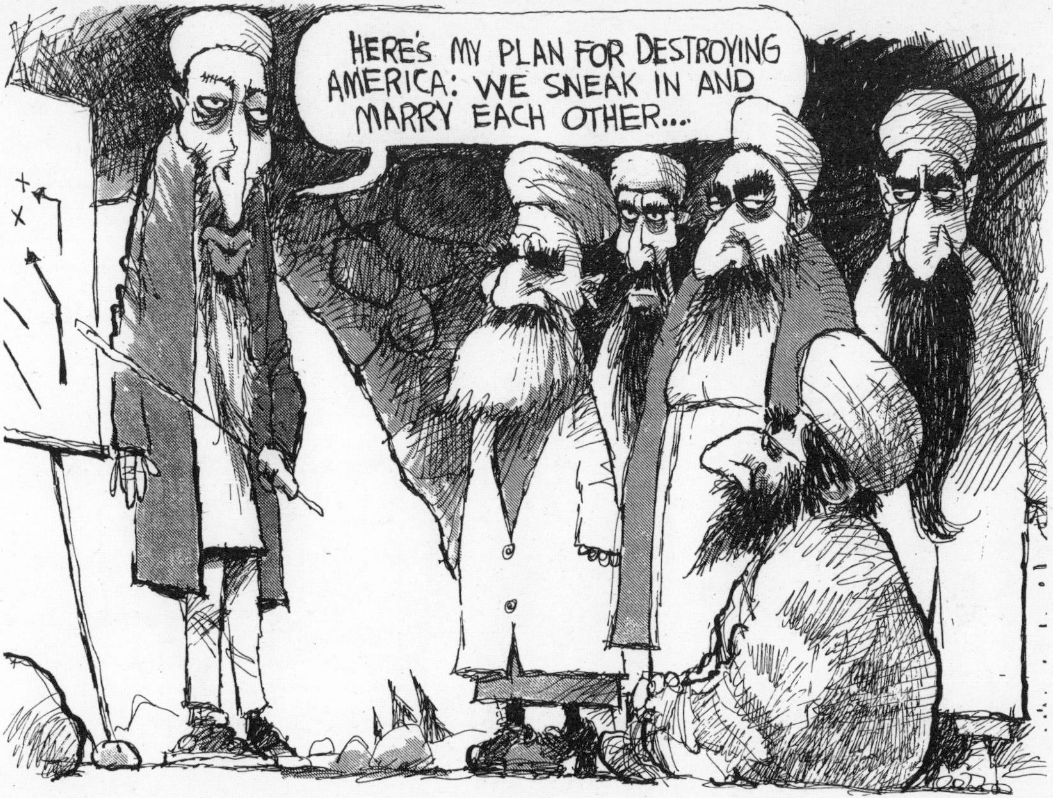
HERE'S MY PLAN FOR DESTROYING AMERICA: WE SNEAK IN AND MARRY EACH OTHER....

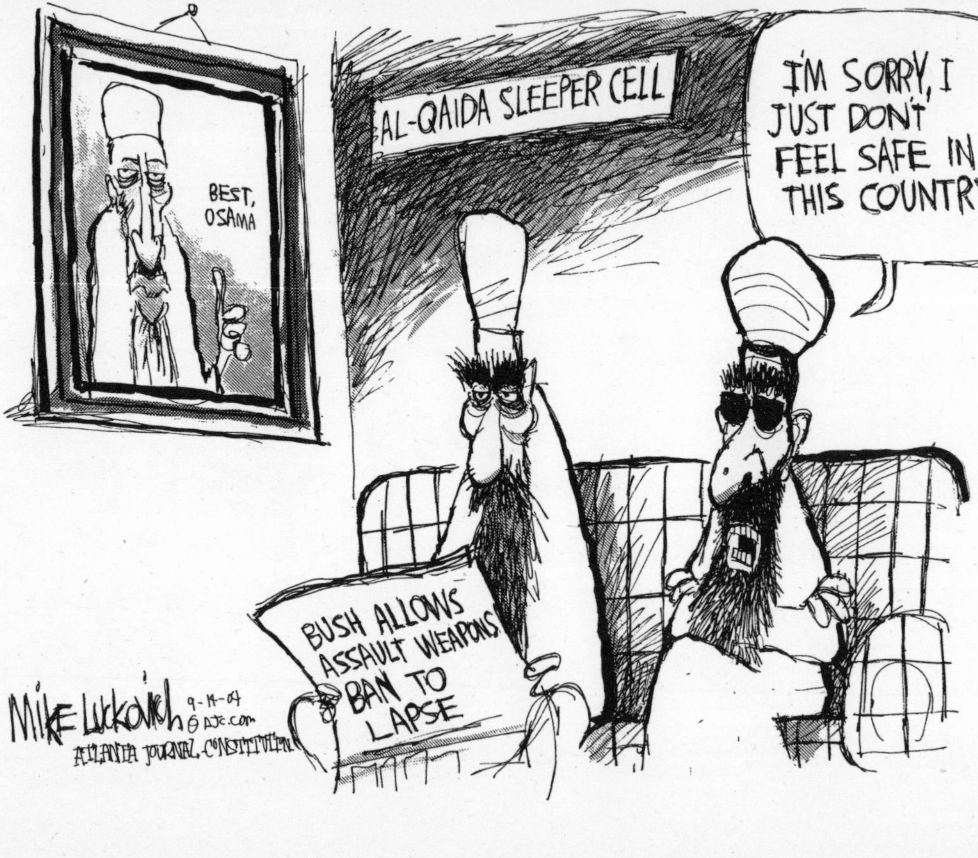
BEST, OSAMA
AL-QAIDA SLEEPER CELL
I'M SORRY, I JUST DON'T FEEL SAFE IN THIS COUNTRY....
BUSH ALLOWS ASSAULT WEAPONS BAN TO LAPSE
MIKE LUCKOVICH 9-14-04 © AJC.com
ATLANTA JOURNAL-CONSTITUTION

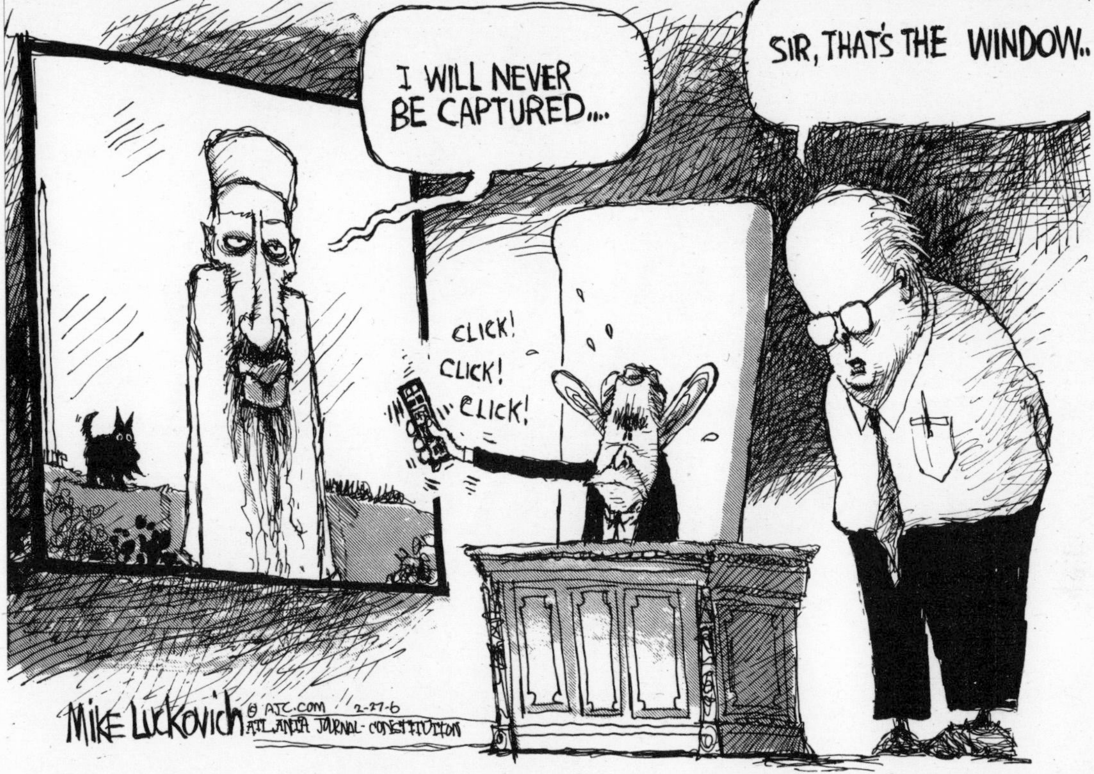
I WILL NEVER BE CAPTURED....
SIR, THAT'S THE WINDOW..
CLICK!
CLICK!
CLICK!
MIKE LUCKOVICH
© AJC.COM
2-27-6
ATLANTA JOURNAL-CONSTITUTION

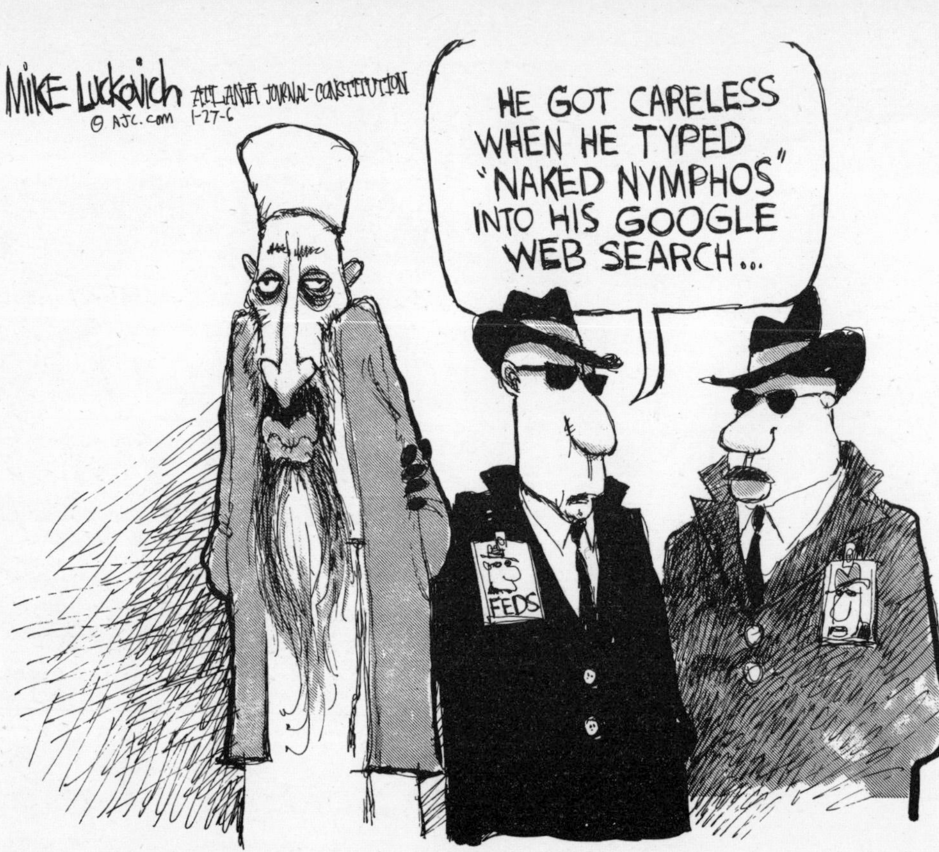
MIKE LUCKOVICH ATLANTA JOURNAL-CONSTITUTION
© AJC.com 1-27-6
HE GOT CARELESS WHEN HE TYPED "NAKED NYMPHOS" INTO HIS GOOGLE WEB SEARCH...
FEDS

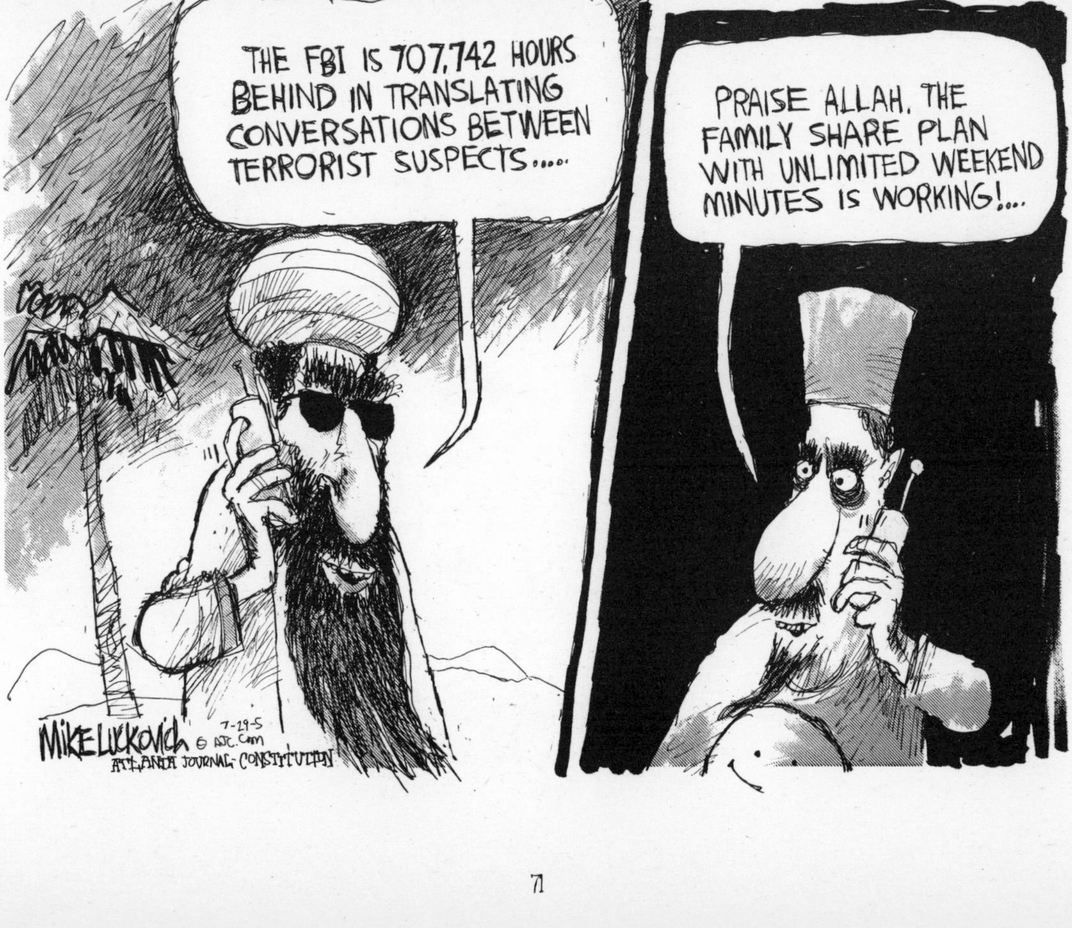
THE FBI IS 707,742 HOURS BEHIND IN TRANSLATING CONVERSATIONS BETWEEN TERRORIST SUSPECTS.....
PRAISE ALLAH. THE FAMILY SHARE PLAN WITH UNLIMITED WEEKEND MINUTES IS WORKING!...
MIKE LUCKOVICH
7-29-5
© AJC.Com
ATLANTA JOURNAL-CONSTITUTION

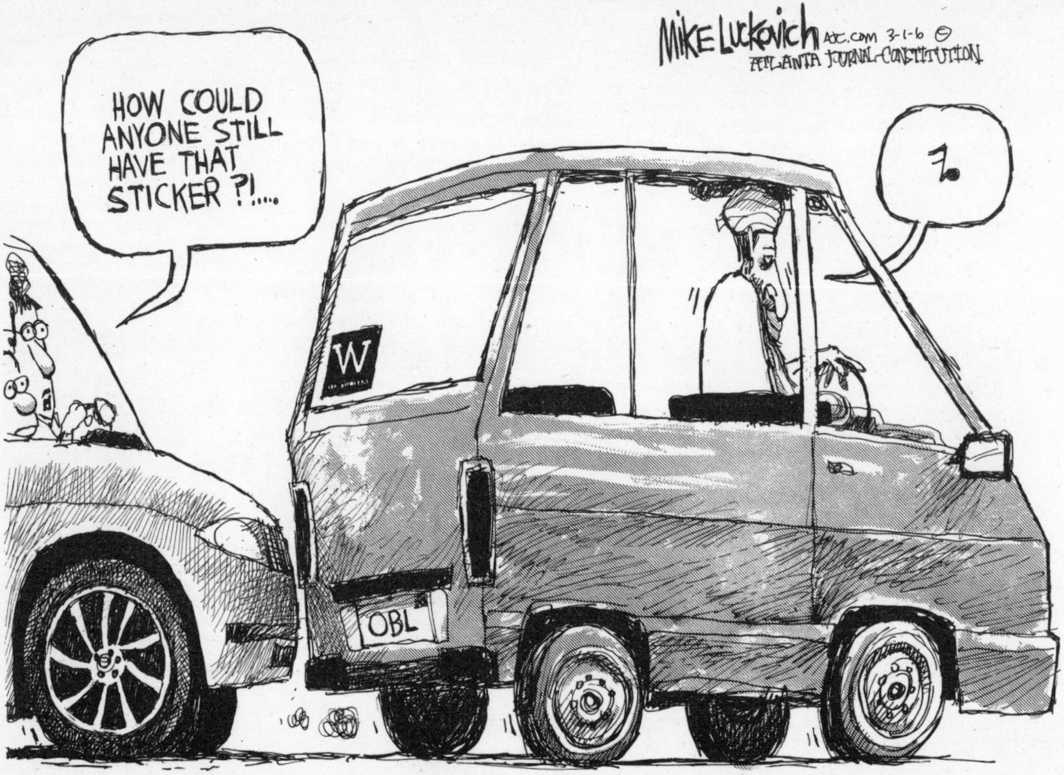
MIKE LUCKOVICH AJC.COM 3-1-6 ©
ATLANTA JOURNAL-CONSTITUTION
HOW COULD ANYONE STILL HAVE THAT STICKER ?!.....
Z
W
OBL

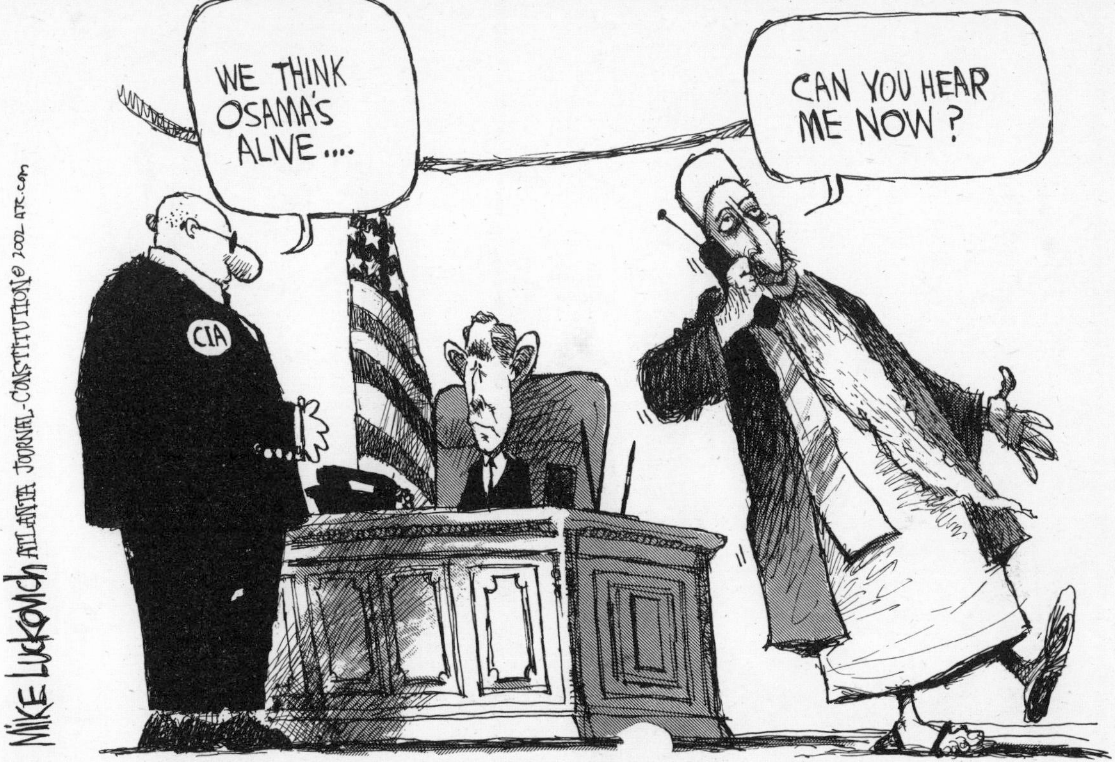
WE THINK OSAMA'S ALIVE....
CAN YOU HEAR ME NOW?
CIA
MIKE LUCKOVICH ATLANTA JOURNAL-CONSTITUTION © 2002 AJC.com

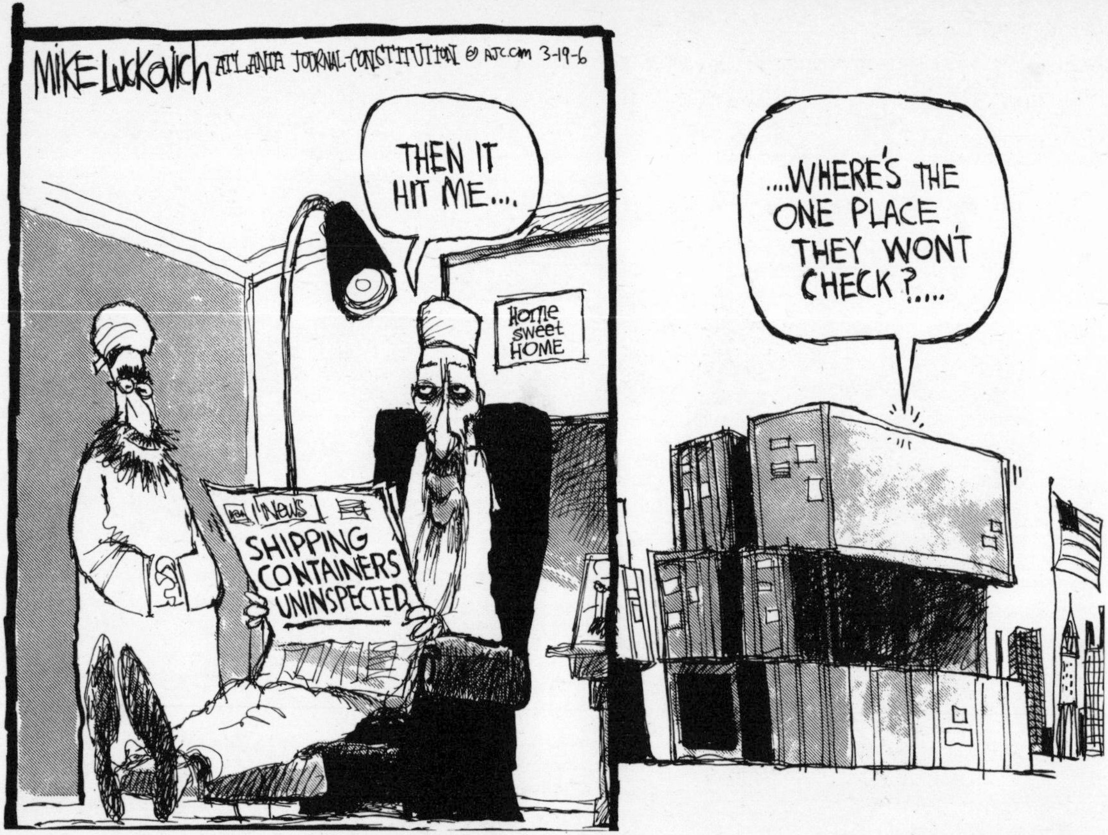
MIKE LUCKOVICH ATLANTA JOURNAL-CONSTITUTION © AJC.com 3-19-6
THEN IT HIT ME....
Home sweet HOME
NEWS
SHIPPING CONTAINERS UNINSPECTED
....WHERE'S THE ONE PLACE THEY WON'T CHECK?.....

The War on Terror

Drat! Early on, Bush let Osama escape from Tora Bora. But that's OK, Bush learns from his mistakes. He sent the U.S. military into Iraq, where they sit, going on four years now, all 135,000 of them, waiting for Bin Laden to get the hankering to visit Basra.

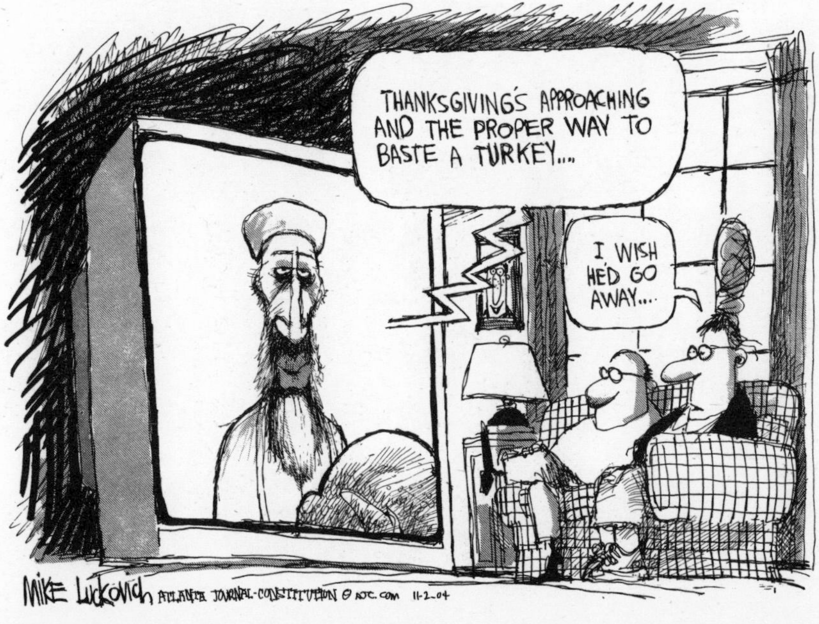
THANKSGIVING'S APPROACHING AND THE PROPER WAY TO BASTE A TURKEY....
I WISH HE'D GO AWAY....
MIKE LUCKOVICH ATLANTA JOURNAL-CONSTITUTION © AJC.COM 11-2-04

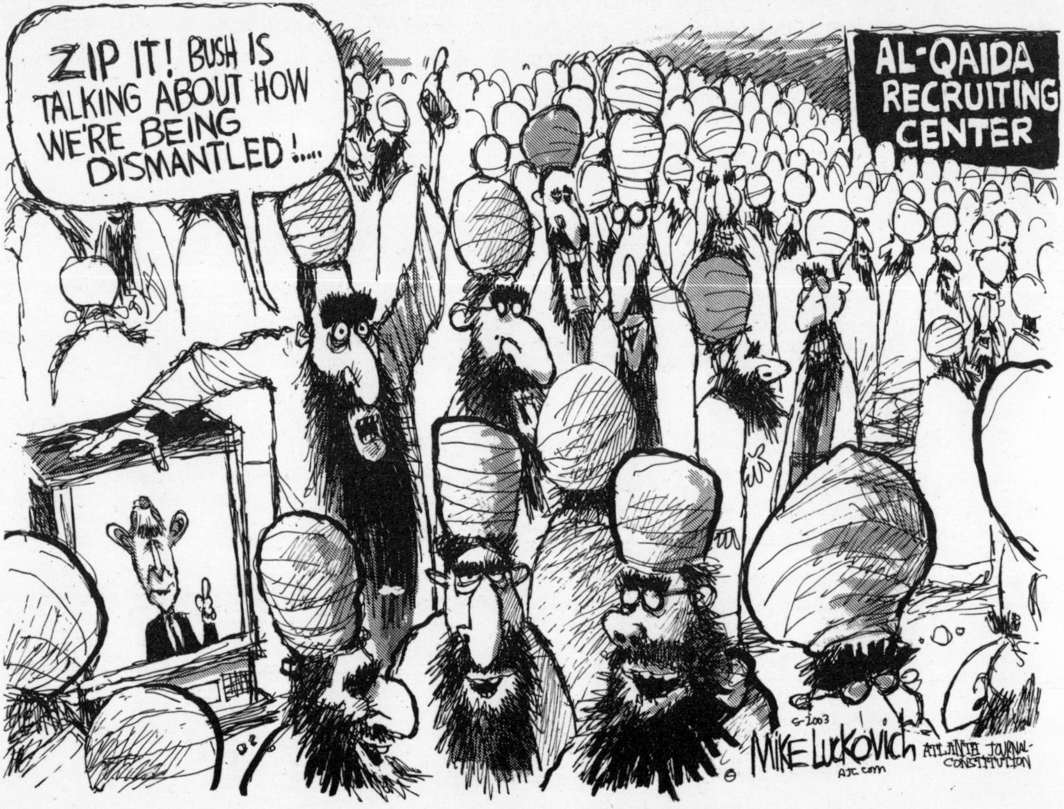
ZIP IT! BUSH IS TALKING ABOUT HOW WE'RE BEING DISMANTLED!....
AL-QAIDA RECRUITING CENTER
5-2003
MIKE LUCKOVICH
AJC.com
ATLANTA JOURNAL-CONSTITUTION

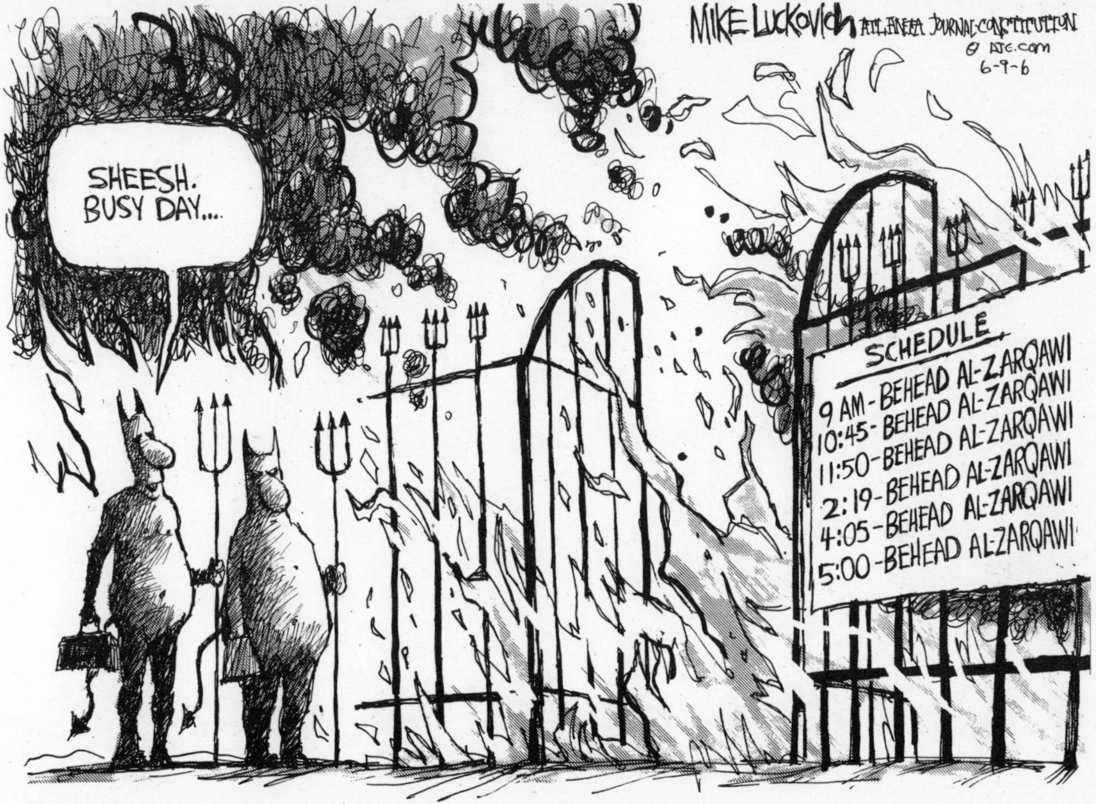
MIKE LUCKOVICH ATLANTA JOURNAL-CONSTITUTION
AJC.com
6-9-6
SHEESH.
BUSY DAY....
SCHEDULE
9 AM - BEHEAD AL-ZARQAWI
10:45 - BEHEAD AL-ZARQAWI
11:50 - BEHEAD AL-ZARQAWI
2:19 - BEHEAD AL-ZARQAWI
4:05 - BEHEAD AL-ZARQAWI
5:00 - BEHEAD AL-ZARQAWI

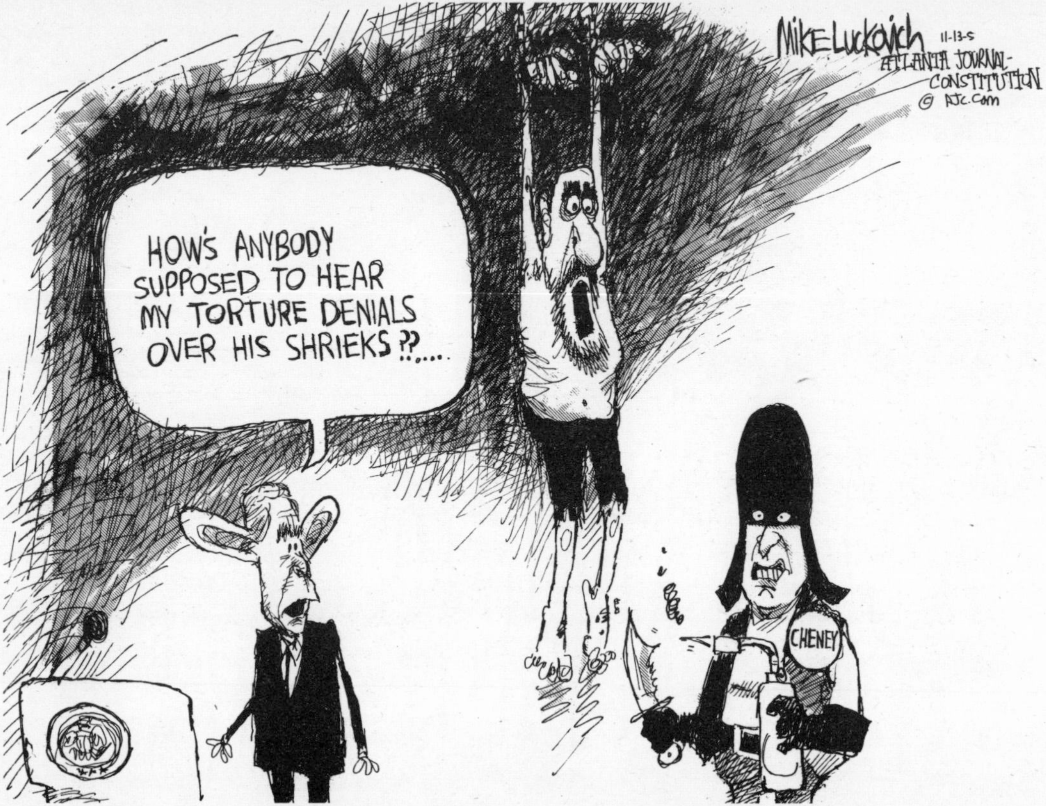
HOW'S ANYBODY SUPPOSED TO HEAR MY TORTURE DENIALS OVER HIS SHRIEKS ??.....
CHENEY
MIKE LUCKOVICH 11-13-5
ATLANTA JOURNAL-CONSTITUTION
© AJC.com

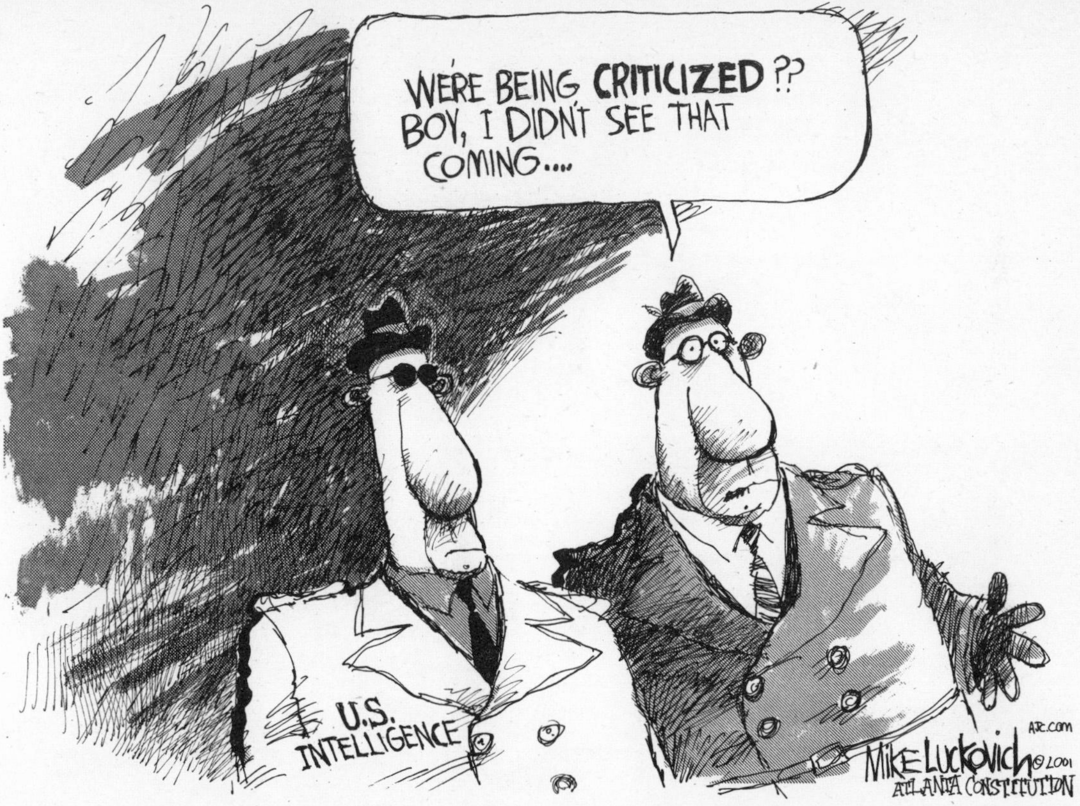
WE'RE BEING CRITICIZED ?? BOY, I DIDN'T SEE THAT COMING....
U.S. INTELLIGENCE
MIKE LUCKOVICH ©2001
ATLANTA CONSTITUTION
AJC.COM

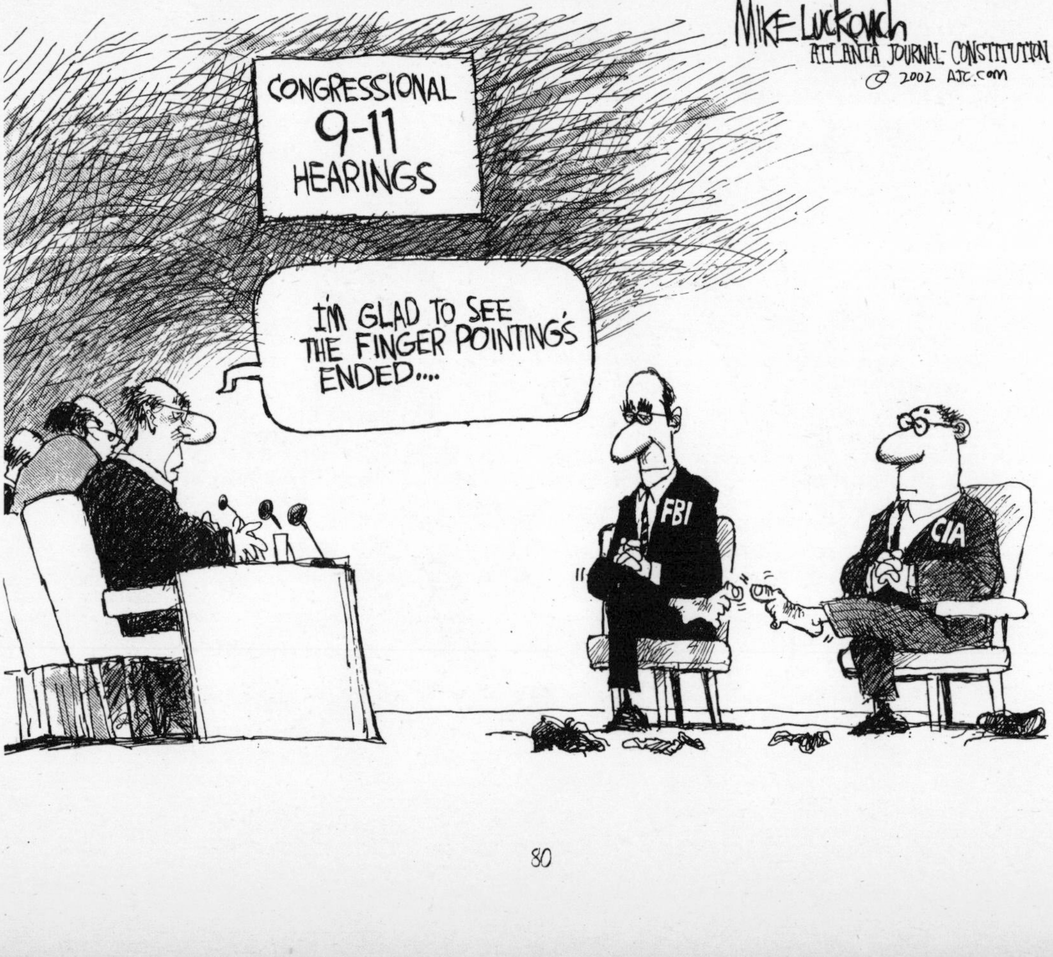
MIKE LUCKOVICH
ATLANTA JOURNAL-CONSTITUTION
© 2002 AJC.com
CONGRESSIONAL
9-11
HEARINGS
I'M GLAD TO SEE THE FINGER POINTING'S ENDED....
FBI
CIA

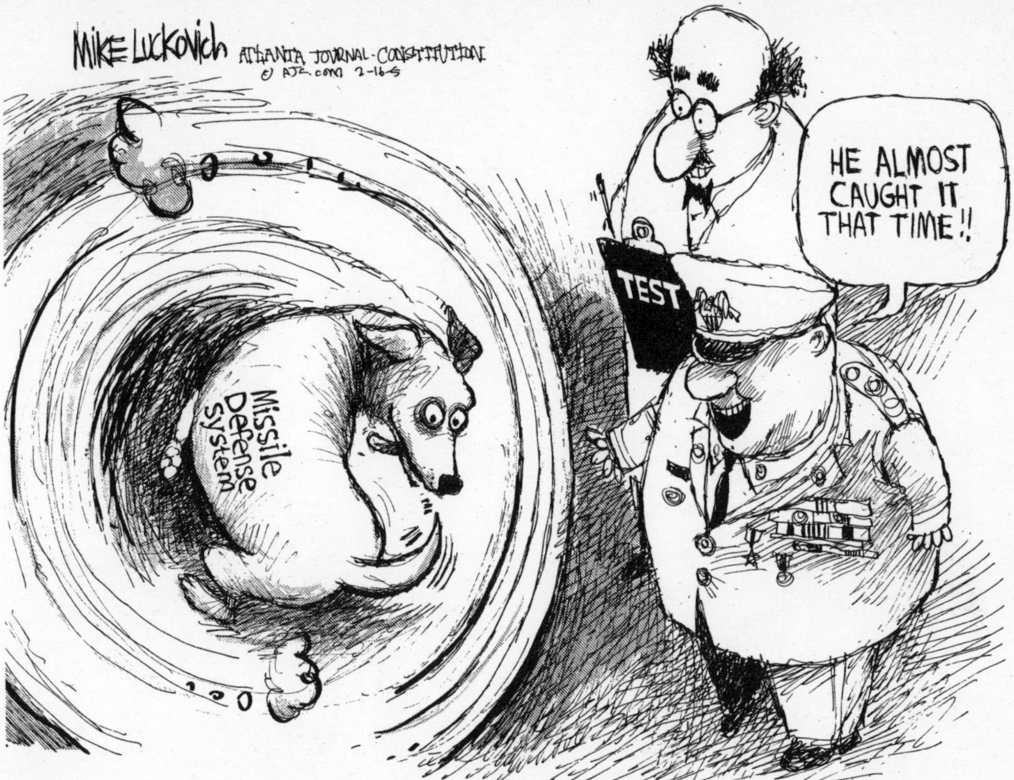
MIKE LUCKOVICH ATLANTA JOURNAL-CONSTITUTION
© AJC.com 2-16-5
Missile Defense System
TEST
HE ALMOST CAUGHT IT THAT TIME!!

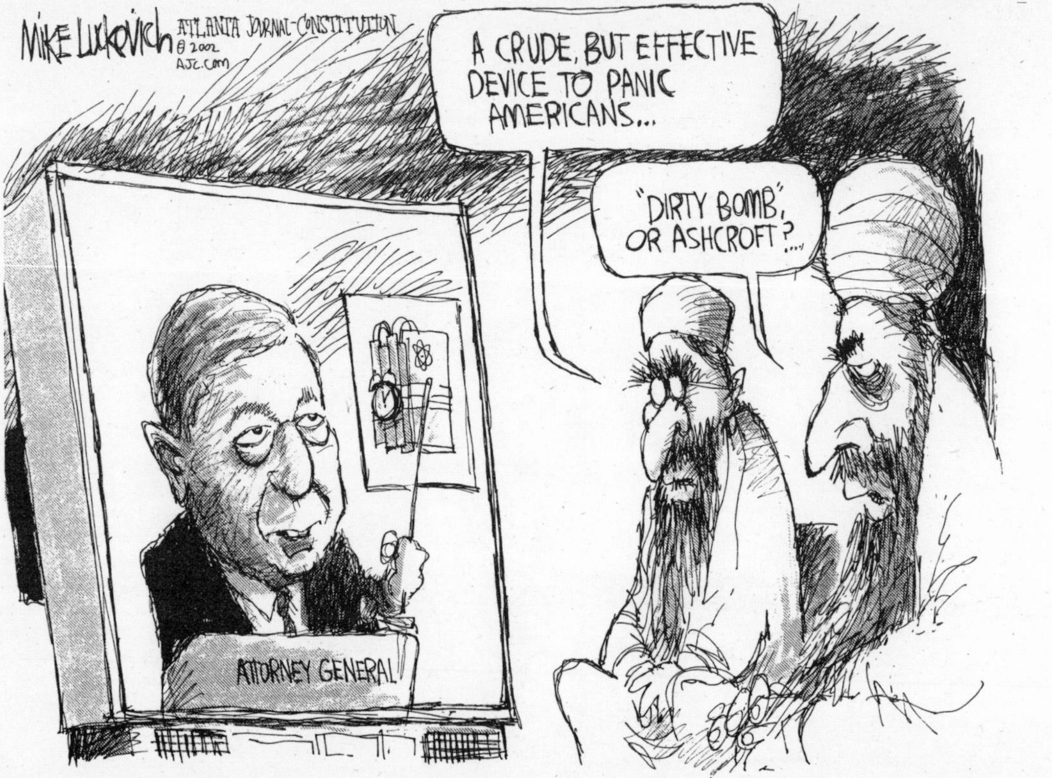
MIKE LUCKOVICH ATLANTA JOURNAL-CONSTITUTION © 2002 AJC.com
A CRUDE, BUT EFFECTIVE DEVICE TO PANIC AMERICANS...
"DIRTY BOMB," OR ASHCROFT?...
ATTORNEY GENERAL

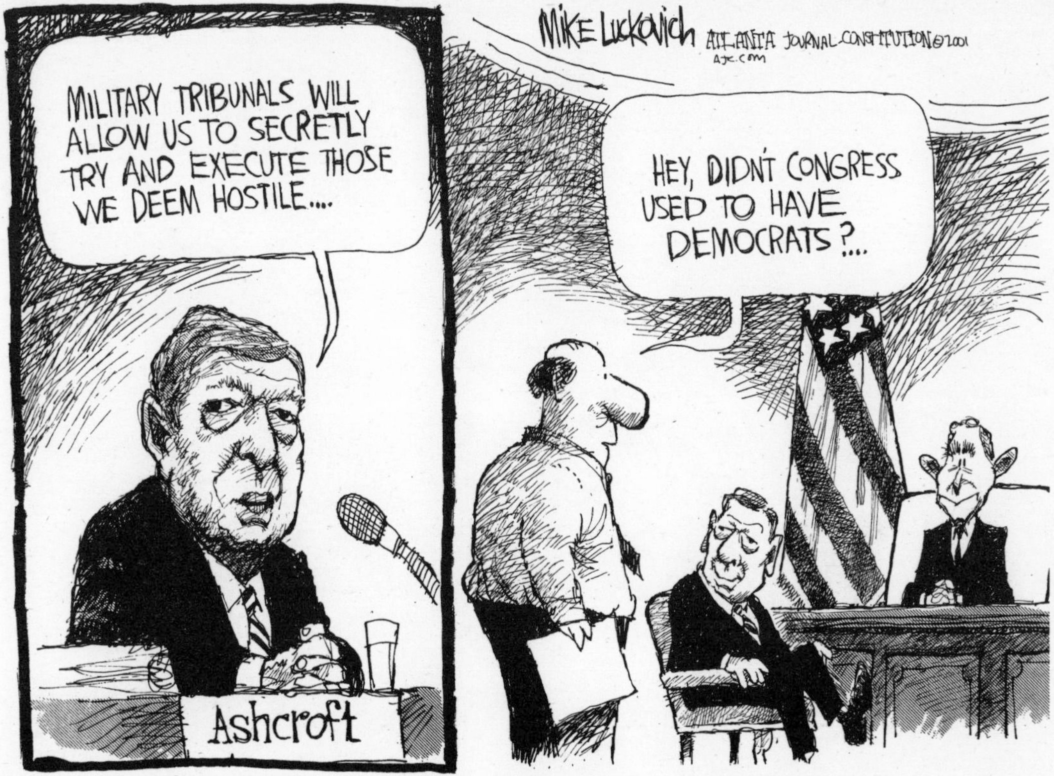
MILITARY TRIBUNALS WILL ALLOW US TO SECRETLY TRY AND EXECUTE THOSE WE DEEM HOSTILE....
Ashcroft
MIKE LUCKOVICH ATLANTA JOURNAL-CONSTITUTION ©2001
ajc.com
HEY, DIDN'T CONGRESS USED TO HAVE DEMOCRATS?...

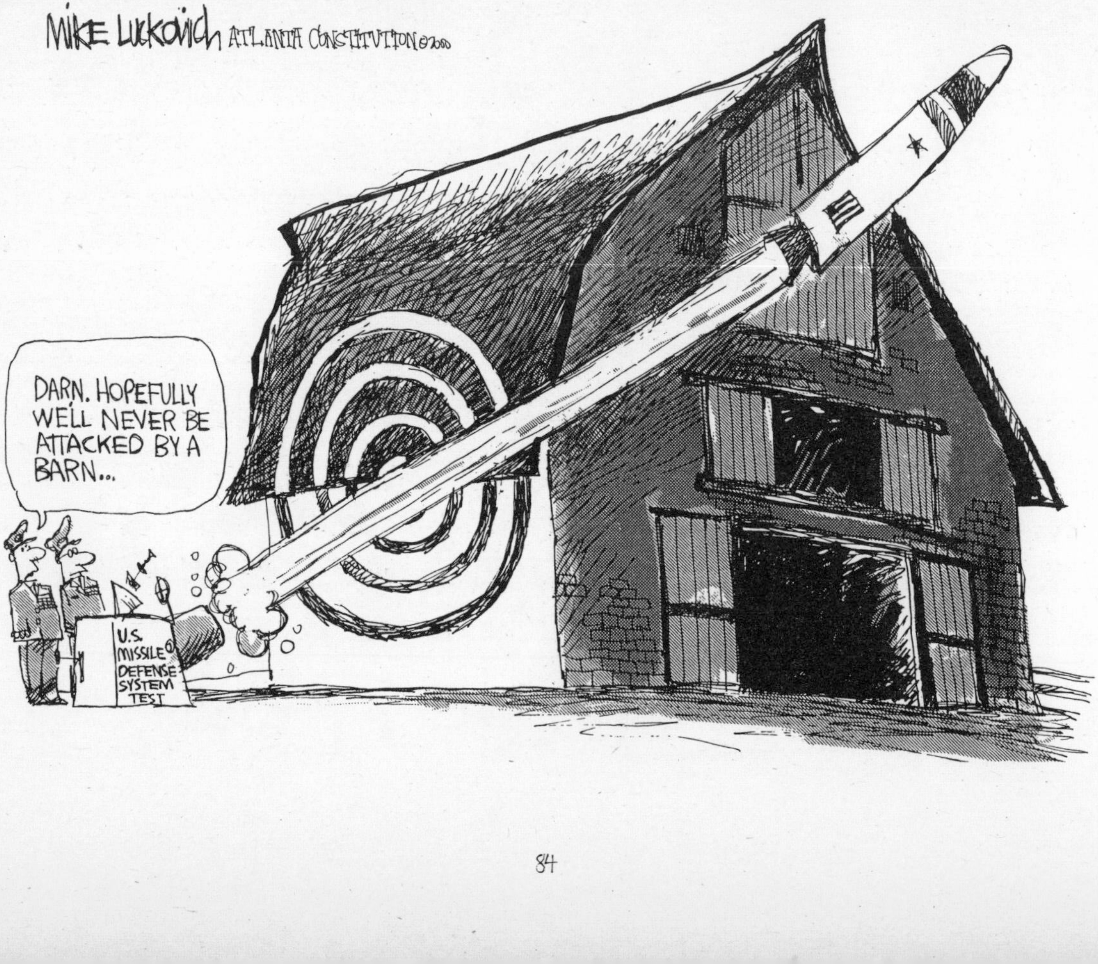
MIKE LUCKOVICH ATLANTA CONSTITUTION ©2000
DARN. HOPEFULLY WE'LL NEVER BE ATTACKED BY A BARN...
U.S. MISSILE DEFENSE SYSTEM TEST

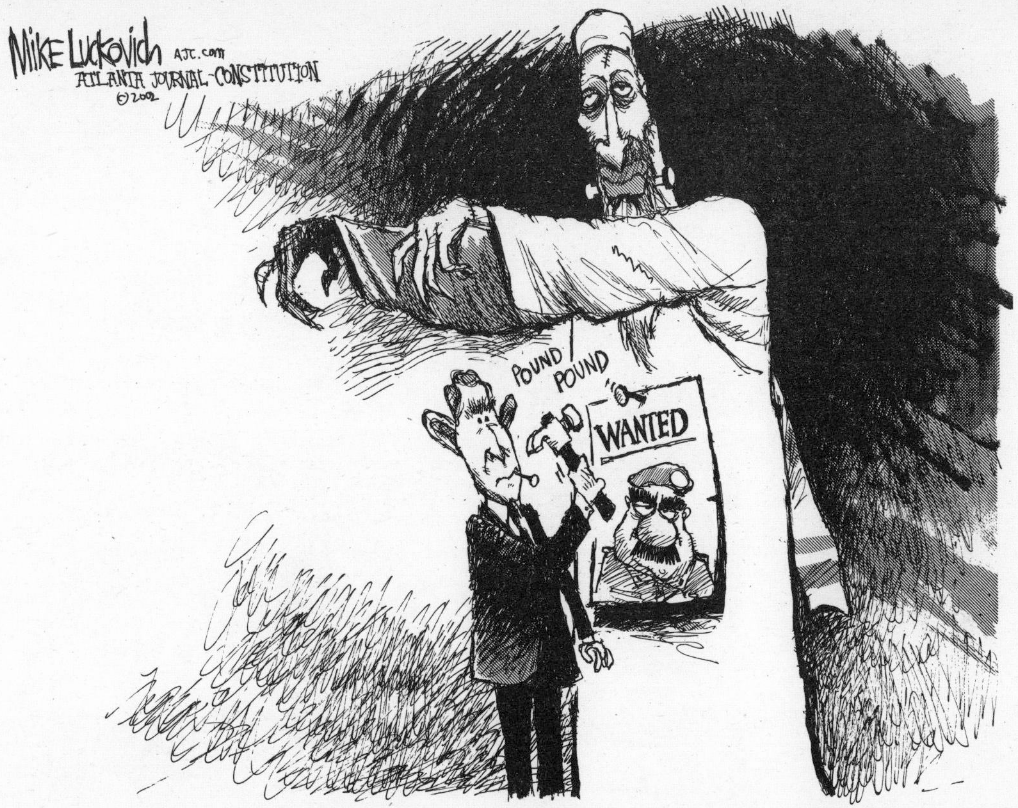
Mike Luckovich AJC.com
ATLANTA JOURNAL-CONSTITUTION
©2002
POUND
POUND
WANTED

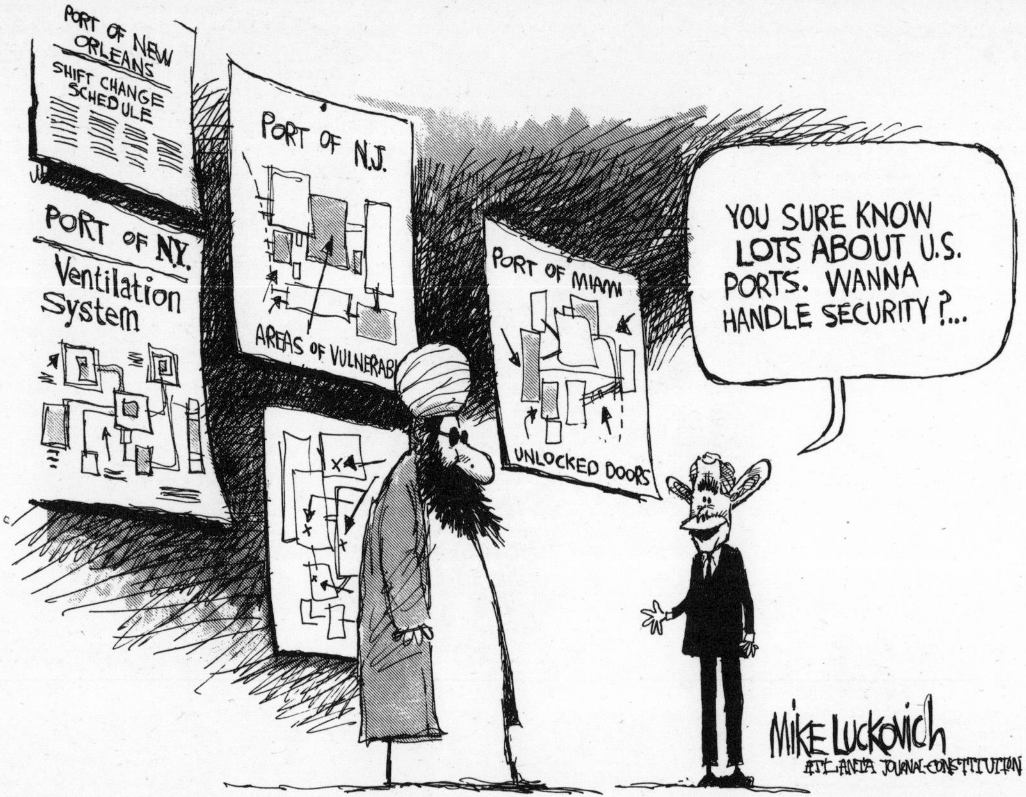
PORT OF NEW ORLEANS
SHIFT CHANGE SCHEDULE
PORT OF N.Y.
Ventilation System
PORT OF N.J.
AREAS OF VULNERAB
PORT OF MIAMI
UNLOCKED DOORS
YOU SURE KNOW LOTS ABOUT U.S. PORTS. WANNA HANDLE SECURITY ?...
MIKE LUCKOVICH
ATLANTA JOURNAL-CONSTITUTION

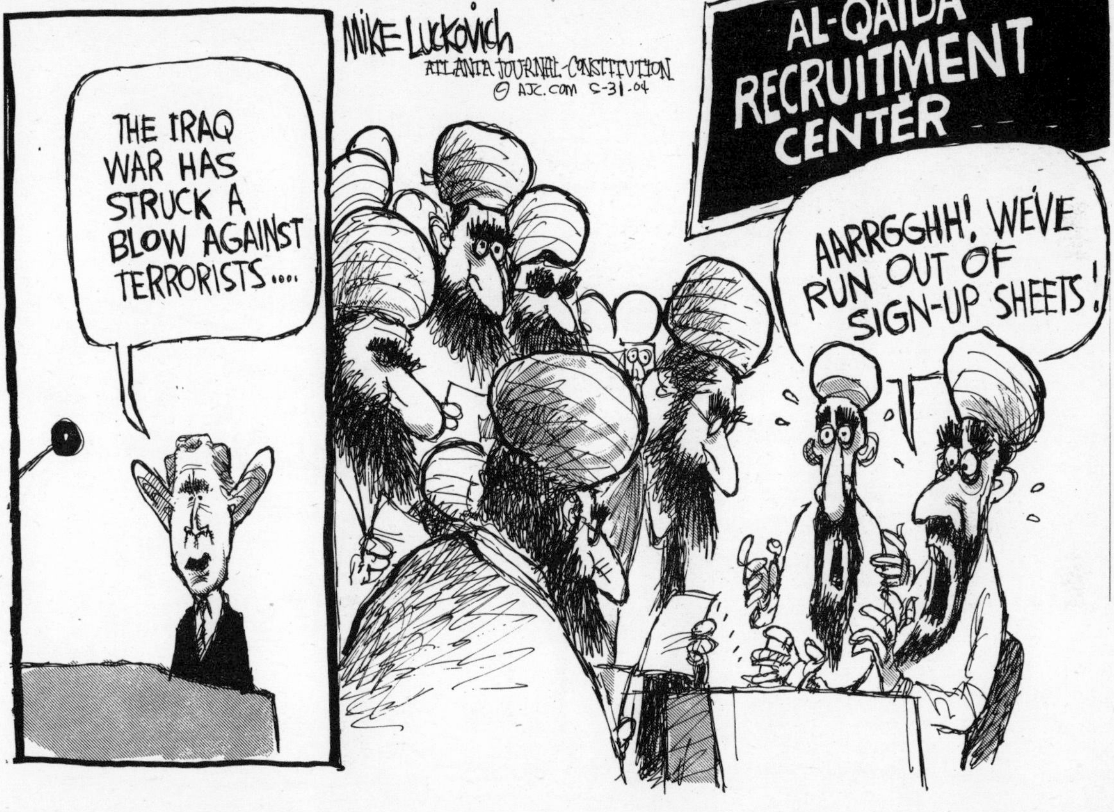
MIKE LUCKOVICH
ATLANTA JOURNAL-CONSTITUTION
© AJC.COM 5-31-04
THE IRAQ WAR HAS STRUCK A BLOW AGAINST TERRORISTS....
AL-QAIDA RECRUITMENT CENTER
AARRGGHH! WE'VE RUN OUT OF SIGN-UP SHEETS!

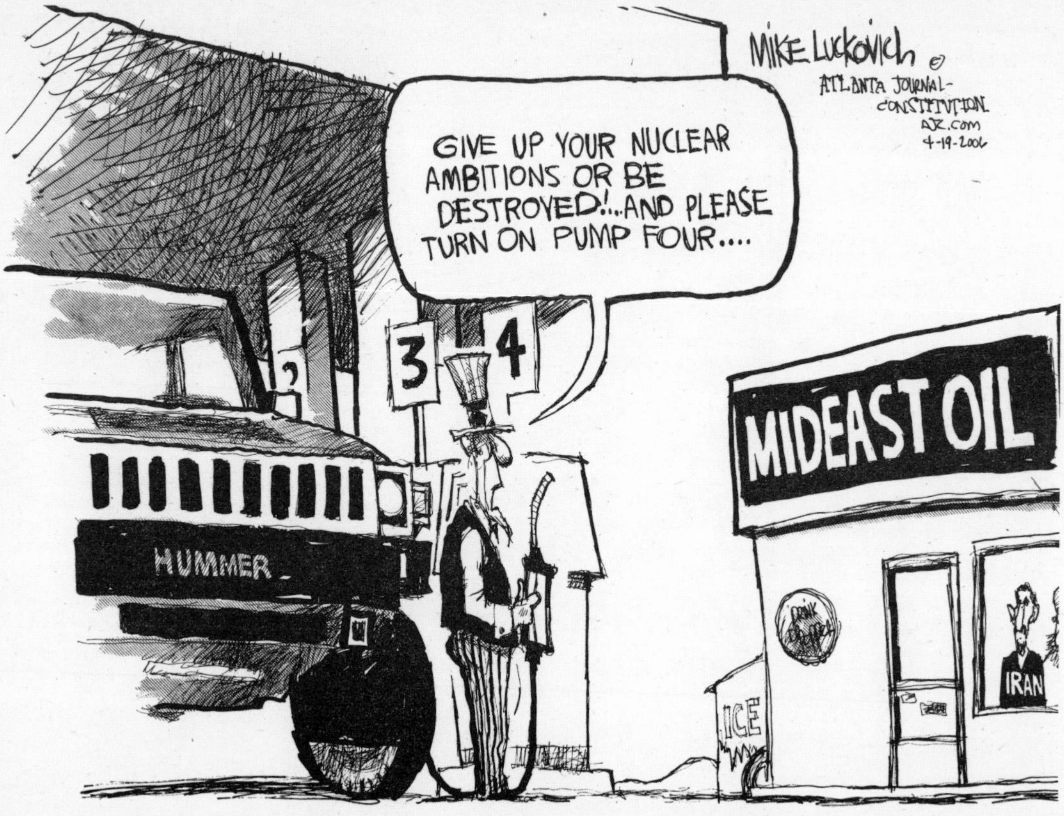
MIKE LUCKOVICH ©
ATLANTA JOURNAL-CONSTITUTION
AJC.com
4-19-2006
GIVE UP YOUR NUCLEAR AMBITIONS OR BE DESTROYED!...AND PLEASE TURN ON PUMP FOUR....
3
4
HUMMER
MIDEAST OIL
IRAN
ICE

Iraq

Iraq may seem like a mess, but it isn't, because according to Bush, we've just turned our 485th corner in the conflict. Not only that, we're making good progress. If those damn journalists would quit getting blown up, they'd be able to report more of the good news from Iraq.

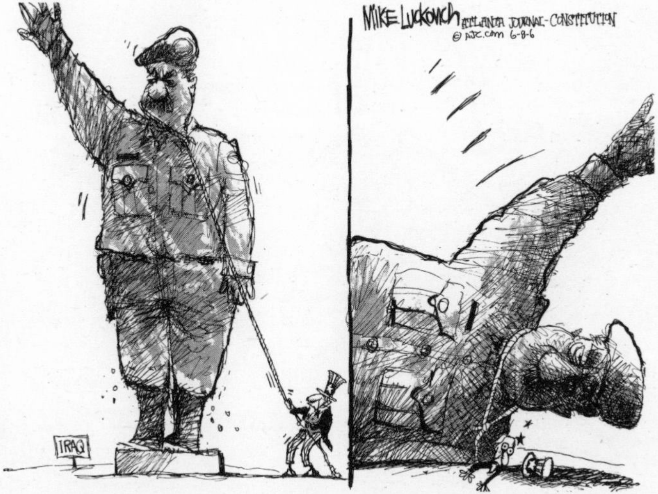
MIKE LUCKOVICH ATLANTA JOURNAL-CONSTITUTION
© AJC.com 6-8-6
IRAQ

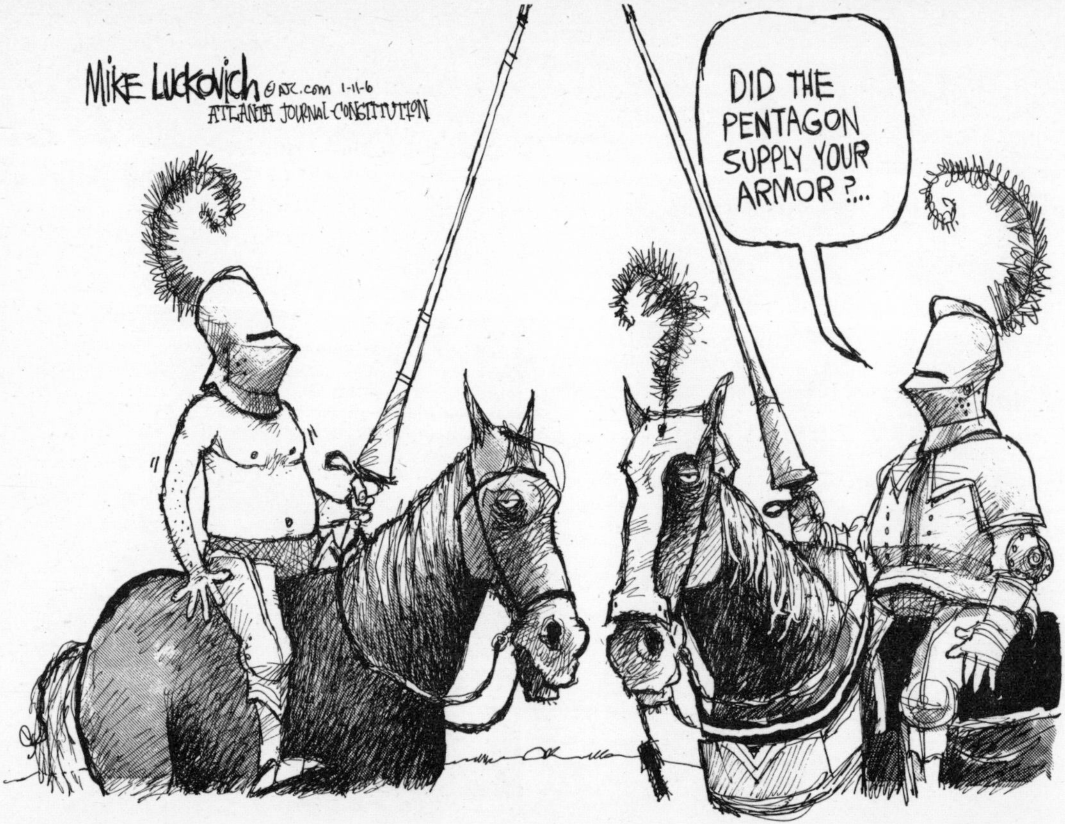
MIKE LUCKOVICH ©AJC.com 1-11-6
ATLANTA JOURNAL-CONSTITUTION
DID THE PENTAGON SUPPLY YOUR ARMOR ?...

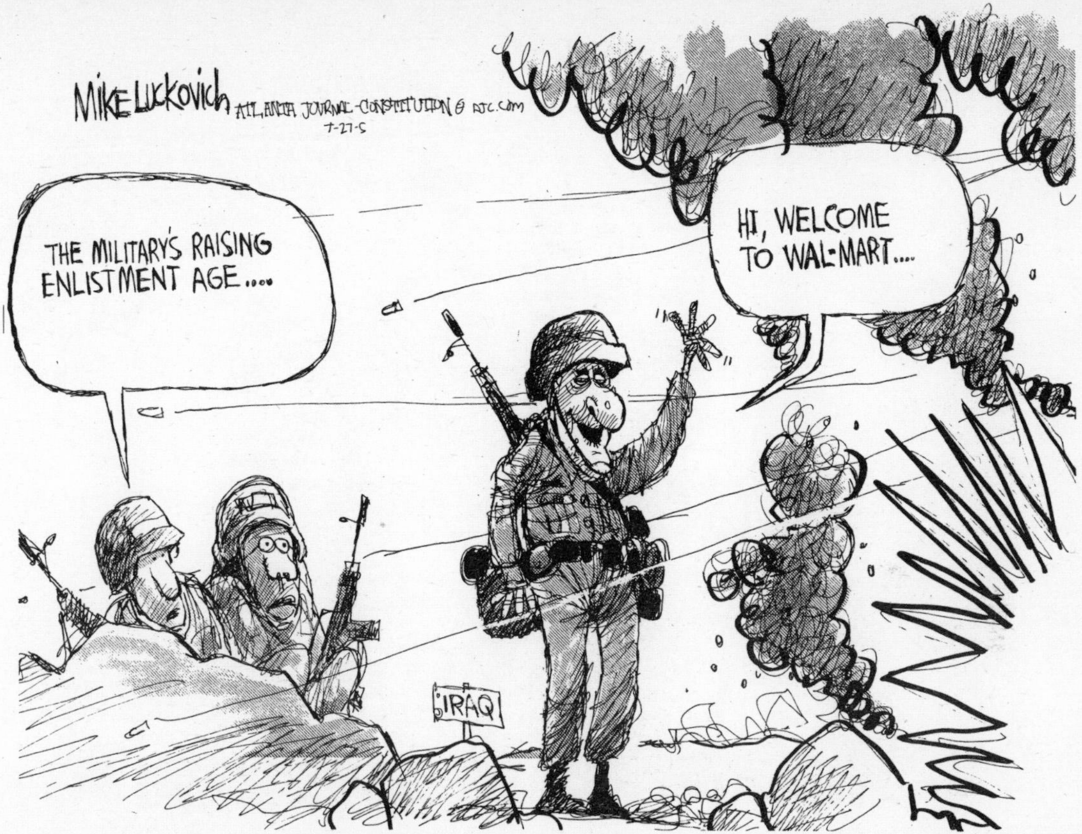
MIKE LUCKOVICH ATLANTA JOURNAL-CONSTITUTION © AJC.COM
7-27-5
THE MILITARY'S RAISING ENLISTMENT AGE....
HI, WELCOME TO WAL-MART....
IRAQ

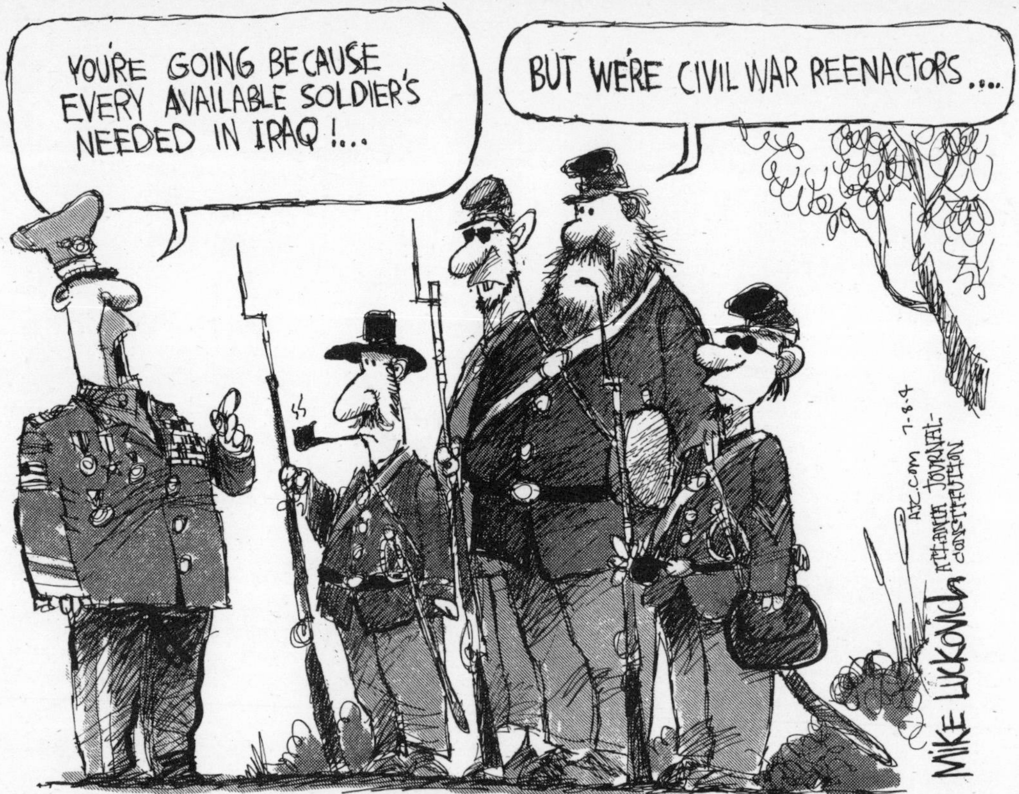
YOU'RE GOING BECAUSE EVERY AVAILABLE SOLDIER'S NEEDED IN IRAQ!...
BUT WE'RE CIVIL WAR REENACTORS....
MIKE LUCKOVICH
ATLANTA JOURNAL-CONSTITUTION
AJC.com
7-8-4

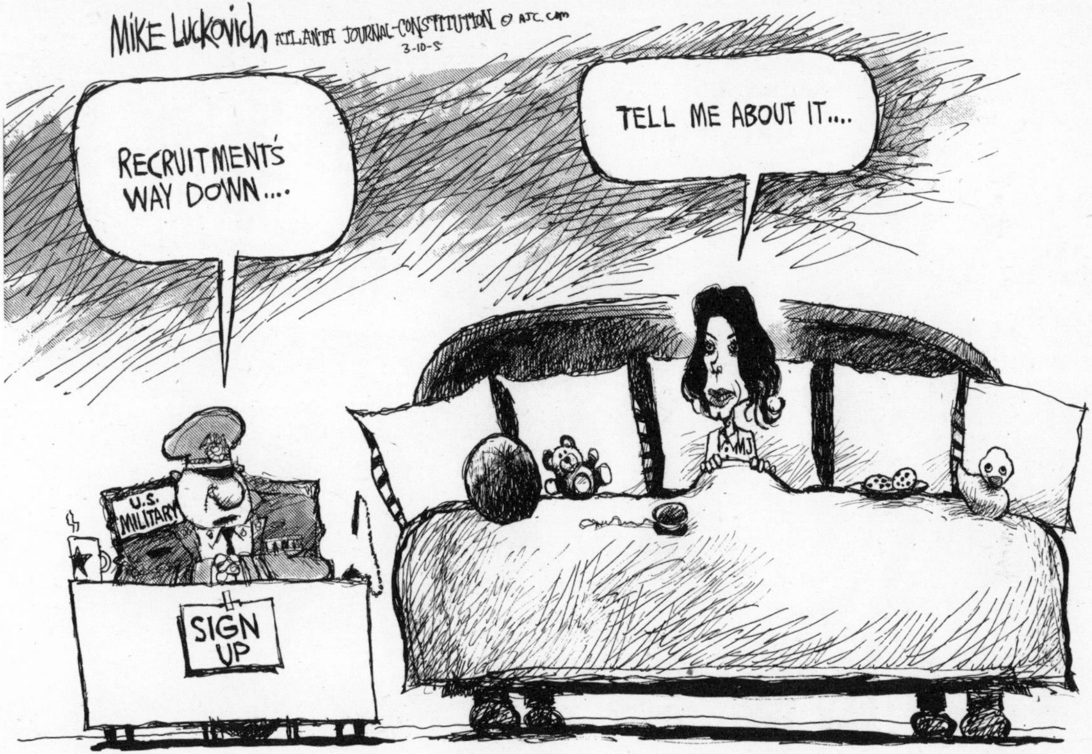
MIKE LUCKOVICH ATLANTA JOURNAL-CONSTITUTION © AJC.com
3-10-5
RECRUITMENT'S WAY DOWN....
TELL ME ABOUT IT....
U.S. MILITARY
SIGN UP
MJ

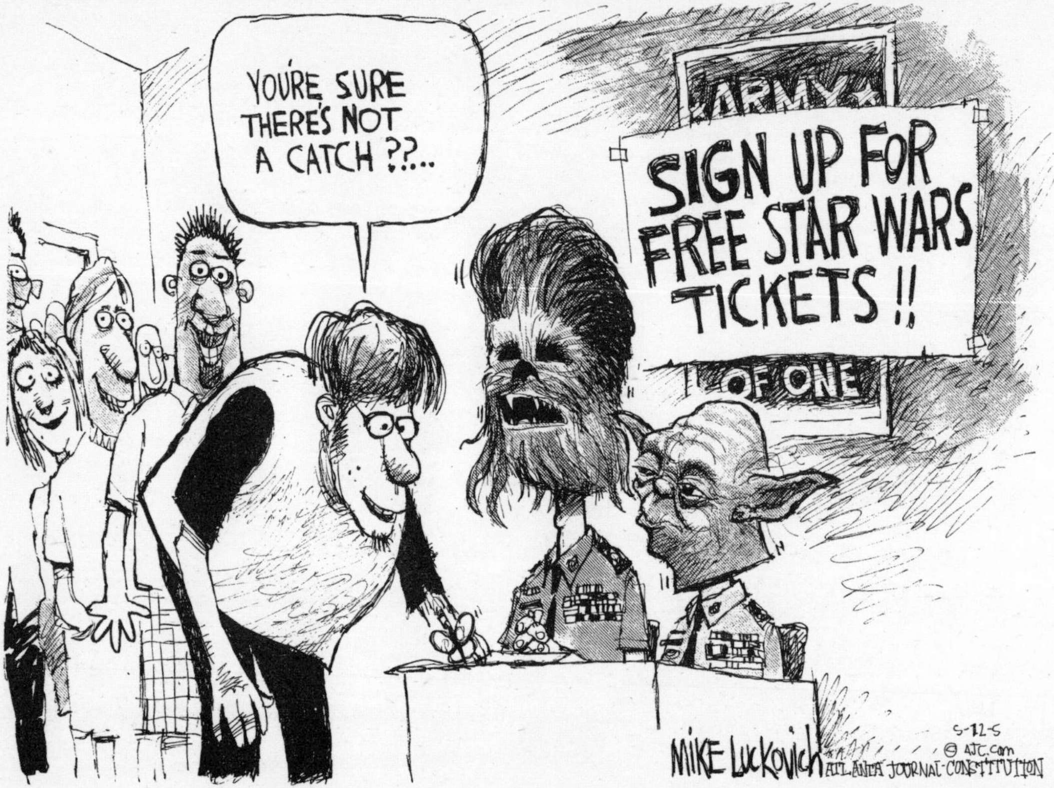
YOU'RE SURE THERE'S NOT A CATCH ??...
ARMY
SIGN UP FOR FREE STAR WARS TICKETS !!
OF ONE
MIKE LUCKOVICH ATLANTA JOURNAL-CONSTITUTION
5-12-5
© AJC.com

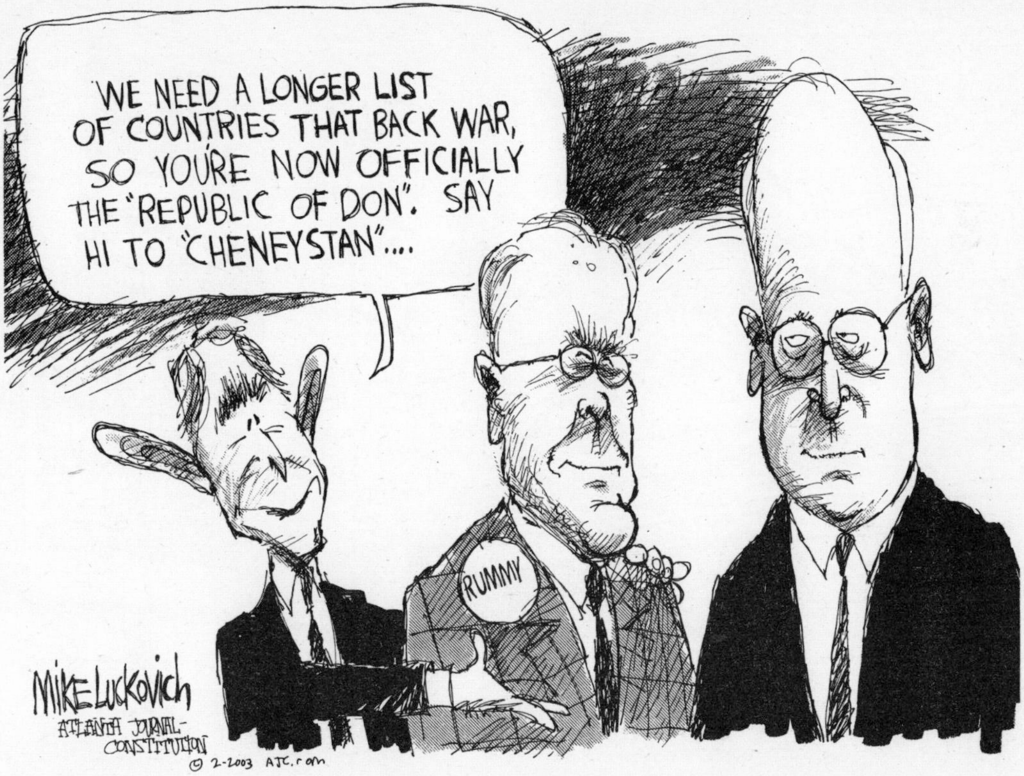
WE NEED A LONGER LIST OF COUNTRIES THAT BACK WAR, SO YOU'RE NOW OFFICIALLY THE "REPUBLIC OF DON". SAY HI TO "CHENEYSTAN"....
RUMMY
MIKE LUCKOVICH
ATLANTA JOURNAL-CONSTITUTION
© 2-2003 AJC.com

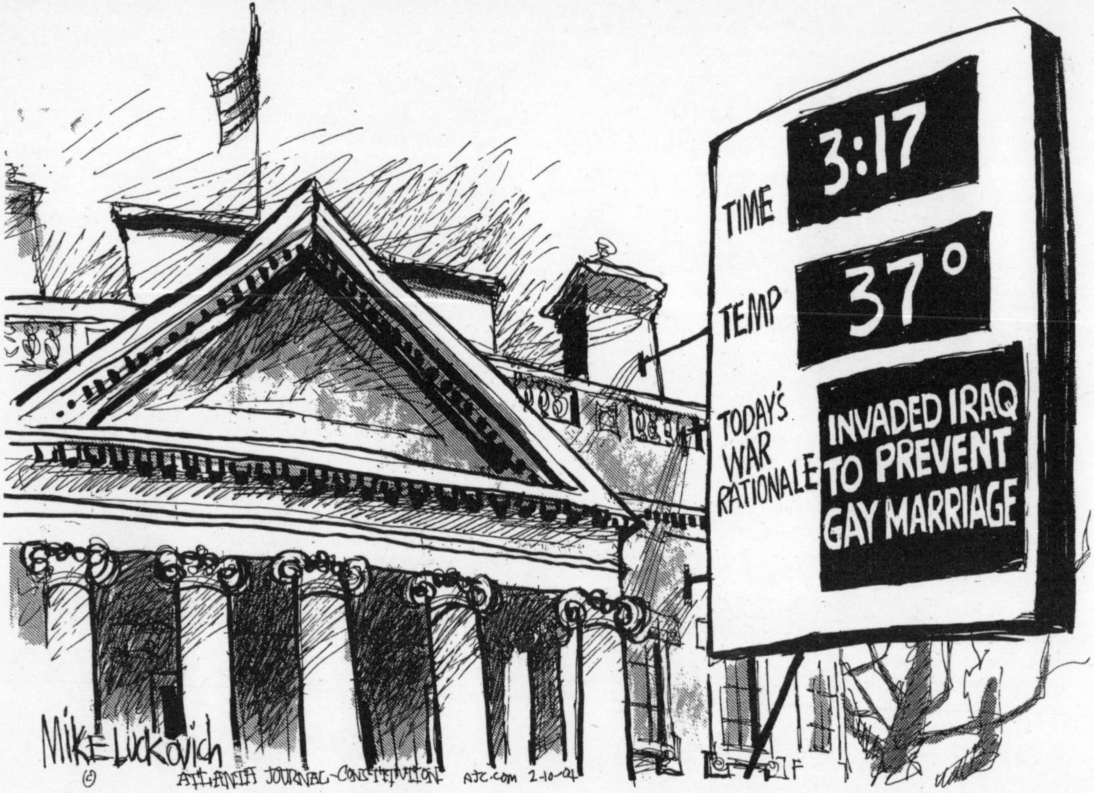
TIME
3:17
TEMP
37°
TODAY'S WAR RATIONALE
INVADED IRAQ TO PREVENT GAY MARRIAGE
MIKE LUCKOVICH
©
ATLANTA JOURNAL-CONSTITUTION AJC.COM 2-10-04

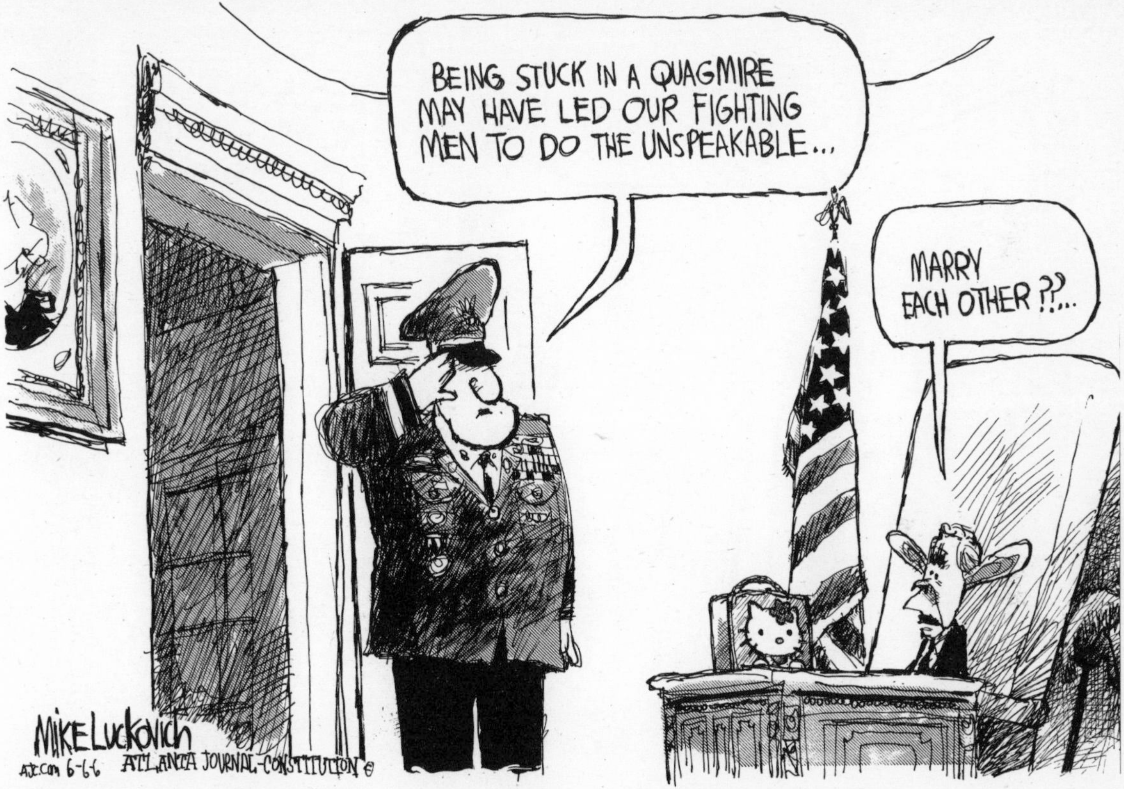
BEING STUCK IN A QUAGMIRE MAY HAVE LED OUR FIGHTING MEN TO DO THE UNSPEAKABLE...
MARRY EACH OTHER ??...
MIKE LUCKOVICH
AJC.COM 6-6-6 ATLANTA JOURNAL-CONSTITUTION ©

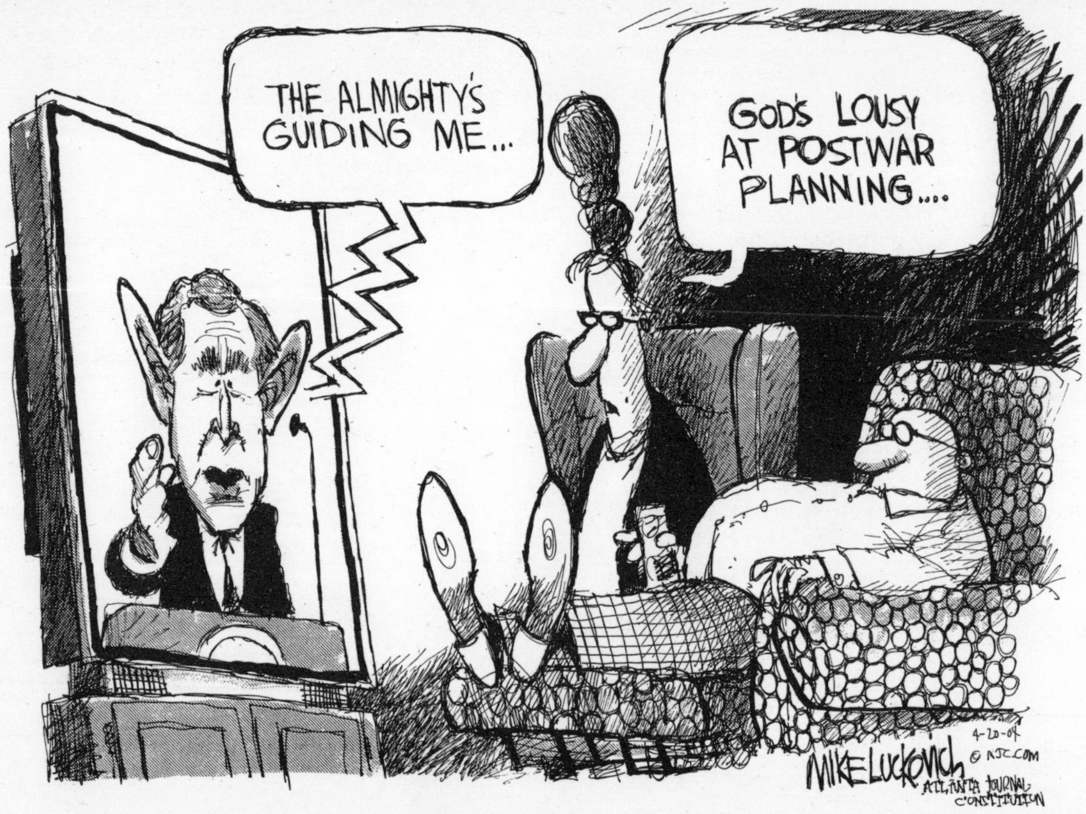
THE ALMIGHTY'S GUIDING ME...
GOD'S LOUSY AT POSTWAR PLANNING....
4-20-04
MIKE LUCKOVICH
© AJC.COM
ATLANTA JOURNAL-CONSTITUTION

Back from Iraq

With three other illustrators, I recently visited Walter Reed Army Medical Center in Washington, DC, to meet wounded GIs. We wanted to go, to talk to them and to do some cartoons for them, to let them know that people are thinking about them. I view these guys as heroes.

This was something we were going to do on our own, but after doing it, we decided we wanted to let people know so that these guys would not be forgotten. People talk about the 2,400 at this point who have died. And that's terrible. But there are more than 17,000 troops who have been injured, some horrifically.

For example, this kid's name was Danny. He was a Navy medic. He was blond, an average-looking kid. I drew his caricature as he talked about what happened. He just talked a blue streak — everything that happened to him the day he got injured. All the people in the Humvee with him were Marines, and he kept referring to them as his Marines. He was packed tightly in the back of the Humvee because he had all of his equipment and he was the medic. The guys in the middle and up front had more room to move around because they needed to be able to use their weapons. They ran over an IED. It killed the two guys up front.

As Danny described it to me, the third casualty was able to be flown back to Walter Reed so he could say his goodbyes to his parents before he died. But there were others who were badly injured. Danny was crawling around the Humvee putting tourniquets on the legs of the wounded soldiers and trying to stabilize them. As he was doing this, he looked down and could see that, from his waist and from his legs, he was bleeding heavily.

He remembered that he had one tourniquet left that he kept on his right shoulder. So he tried grabbing for the tourniquet repeatedly, and he couldn't get it. He looked down at his left hand and found that the tops of his fingers had all been blown off. That's why he couldn't grab the thing.

The troops he had stabilized told him afterwards that he looked down at his hand and just started laughing. He was trying to grab this tourniquet and couldn't, and at the time it just seemed funny to him. You have to imagine: this guy's in the middle of a war, and his comrades are all around him, dead or injured, and he sees his hand; it was just like a release for him too.

There were one or two soldiers from Afghanistan, but the majority had been fighting in Iraq. All but two were involved in IED explosives detonating while they were in their Humvees. What was interesting was they all wanted to talk about what happened and relive what they had gone through. They just wanted someone to listen to them. And many of them wanted to go back to Iraq to support the buddies they had left behind. It was really amazing, especially to look at these kids, missing legs, lying in hospital beds, talking about their friends who are still over there.

There was another young man whose chest area was exposed because of his hospital gown, and he just looked so slight. He wasn't a big guy. He had red hair and glasses — I mean, this was not Rambo. His right leg was pinned in various places. He had a very large wound across his thigh, open, and I don't know what he had suffered there exactly. He didn't really talk too much; he seemed like he was probably on morphine. He was missing his other leg up to his pelvic bone. There was nothing there. And this is a young kid, with his mom sitting next to his bed. You know, she was smiling, she was happy that we were in to see him. She was talkative. But it must be so hard. I'm sure she is very happy that he's still with her, but he will have a very large cross to bear for the rest of his life.

There was one kid, named Eric — another red-headed kid, with an upturned nose. These were just average kids. I came into his room. He had his six-year-old sister with him, and his mom, who was originally from Germany. She still had a light accent, and was very upbeat. Eric was looking at me, following my face. He had a tube in his throat, so he couldn't talk. He was in Mosul, operating a .50-caliber machine gun, and he somehow poked his head up from behind the thing. A sniper shot through his helmet, apparently, and blew off the back of his head.

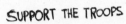

SUPPORT THE TROOPS

Mike Luckovich 2006

And he was lying in bed. His head was on the pillow, but they put in some sort of metal piece. I didn't see the back of his head, but I could tell there was something there.

Physically he looked fabulous. His mom was talking about how another former soldier had come in. He had been shot in the head and come back to say, "I recovered, I'm back to normal." I don't know what lies ahead for Eric. I do know that he needs all the prayers and support he can get.

We would talk to the soldiers and do some sketches. I tried to sketch one, but I couldn't — he got a phone call from his sergeant on the ground in Iraq, who was calling to make sure he was doing all right.

We were seeing these kids fresh off the battlefield. They got blown up, were taken to a staging area in Iraq, stabilized, flown immediately to Germany, and from Germany brought to the United States. So we saw some kids who, five days before, were fighting in Iraq. And now here they were, lying there with pieces missing.

Something I was told by the USO volunteer is that it's like a conveyor belt because they are getting more injured in all the time. As soon as possible, they would transfer these soldiers to dorms or hotel-like rooms that they have around the hospital. And according to this woman from the USO, there are literally hundreds of soldiers with injuries like the ones we saw — trying to learn to live with their new prosthetics and adjust.

It never came up whether these guys supported the war or not, and I didn't feel like it was my place to get into a discussion about that. They were recovering from wounds; they're going to have to deal with that issue and come to their own conclusions. When we visited these guys — kids, most of them, 19, 20, 21 — it was never to discuss whether the war was right or wrong. It was just to be there for them and to thank them for serving their country.

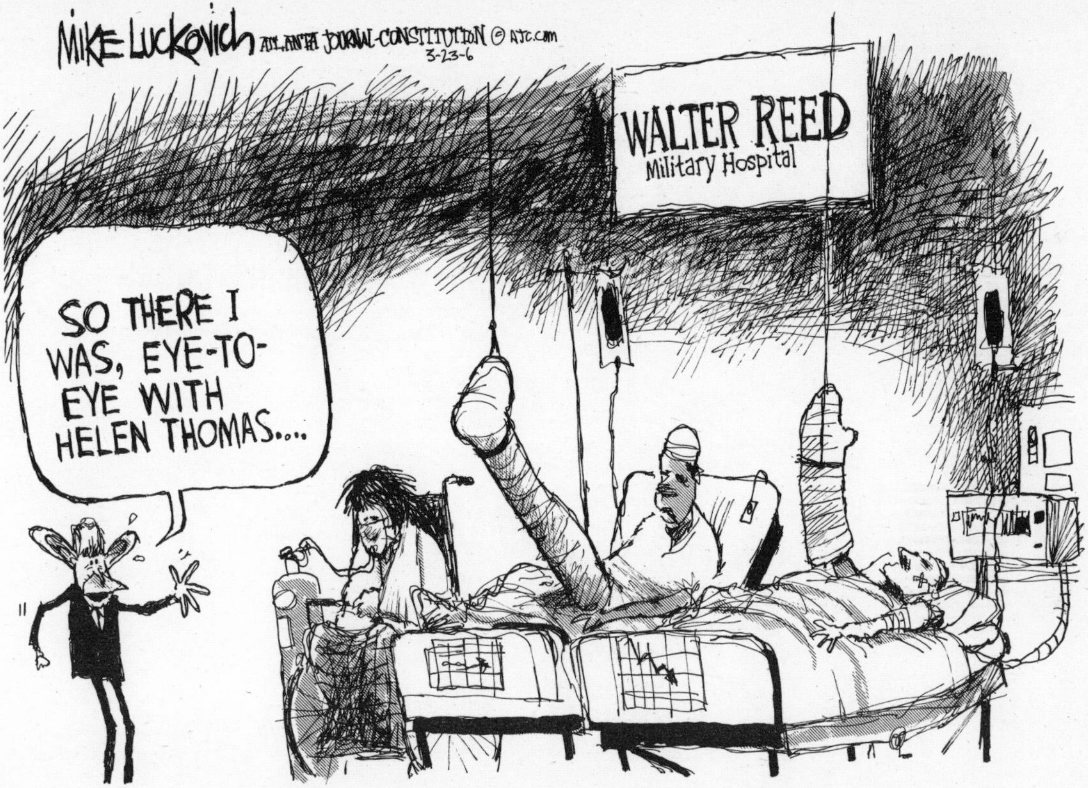
MIKE LUCKOVICH ATLANTA JOURNAL-CONSTITUTION © AJC.com
3-23-6
WALTER REED
Military Hospital
SO THERE I WAS, EYE-TO-EYE WITH HELEN THOMAS....

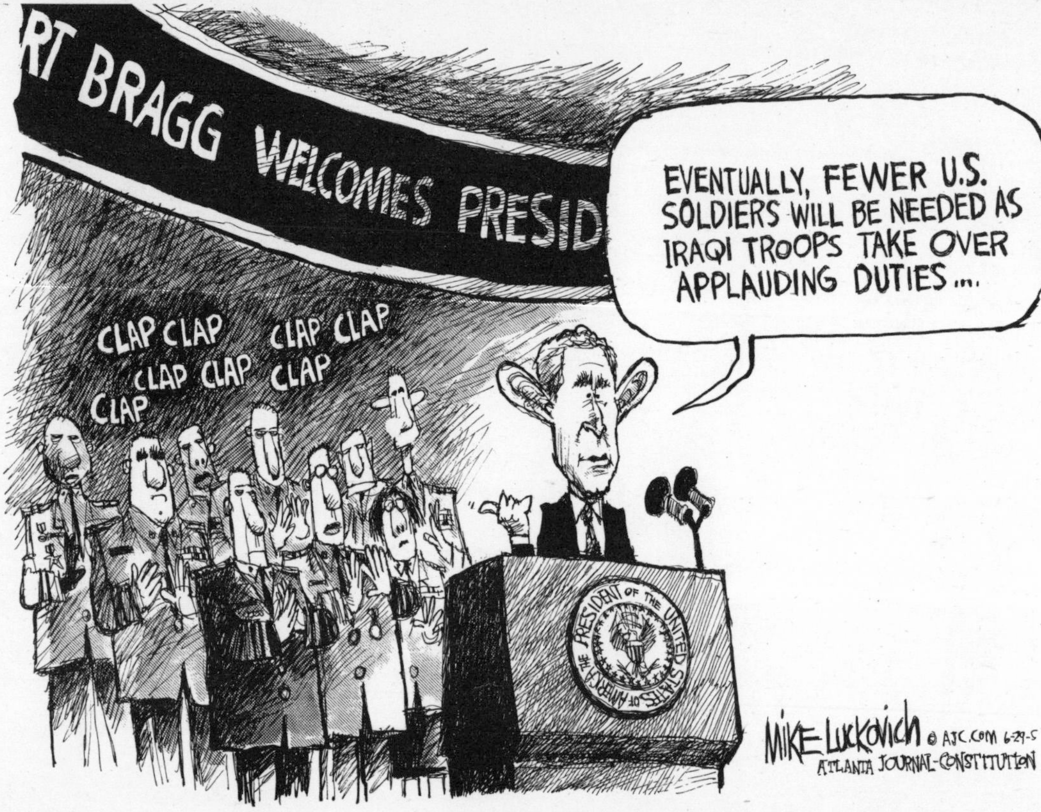
RT BRAGG WELCOMES PRESID
EVENTUALLY, FEWER U.S. SOLDIERS WILL BE NEEDED AS IRAQI TROOPS TAKE OVER APPLAUDING DUTIES....
CLAP CLAP
CLAP CLAP
CLAP CLAP
CLAP CLAP
CLAP
THE PRESIDENT OF THE UNITED STATES OF AMERICA
MIKE LUCKOVICH © AJC.COM 6-29-5
ATLANTA JOURNAL-CONSTITUTION

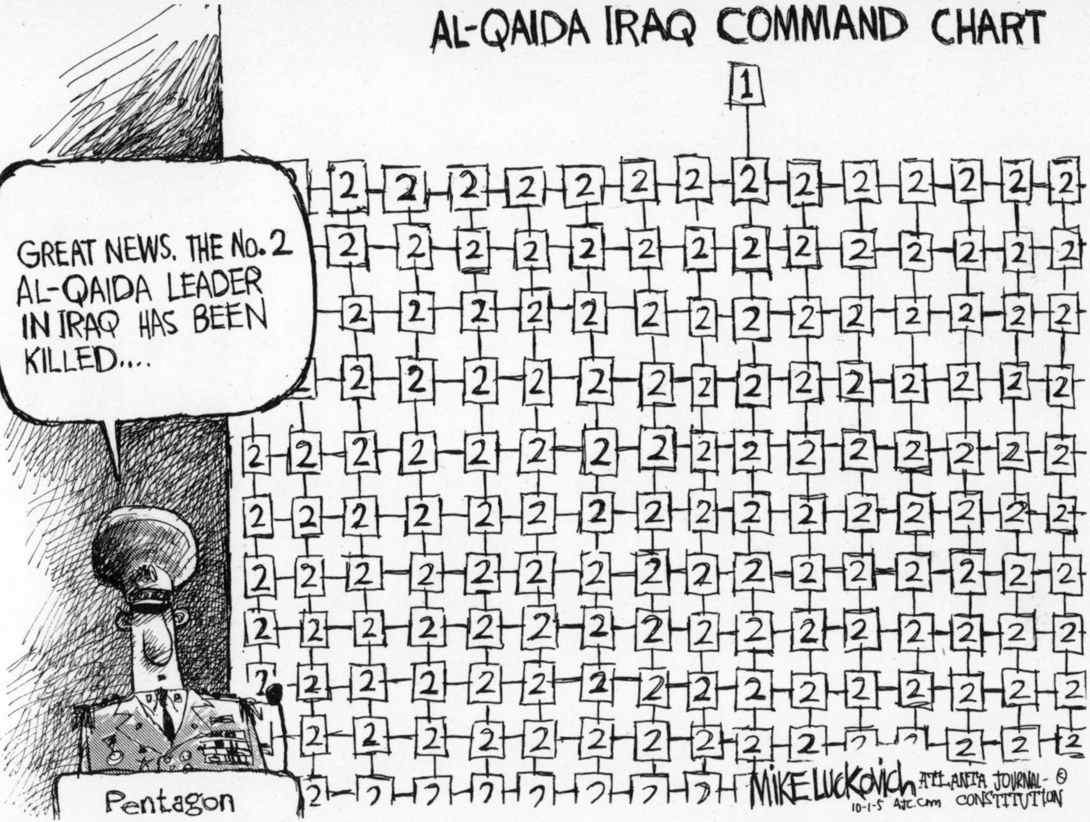
AL-QAIDA IRAQ COMMAND CHART
GREAT NEWS. THE No. 2 AL-QAIDA LEADER IN IRAQ HAS BEEN KILLED....
Pentagon
MIKE LUCKOVICH ATLANTA JOURNAL-CONSTITUTION ©
10-1-5 Ajc.com

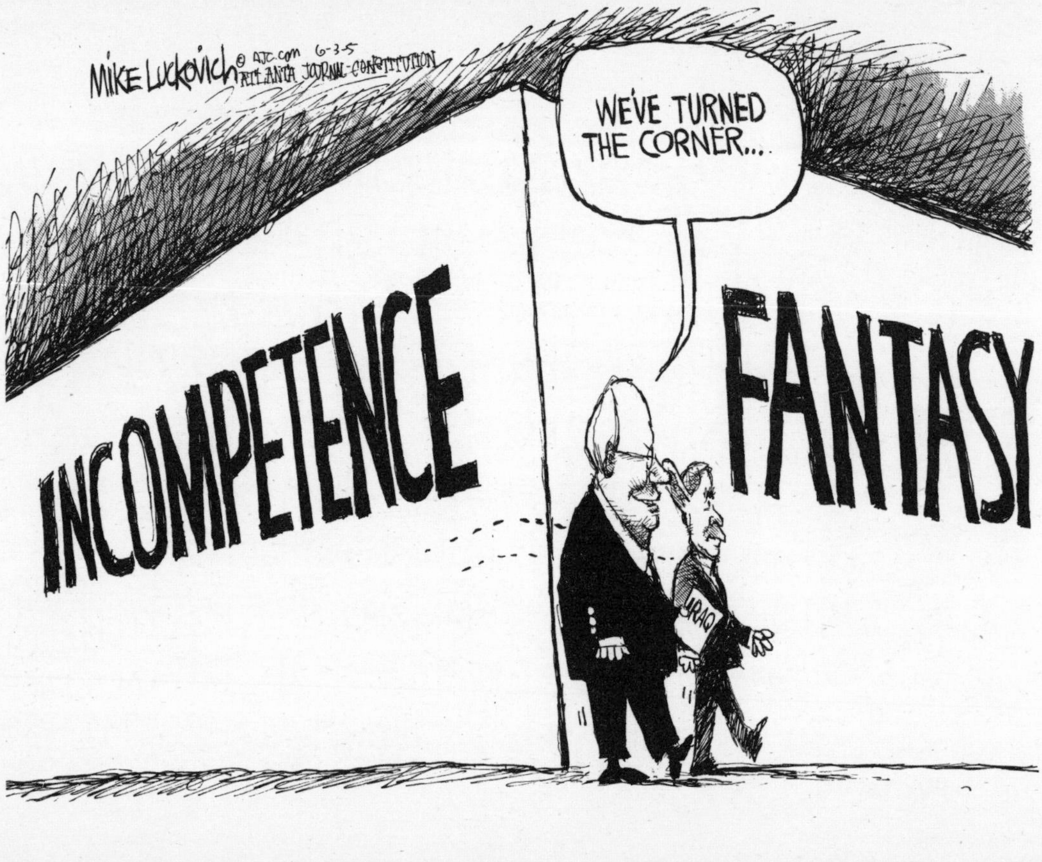
MIKE LUCKOVICH © AJC.com 6-3-5 ATLANTA JOURNAL-CONSTITUTION
WE'VE TURNED THE CORNER....
INCOMPETENCE
FANTASY
IRAQ

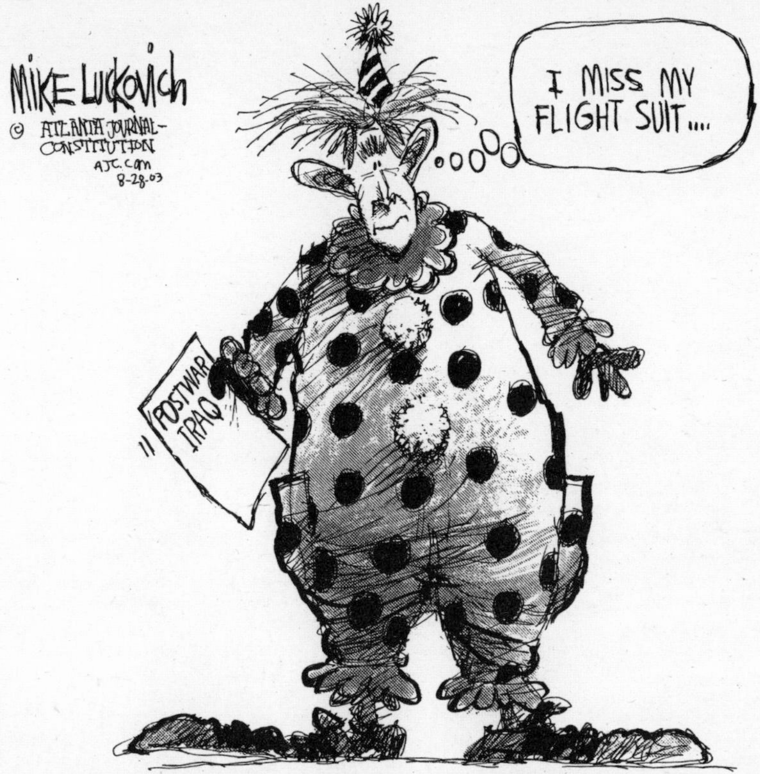
MIKE LUCKOVICH
© ATLANTA JOURNAL-CONSTITUTION
AJC.com
8-28-03
I MISS MY FLIGHT SUIT....
POSTWAR IRAQ

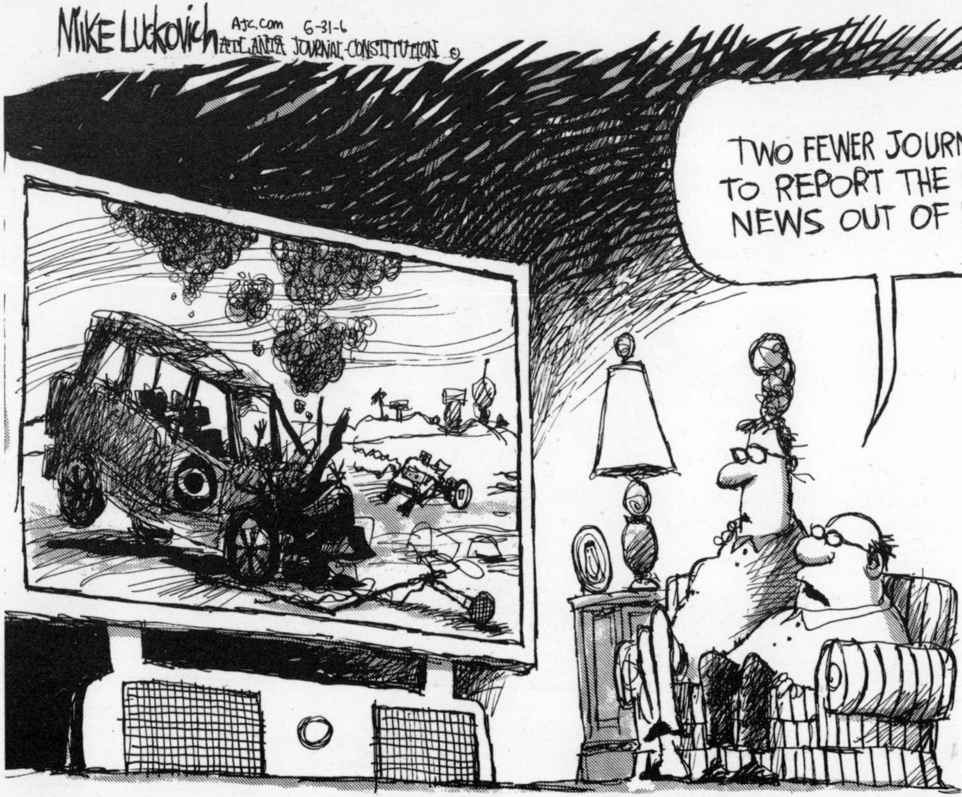
MIKE LUCKOVICH AJC.com 6-31-6 ATLANTA JOURNAL-CONSTITUTION ©
TWO FEWER JOURNALISTS TO REPORT THE GOOD NEWS OUT OF IRAQ....

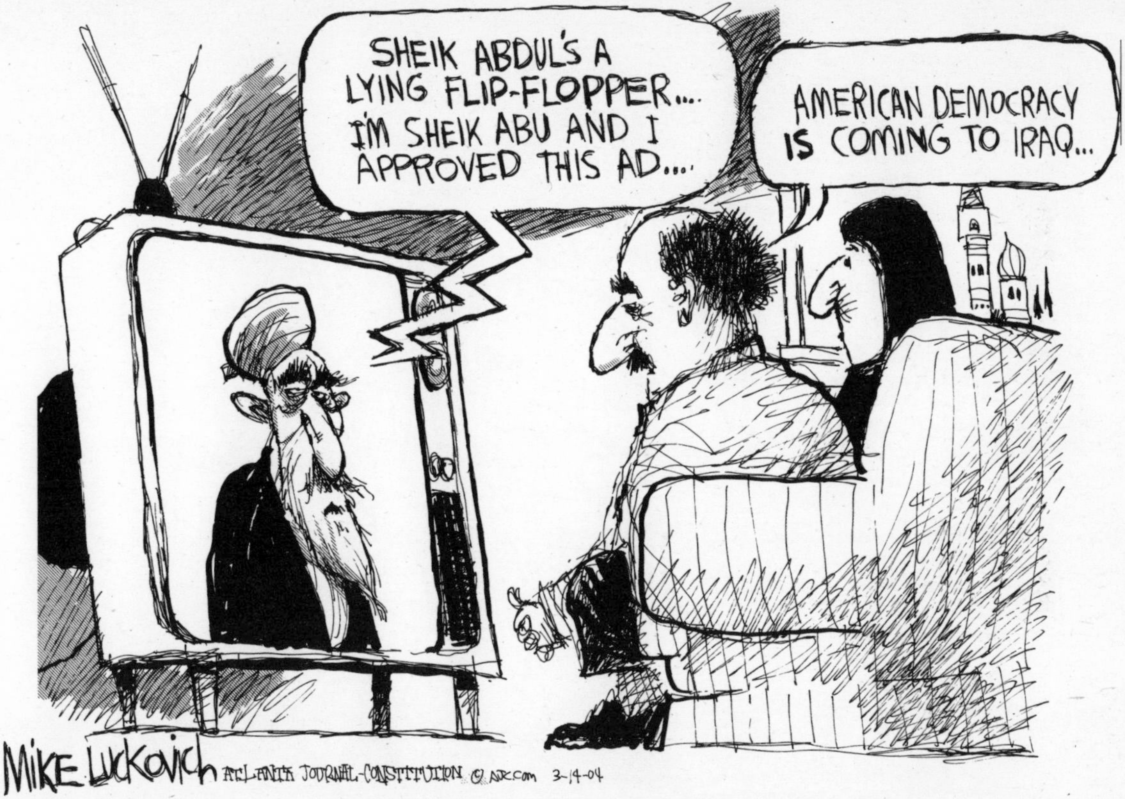
SHEIK ABDUL'S A LYING FLIP-FLOPPER.... I'M SHEIK ABU AND I APPROVED THIS AD....
AMERICAN DEMOCRACY IS COMING TO IRAQ...
MIKE LUCKOVICH ATLANTA JOURNAL-CONSTITUTION © AJC.com 3-14-04

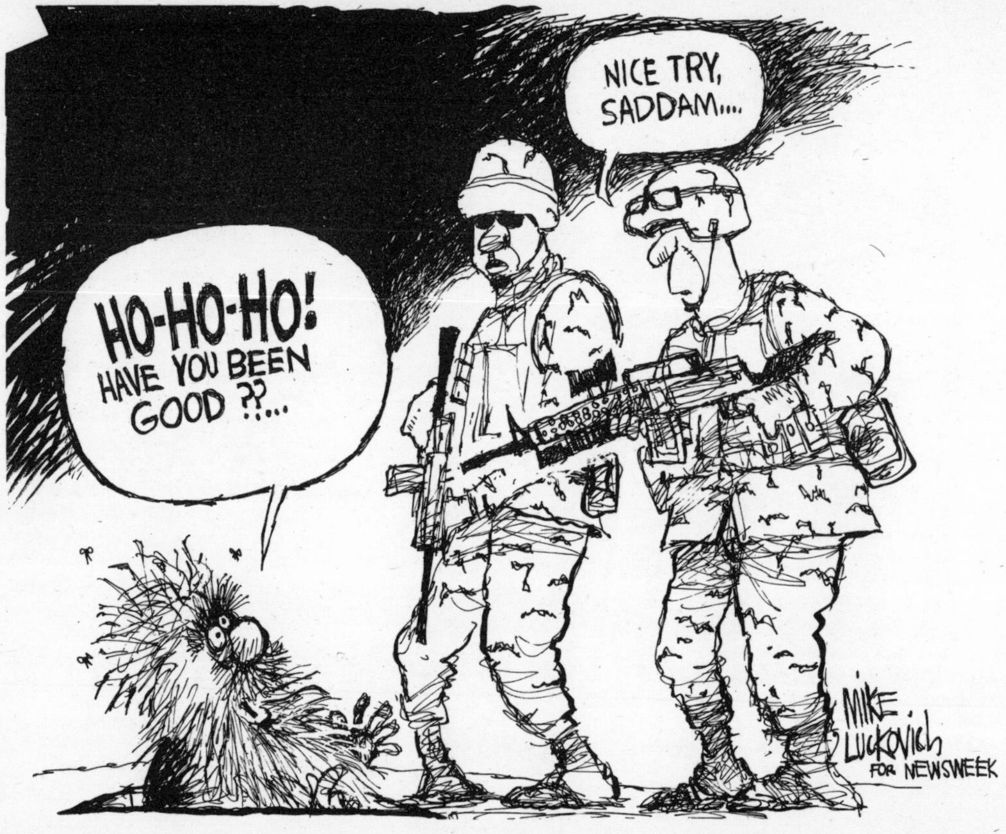
HO-HO-HO! HAVE YOU BEEN GOOD ??...
NICE TRY, SADDAM....
MIKE LUCKOVICH FOR NEWSWEEK

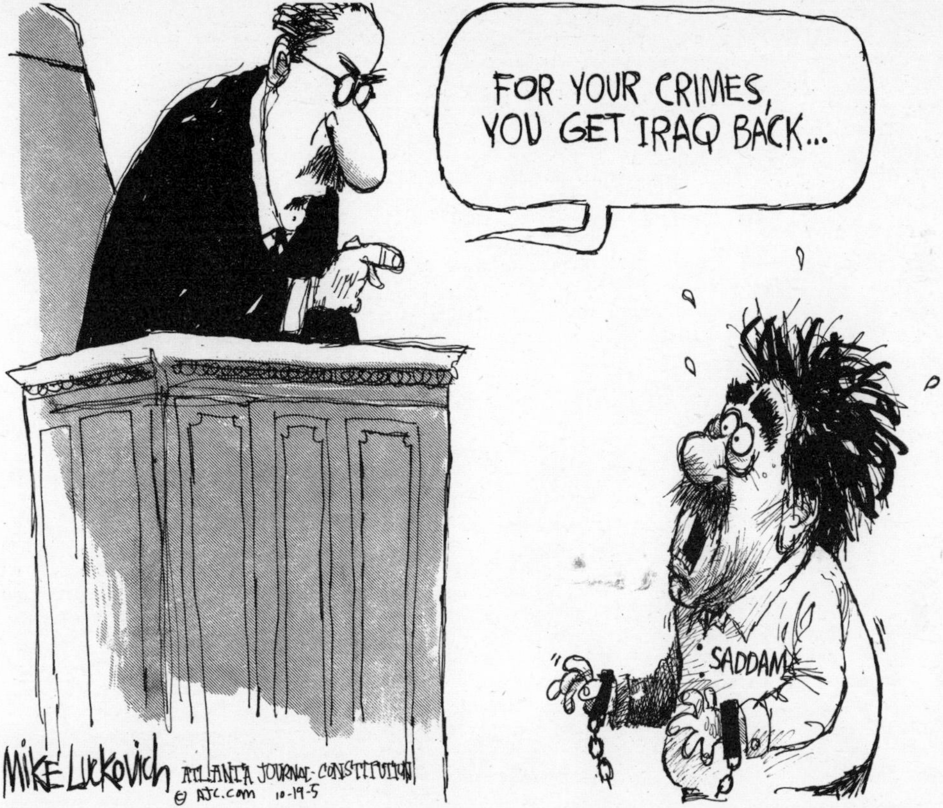
FOR YOUR CRIMES,
YOU GET IRAQ BACK...
SADDAM
MIKE LUCKOVICH ATLANTA JOURNAL-CONSTITUTION
© AJC.com 10-19-5

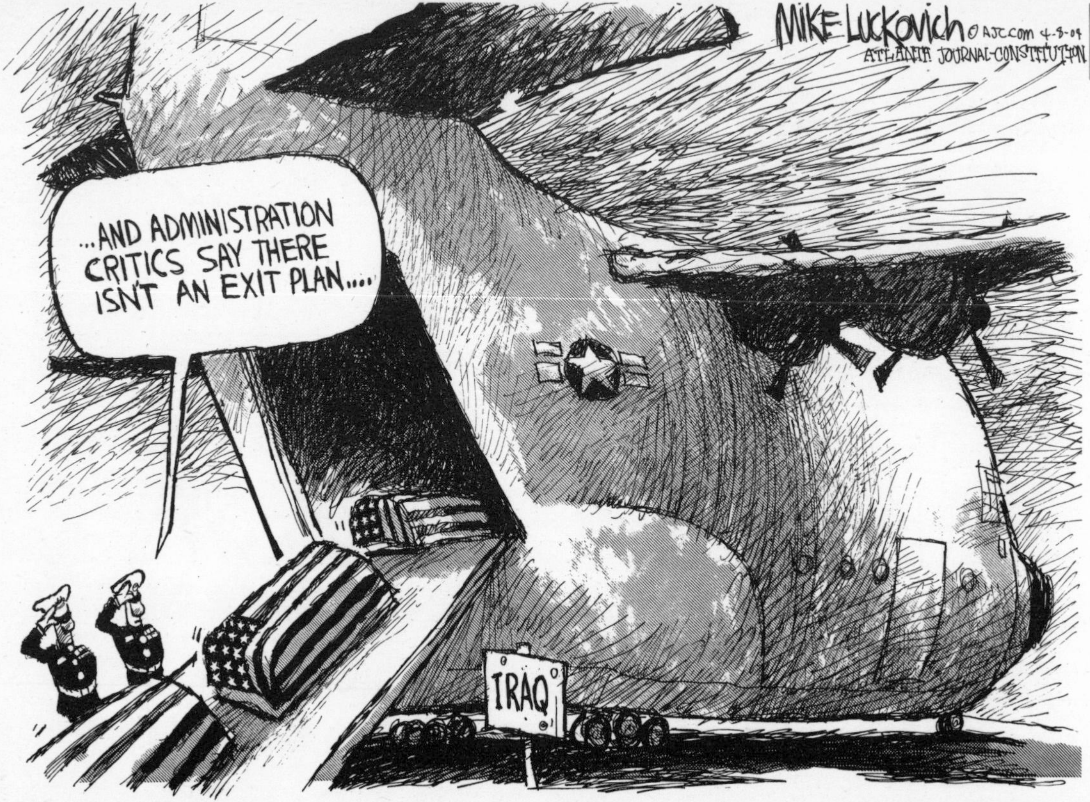
MIKE LUCKOVICH © AJC.COM 4-8-04
ATLANTA JOURNAL-CONSTITUTION
...AND ADMINISTRATION CRITICS SAY THERE ISN'T AN EXIT PLAN....
IRAQ

Bush Administration

What a zany cast of incompetent ideologues. The less able they are, the bigger medals of honor George W. gives them. Historically, presidents have wanted to be surrounded by the best and the brightest. Bush prefers the worst and the dimmest.

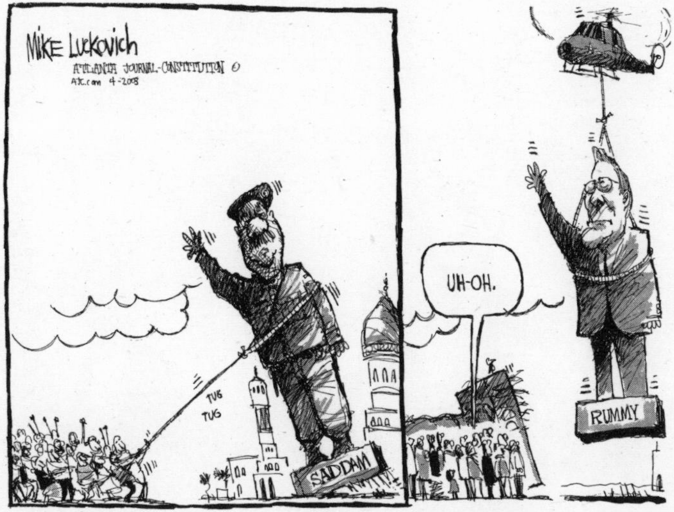
MIKE LUCKOVICH
ATLANTA JOURNAL-CONSTITUTION
AJC.com 4-2008
TUG
TUG
SADDAM
UH-OH.
RUMMY

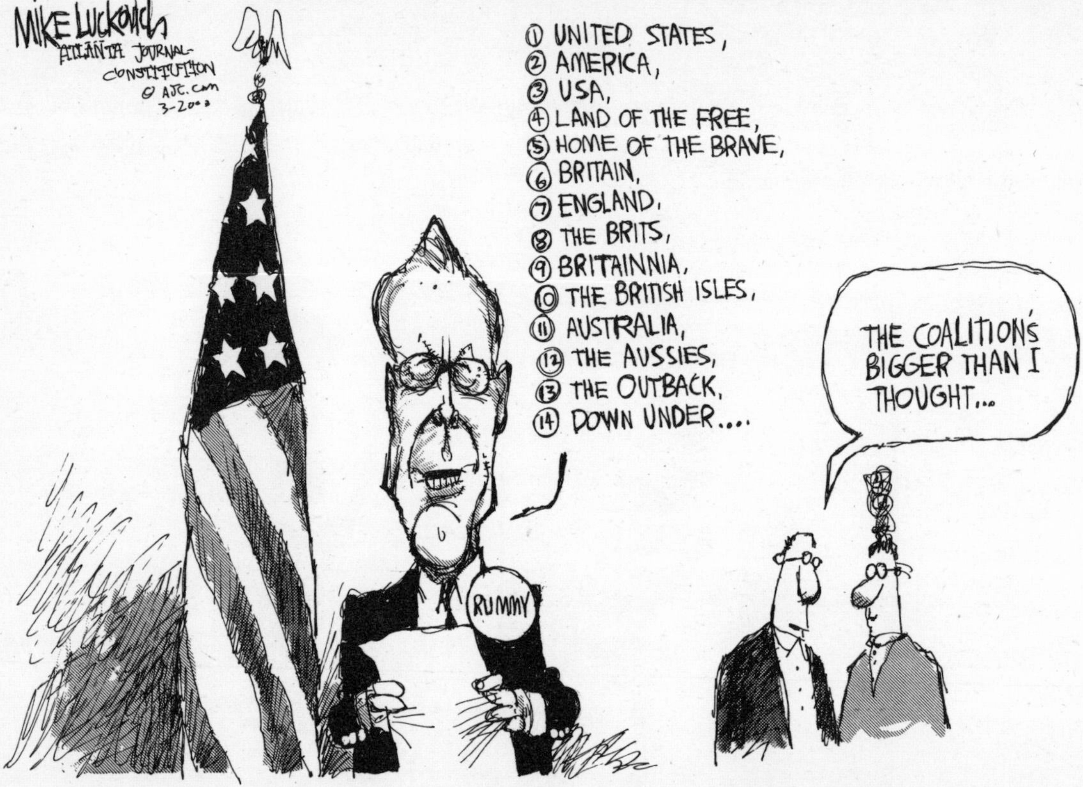
MIKE LUCKOVICH
ATLANTA JOURNAL-CONSTITUTION
© AJC.com
3-2003
① UNITED STATES,
② AMERICA,
③ USA,
④ LAND OF THE FREE,
⑤ HOME OF THE BRAVE,
⑥ BRITAIN,
⑦ ENGLAND,
⑧ THE BRITS,
⑨ BRITAINNIA,
⑩ THE BRITISH ISLES,
⑪ AUSTRALIA,
⑫ THE AUSSIES,
⑬ THE OUTBACK,
⑭ DOWN UNDER....
RUMMY
THE COALITION'S BIGGER THAN I THOUGHT...

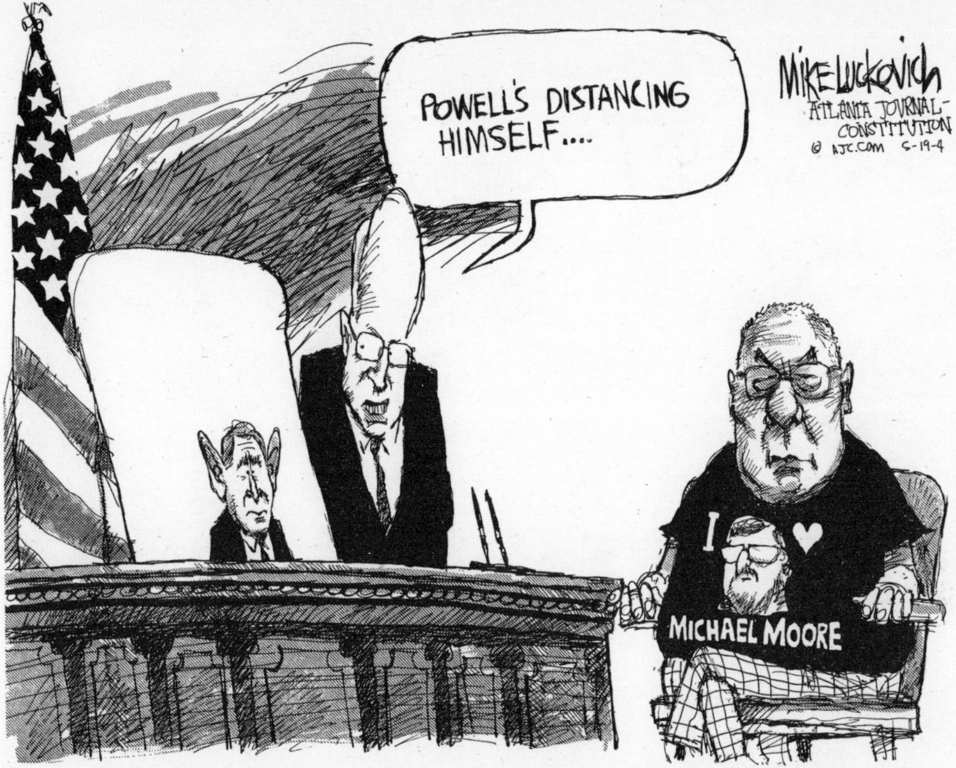
POWELL'S DISTANCING HIMSELF....
MIKE LUCKOVICH
ATLANTA JOURNAL-CONSTITUTION
© AJC.COM 5-19-4
I ♥
MICHAEL MOORE

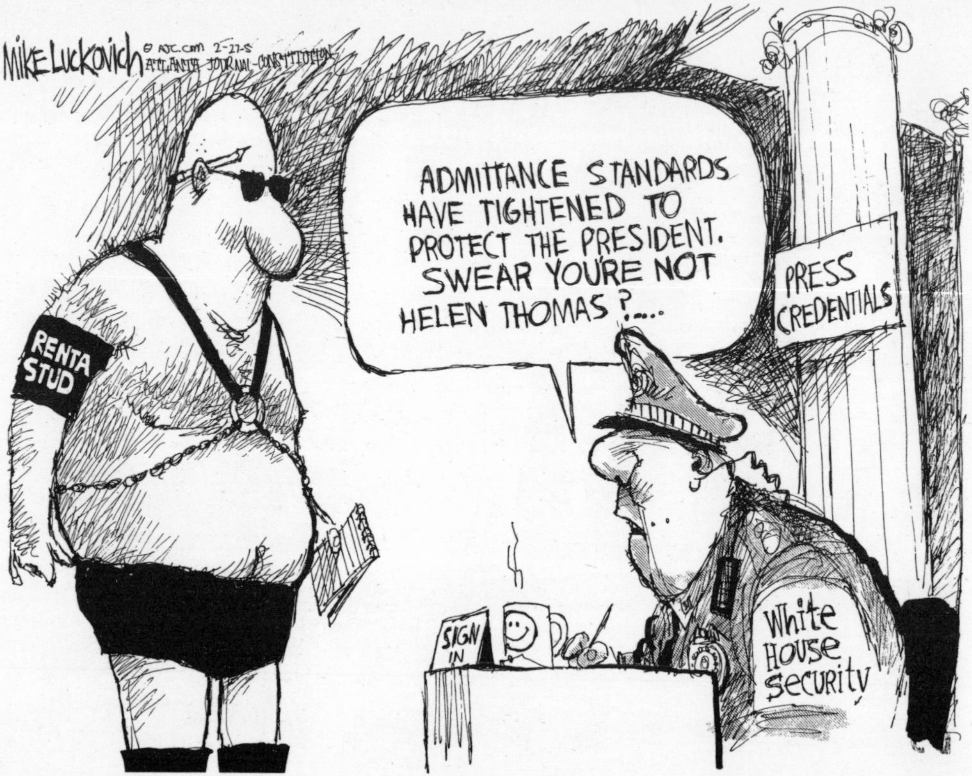
MIKE LUCKOVICH © AJC.com 2-27-5 ATLANTA JOURNAL-CONSTITUTION
ADMITTANCE STANDARDS HAVE TIGHTENED TO PROTECT THE PRESIDENT. SWEAR YOU'RE NOT HELEN THOMAS ?....
PRESS CREDENTIALS
RENTA STUD
SIGN IN
White House Security

I ADMIT TO ACCEPTING PAYMENTS FROM THE WHITE HOUSE TO CLAIM SPRING'S AROUND THE CORNER....
GROUNDHOG
MIKE LUCKOVICH © AJC.com
ATLANTA JOURNAL-CONSTITUTION
1-27-5

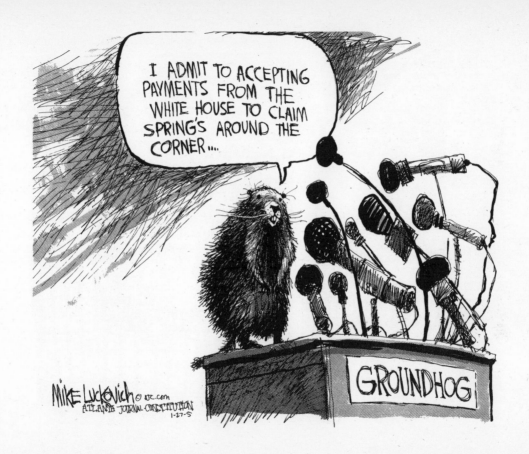

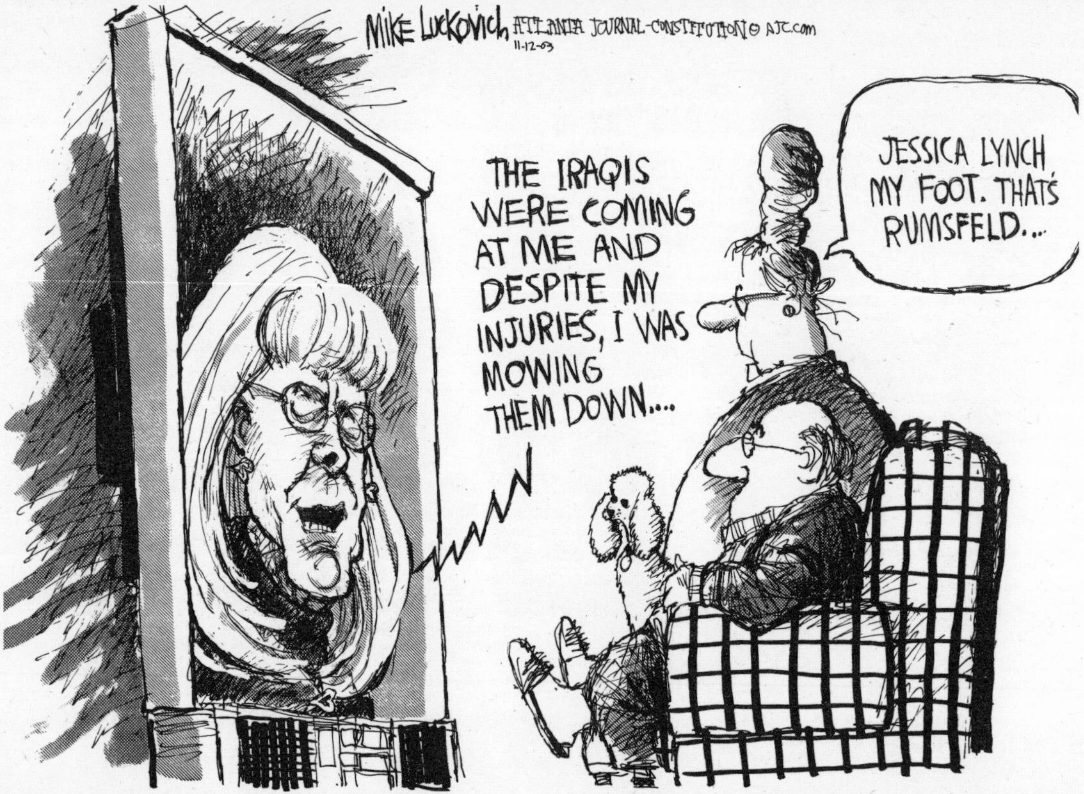
MIKE LUCKOVICH, ATLANTA JOURNAL-CONSTITUTION © AJC.com
11-12-03
THE IRAQIS WERE COMING AT ME AND DESPITE MY INJURIES, I WAS MOWING THEM DOWN....
JESSICA LYNCH MY FOOT. THAT'S RUMSFELD....

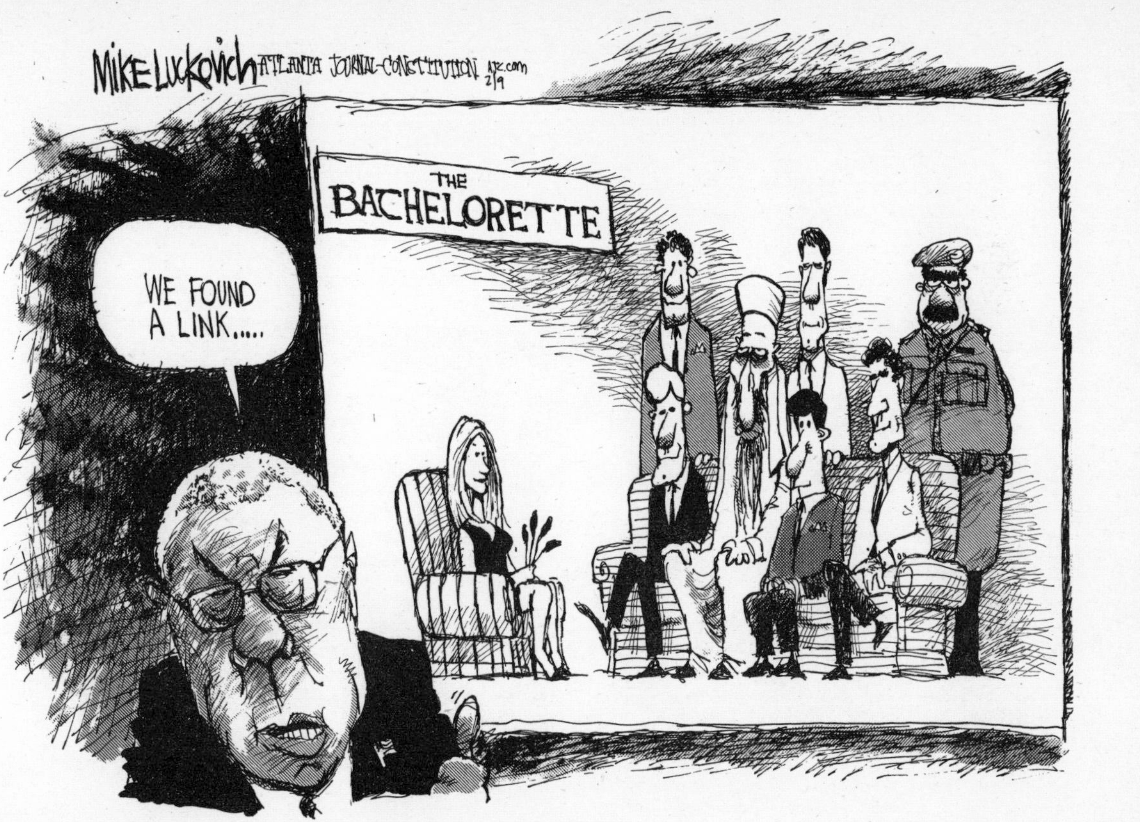
MIKE LUCKOVICH ATLANTA JOURNAL-CONSTITUTION AJC.com 2/9
THE BACHELORETTE
WE FOUND A LINK.....

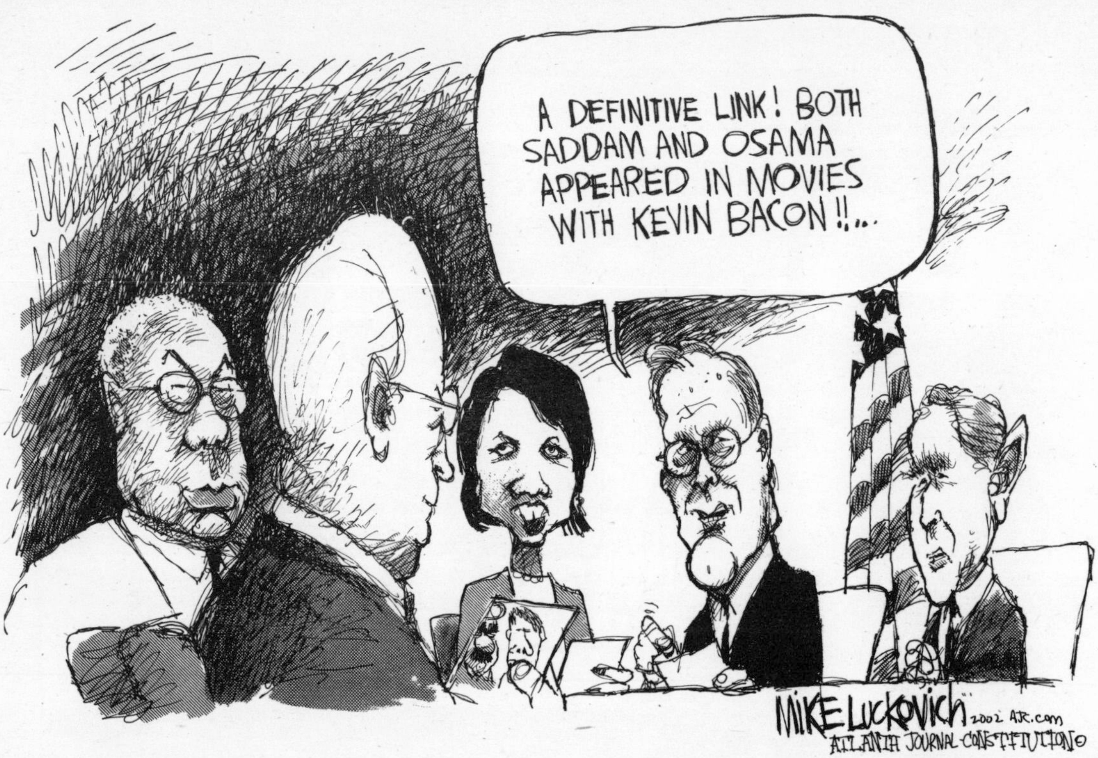
A DEFINITIVE LINK! BOTH SADDAM AND OSAMA APPEARED IN MOVIES WITH KEVIN BACON!!...
MIKE LUCKOVICH 2002 AJC.com
ATLANTA JOURNAL-CONSTITUTION©

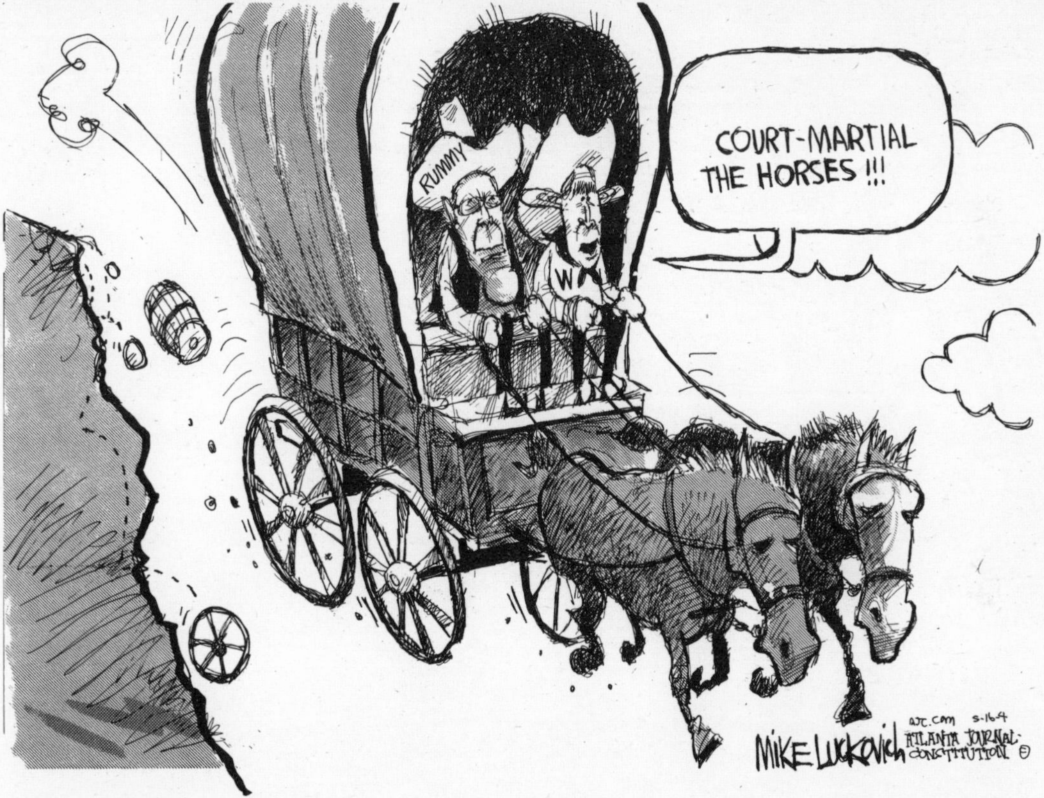
COURT-MARTIAL THE HORSES !!!
RUMMY
W
MIKE LUCKOVICH
ajc.com 5-16-4
ATLANTA JOURNAL-CONSTITUTION

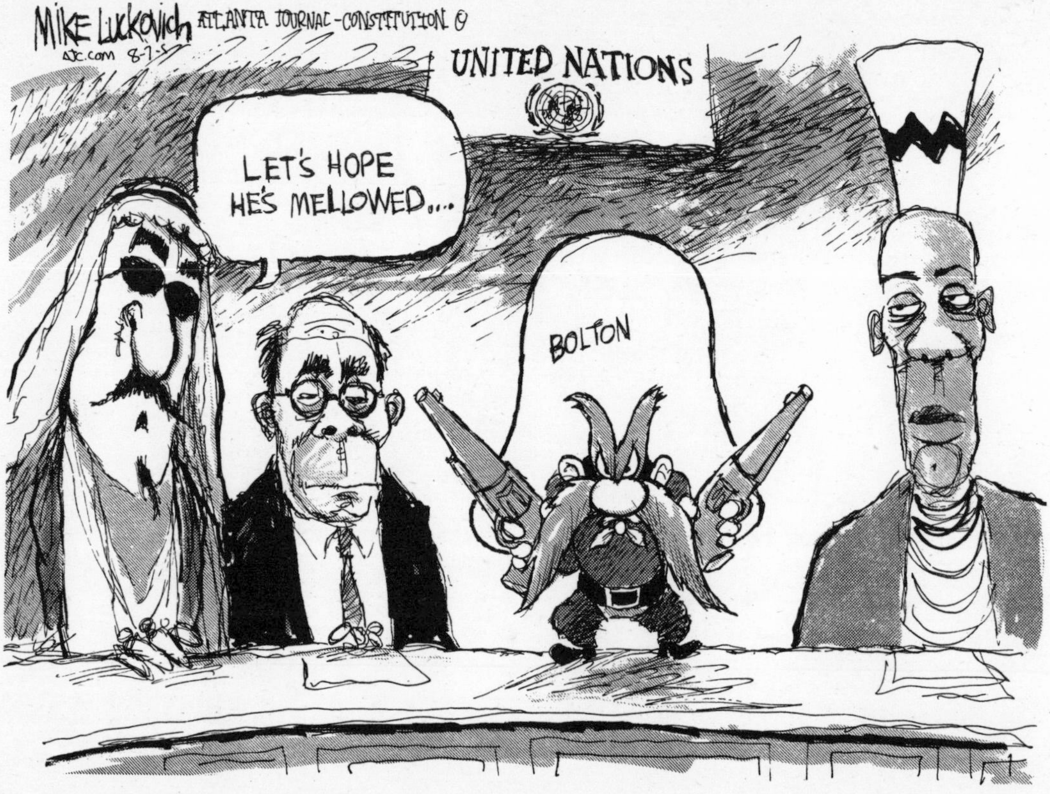
MIKE LUCKOVICH ATLANTA JOURNAL-CONSTITUTION ©
AJC.COM 8-7-5
UNITED NATIONS
LET'S HOPE HE'S MELLOWED....
BOLTON

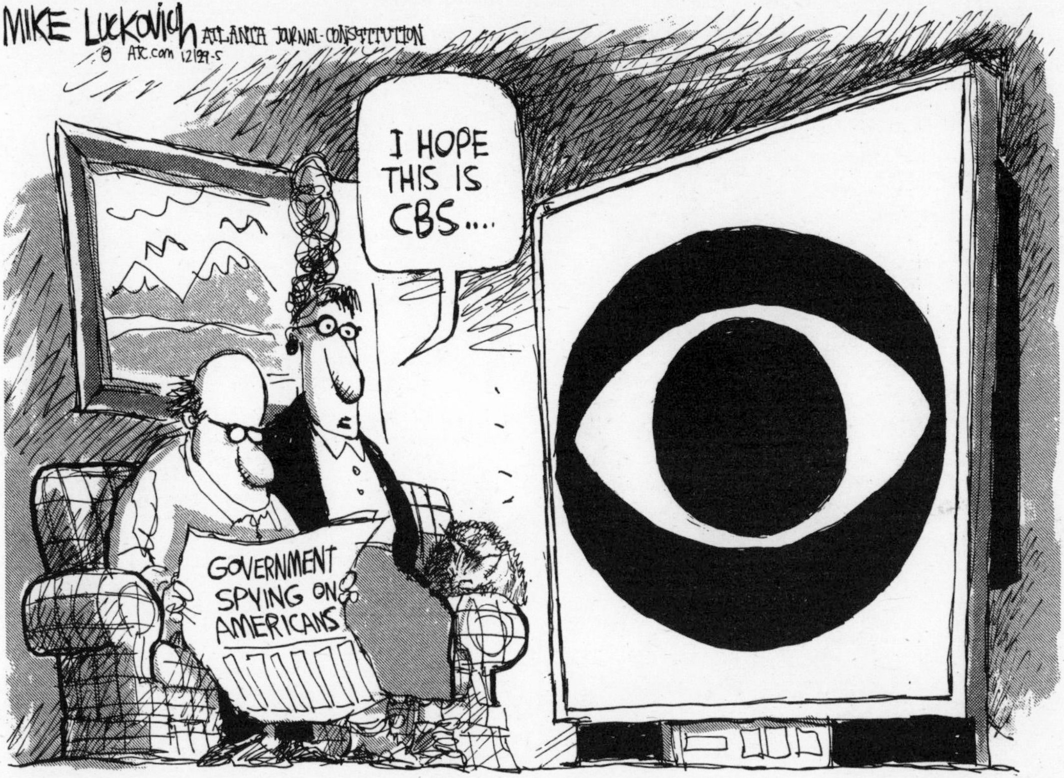
MIKE LUCKOVICH ATLANTA JOURNAL-CONSTITUTION
© AJC.com 12/29-5
I HOPE THIS IS CBS....
GOVERNMENT SPYING ON AMERICANS

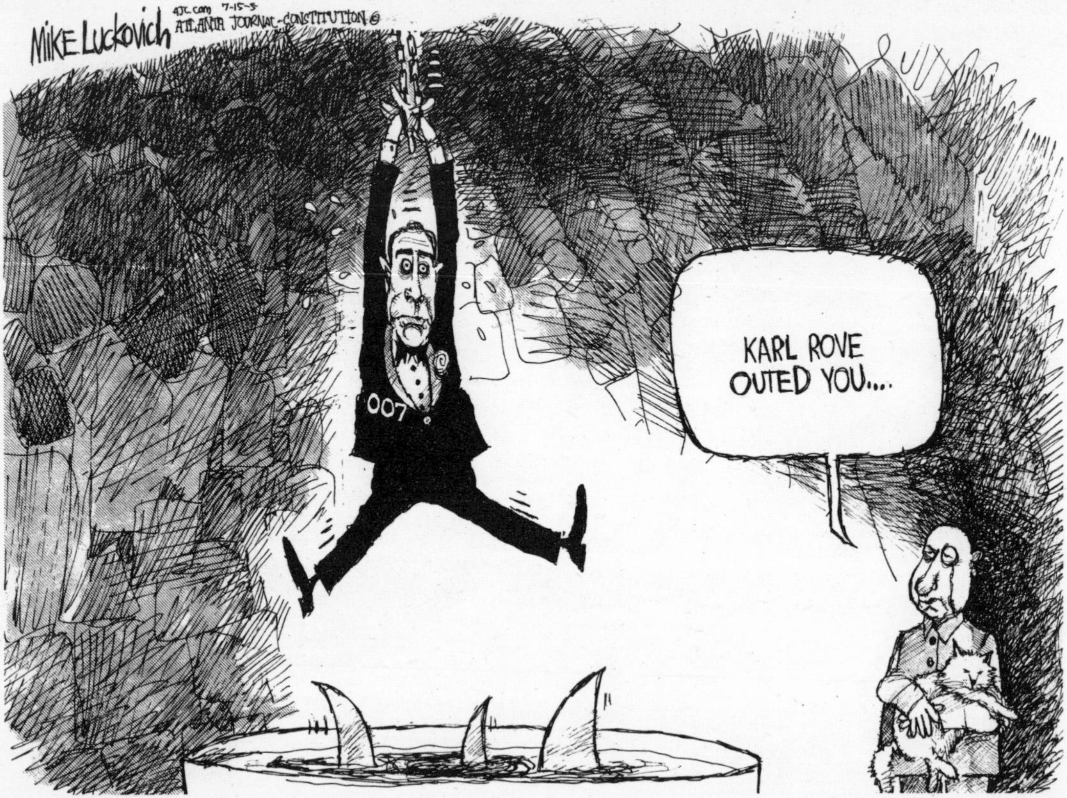
MIKE LUCKOVICH
ajc.com 7-15-5
ATLANTA JOURNAL-CONSTITUTION ©
007
KARL ROVE OUTED YOU....

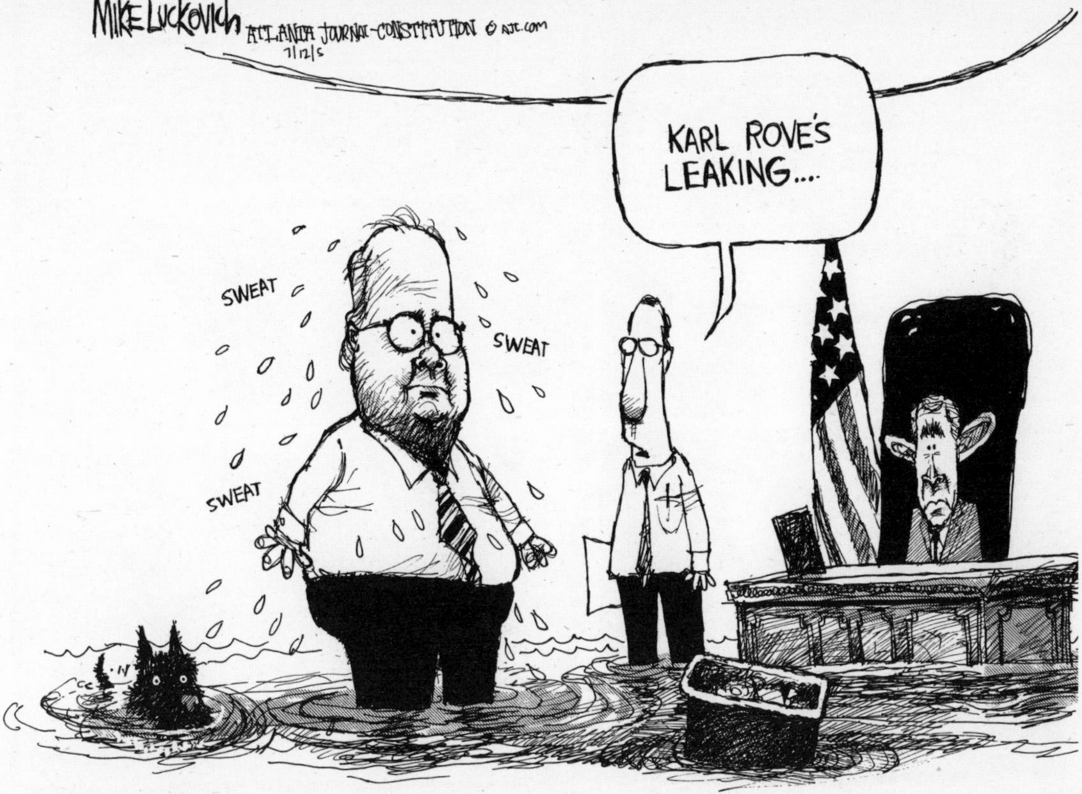
MIKE LUCKOVICH ATLANTA JOURNAL-CONSTITUTION © AJC.COM
7/12/5
KARL ROVE'S LEAKING....
SWEAT
SWEAT
SWEAT

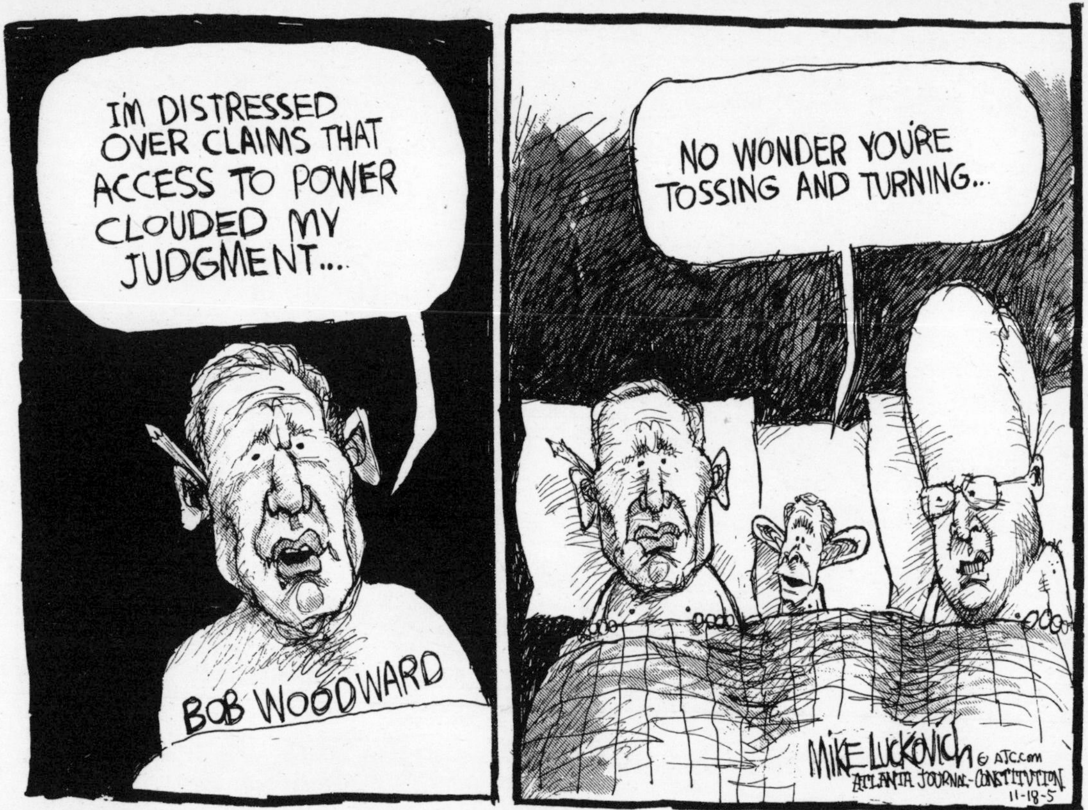
I'M DISTRESSED OVER CLAIMS THAT ACCESS TO POWER CLOUDED MY JUDGMENT....
BOB WOODWARD
NO WONDER YOU'RE TOSSING AND TURNING...
MIKE LUCKOVICH © AJC.com
ATLANTA JOURNAL-CONSTITUTION
11-18-5

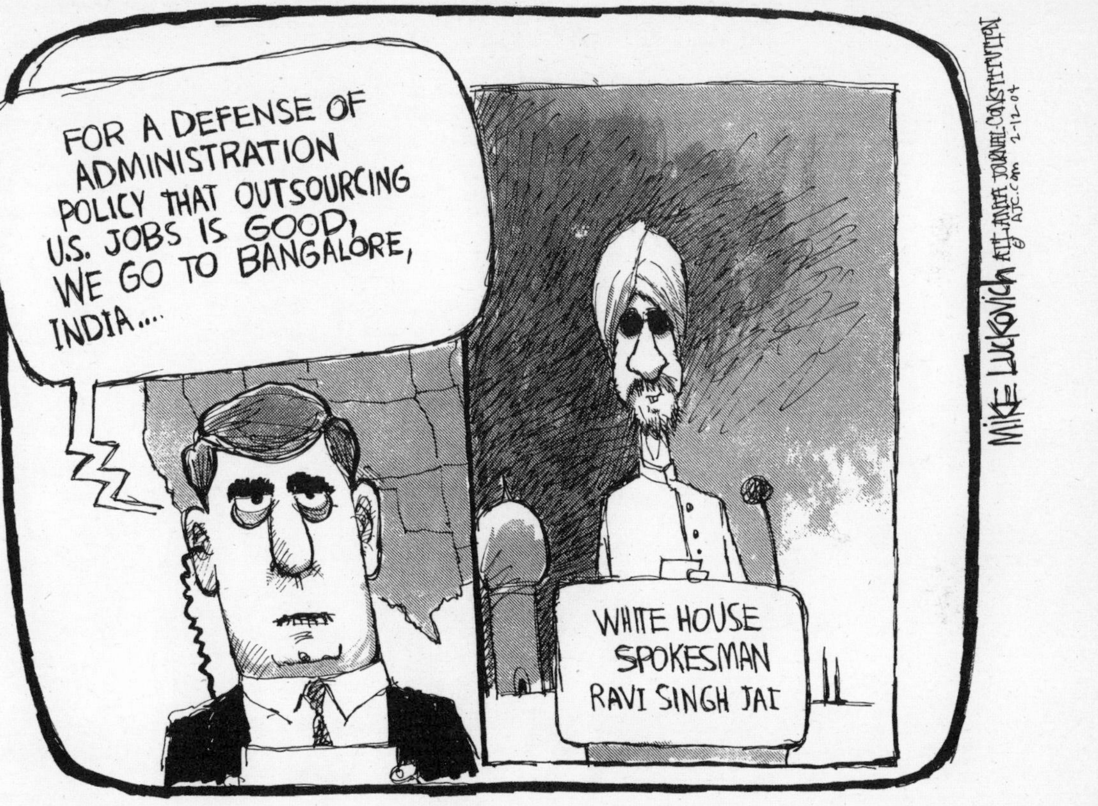
FOR A DEFENSE OF ADMINISTRATION POLICY THAT OUTSOURCING U.S. JOBS IS GOOD, WE GO TO BANGALORE, INDIA....
WHITE HOUSE SPOKESMAN RAVI SINGH JAI
MIKE LUCKOVICH
ATLANTA JOURNAL-CONSTITUTION
© AJC.com 2-12-04

TREASURY SECRETARY O'NEILL & BONO IN AFRICA

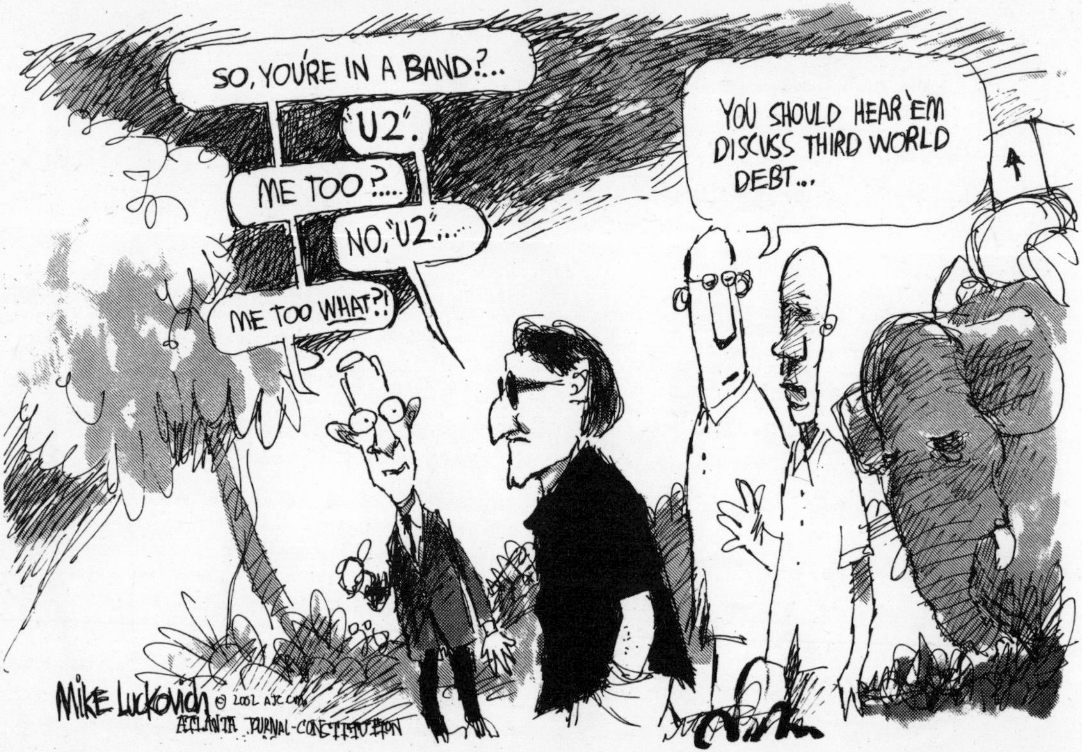
SO, YOU'RE IN A BAND?...
"U2".
ME TOO?....
NO, "U2"....
ME TOO WHAT?!
YOU SHOULD HEAR 'EM DISCUSS THIRD WORLD DEBT...
MIKE LUCKOVICH
ATLANTA JOURNAL-CONSTITUTION

Rumsfeld's Rules

Defense Secretary Donald Rumsfeld had requested the original drawings of a couple cartoons I had done recently, and I had been glad to oblige. So with the war now on, Torie Clarke, the assistant secretary of defense for public affairs, invited me to come up to Washington for a visit.

I guess she thought that having a cartoonist hanging around the Pentagon might lighten the mood a bit. She also mentioned something about a one-armed push-up contest with a marine in her office.

After arriving and waiting to attend my first briefing, a massively muscled marine asked if I was ready for "the contest." I thought Clarke had been joking, but I thought wrong. So, in the middle of her office, the one-armed competition began. I did six more than the marine.

Short cartoonists are so often underestimated.

As it happened, President Bush was coming to the Pentagon that morning to give a pep talk to the assembled brass. Alongside him at the podium would be Rumsfeld, Rumsfeld's right-hand man Paul Wolfowitz, and six or eight generals.

The best part of the event was watching the preparation, because I had no idea it would be so choreographed. White House advance personnel spent forty-five minutes rearranging pieces of masking tape on the floor. The tape contained the names of all the generals, and the advance crew had to make sure they'd all fit in the camera angle with Bush.

After the speech, I was standing in the hall when Rumsfeld, his aides, and a photographer friend of mine, David Kennerly, walked by. "C'mon," Kennerly said, and I followed. Rumsfeld saw me and said, "What's he doing here?"

For the rest of the day, he said the same thing whenever he saw me.

We went to Rumsfeld's office. I was told to make sure my cellphone was off because of security reasons.

Alarms sound if a cellphone is on in his office. We walked past Rumsfeld's desk and into a small side bathroom. Rumsfeld showed me early photos of himself with the German rocket designer Wernher von Braun and past presidents. On the adjacent wall were cartoons. Rumsfeld pointed out two of mine that I'd recently sent.

I was escorted out shortly after that, as if he had more important things to do. Sheesh.

At 11:30, I was brought back to Rumsfeld's office to watch a "pre-briefing" to prepare Rumsfeld for the actual press briefing he would be giving twenty minutes later. Besides Rumsfeld, the meeting included Clarke, General Richard Myers (then chairman of the Joint Chiefs of Staff), Paul Wolfowitz, and four or five other aides. The purpose of such a gathering is to anticipate what the press will ask and go over the best answers.

"What's he doing here?" Rumsfeld asked as soon as he saw me. "Draw us however you want, but whatever you do, don't make General Myers look bad."

Clarke threw questions at Rumsfeld: "Wasn't this war supposed to be a cakewalk?" Then Rumsfeld, Clarke, and Myers decided on an appropriate response — in this case, stressing that the war had been going on only a few days.

Rumsfeld has a desk in his office, but he doesn't use it. Instead he stands at a chest-high table. As I drew this scene, Wolfowitz inquired whether I might be able to come by his office later to do a sketch.

As the pre-briefing ended, I showed Rumsfeld my drawing and pointed out how "pretty" I'd made Myers.

We left Rumsfeld's office and headed to the briefing. Clarke had been right; many of the questions she had asked Rumsfeld were asked by the press as well.

After the briefing, Rumsfeld, Clarke, the general, assorted aides, my photographer friend, and I all headed back to the defense secretary's office. I moved up next to Rumsfeld as he conversed with Myers and

Clarke. I leaned in as if I were part of the discussion, hoping Kennerly would take a picture. Rumsfeld stopped and pointed to a photo in the Pentagon hallway of him and some old dude.

"Who am I with?" he asked me.

"That's Eisenhower," I answered.

And we walked on.

At 1:15, I was ushered into a lunch meeting with former defense secretaries and national security officers. Madeleine Albright, Frank Carlucci, James Schlesinger, Zbigniew Brzezinski, Robert McNamara, William Cohen, and R. James Woolsey were being briefed on the administration's vision of a postwar Iraq.

They were hard to draw because they were all chewing.

That was my last official event, so I wandered over to Wolfowitz's office. He's the architect of "pre-emptive" war. He asked if I'd draw some of his staff. I said sure, if he'd draw a cartoon of himself.

He reluctantly agreed, so it was Wolfowitz and me seated side by side at a little round table in his office drawing cartoons. I ended up drawing him, his entire staff, and spending an hour with him. We discussed Iraq and North Korea. I think I straightened him out.

He gave me a little blue hardcover book called *Rumsfeld's Rules* by the defense secretary. When I got back to Atlanta I opened it up and noticed it was signed, "To Paul for all you do and do so well — Donald Rumsfeld." Maybe he gave me the wrong one.

At 3:30, I left Wolfowitz and went back to Clarke's office to say goodbye and to thank her. You have to be escorted out of the Pentagon. The sergeant who escorted me out said, "This is the most fun we've had here."

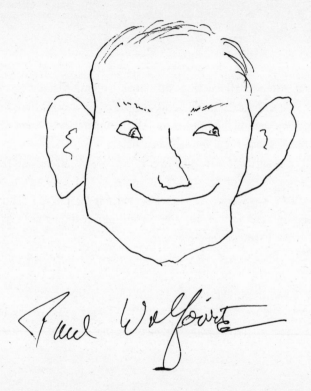

Paul Wolfowitz

ONE ARMED PUSH-UP CONTEST IN TORIE CLARK'S OFFICE

PRE-BRIEFING IN RUMMY'S OFFICE

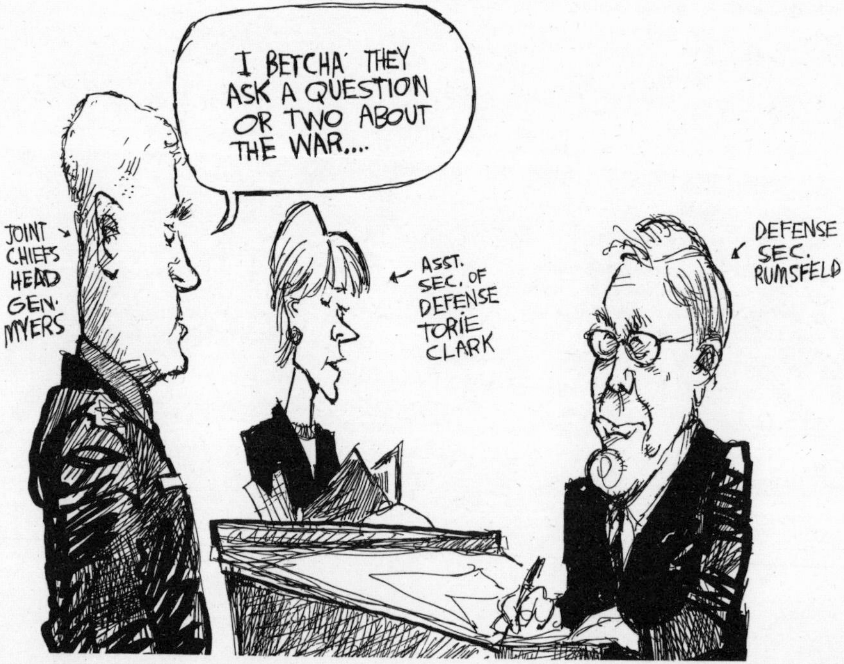
I BETCHA' THEY ASK A QUESTION OR TWO ABOUT THE WAR....
JOINT CHIEFS HEAD GEN. MYERS
ASST. SEC. OF DEFENSE TORIE CLARK
DEFENSE SEC. RUMSFELD

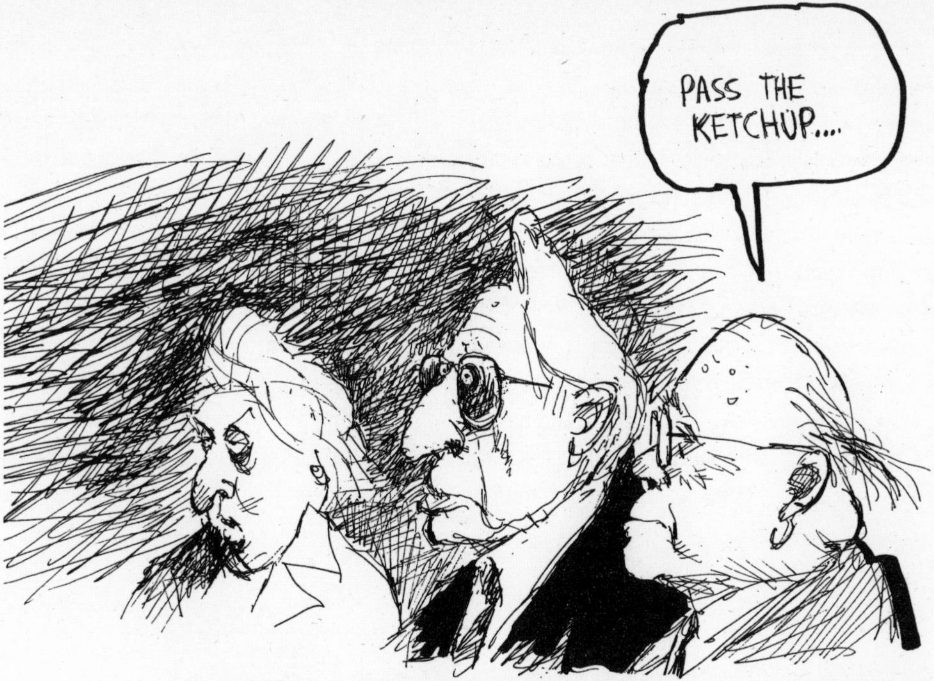
PASS THE KETCHUP....

ALBRIGHT, CARLUCCI & MACNAMARA AT A LUNCHEON FOR FORMER DEFENSE SECRETARIES & NATL. SECURITY ADVISERS

Rummy and I

I got a call from a general at the Pentagon, requesting copies of a couple of cartoons I had done on Rumsfeld. These cartoons weren't flattering, but he requested them anyway. Some politicians don't care whether you take shots at them in cartoons. Rumsfeld fits in that category. Other politicians get greatly offended. Newt Gingrich is that type, which is the type I prefer. The general told me that if I sent an extra copy, Rumsfeld would sign it and send it back to me.

"Big deal," I thought, "why would I want a Rumsfeld-signed copy of my own cartoon?" Instead, I drew an official-looking memo that had a seal in the top left-hand corner that said Rummy with Rumsfeld's face in it and across the top I wrote, "From the Office of Defense Secretary Rumsfeld." In the middle I wrote, "This entitles super-patriot, Mike Luckovich, unlimited use of one gassed-up M1 Abram's tank and free lunch at the Pentagon cafeteria." At the bottom, I drew a line for Rumsfeld's signature.

A cartoonist friend of mine said Rumsfeld would never sign something like that, but a week later I received it back signed by Rumsfeld with two addendums. First, the Pentagon lunch wouldn't be at taxpayers' expense and second, the tank I'd be using would be in a country of their choosing.

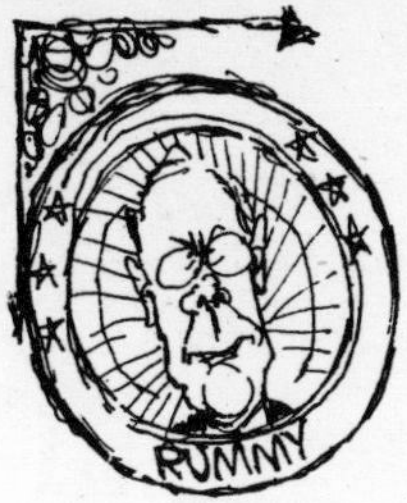
RUMMY

From the Desk of Defense Secretary Donald Rumsfeld

★ OFFICIAL ★

THIS ENTITLES AMERICAN PATRIOT, MIKE LUCKOVICH, WEEKEND USE OF GASSED-UP M1 ABRAMS' TANK,(1) PLUS FREE LUNCH AT PENTAGON CAFETERIA(2)

SIGNED ____________
DEFENSE SECRETARY

(1) In a country of our choice

(2) But not at taxpayer's expense

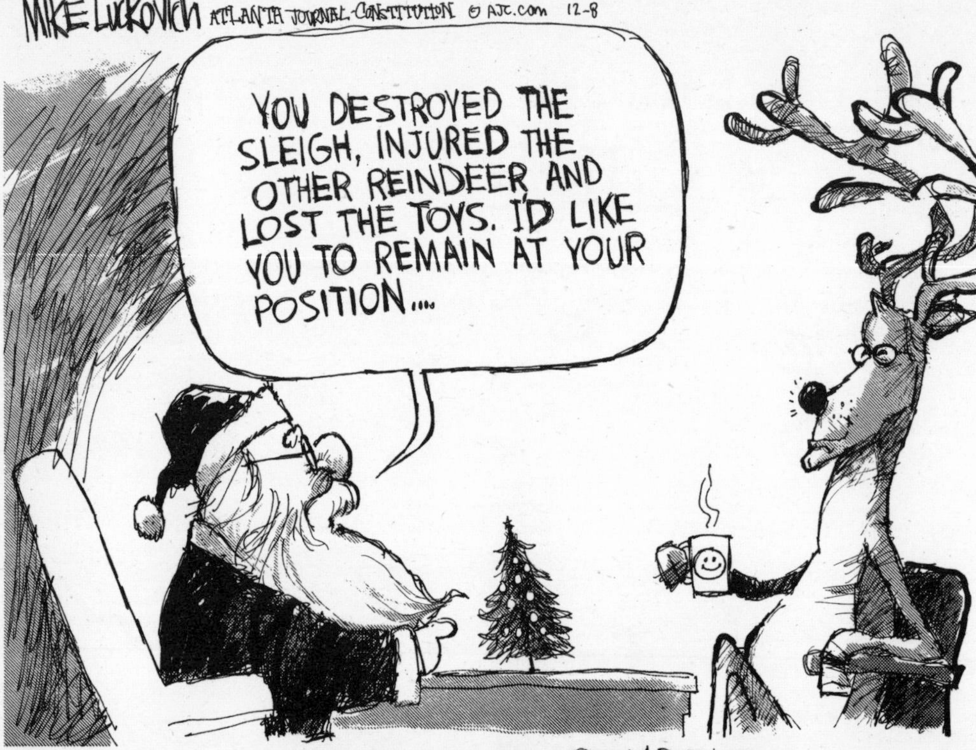
MIKE LUCKOVICH ATLANTA JOURNAL-CONSTITUTION © AJC.com 12-8
YOU DESTROYED THE SLEIGH, INJURED THE OTHER REINDEER AND LOST THE TOYS. I'D LIKE YOU TO REMAIN AT YOUR POSITION....

RUMSFELD THE REINDEER

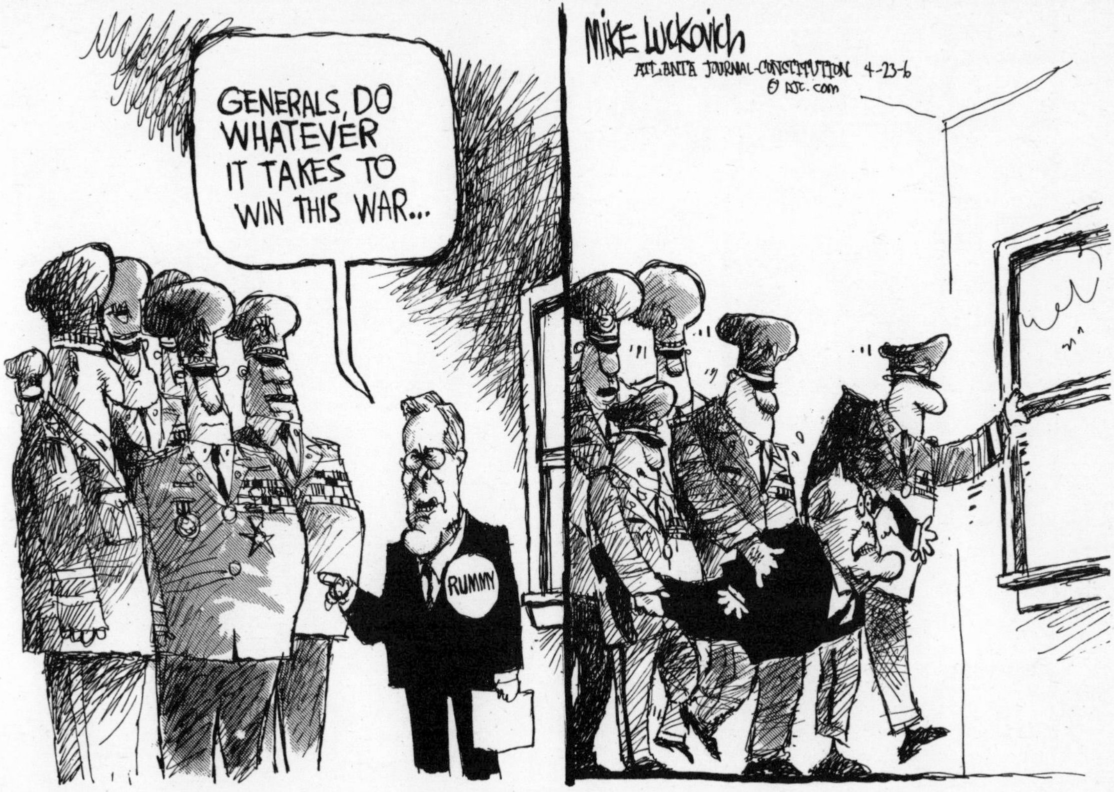
GENERALS, DO WHATEVER IT TAKES TO WIN THIS WAR...
RUMMY
MIKE LUCKOVICH
ATLANTA JOURNAL-CONSTITUTION 4-23-6
© AJC.com

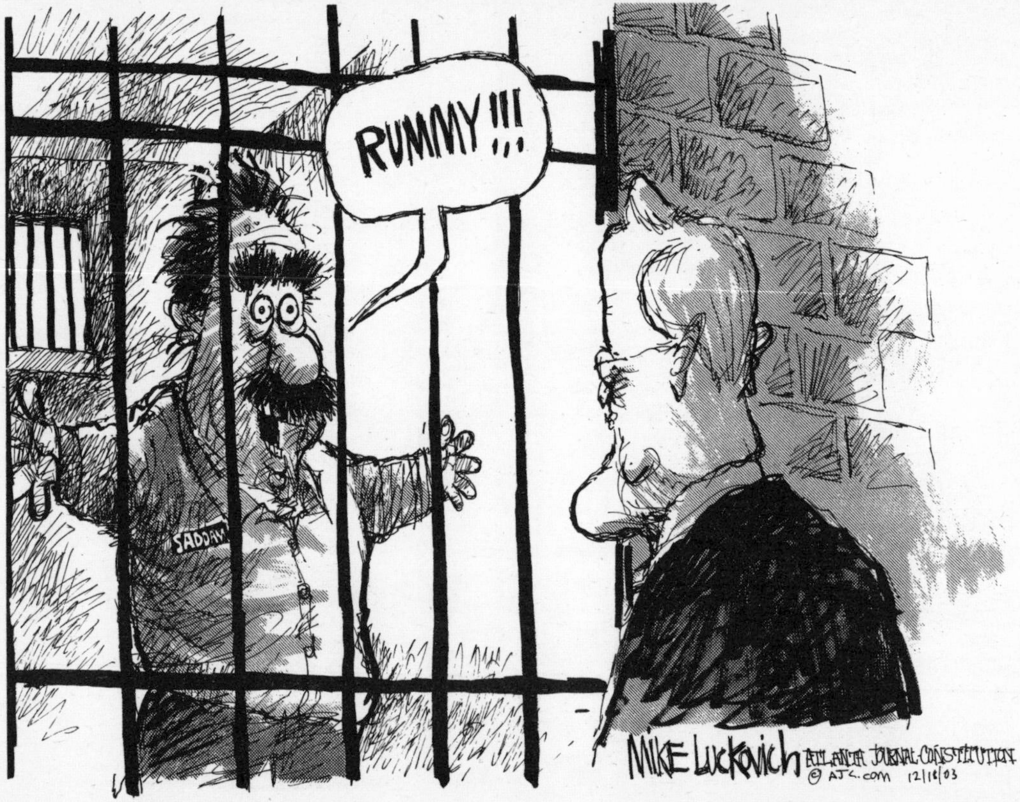
RUMMY!!!
SADDAM
MIKE LUCKOVICH ATLANTA JOURNAL-CONSTITUTION
© AJC.com 12/18/03

Campaign 2004

The 2004 campaign was depressing. The way Bush and Karl Rove, in conjunction with the Swift Boaters, smeared John Kerry, a genuine war hero, was sickening. And Kerry's seeming inability to respond forcefully enough to the smears was disappointing.

The Republicans are good at coming up with issues that get people stirred up but actually have no direct impact on their lives, like gay marriage. So instead of being concerned about things that really affect them and their families, such as affordable health care, they get caught up in whatever straw man the GOP has come up with. And as soon as the election is over, the issue disappears.

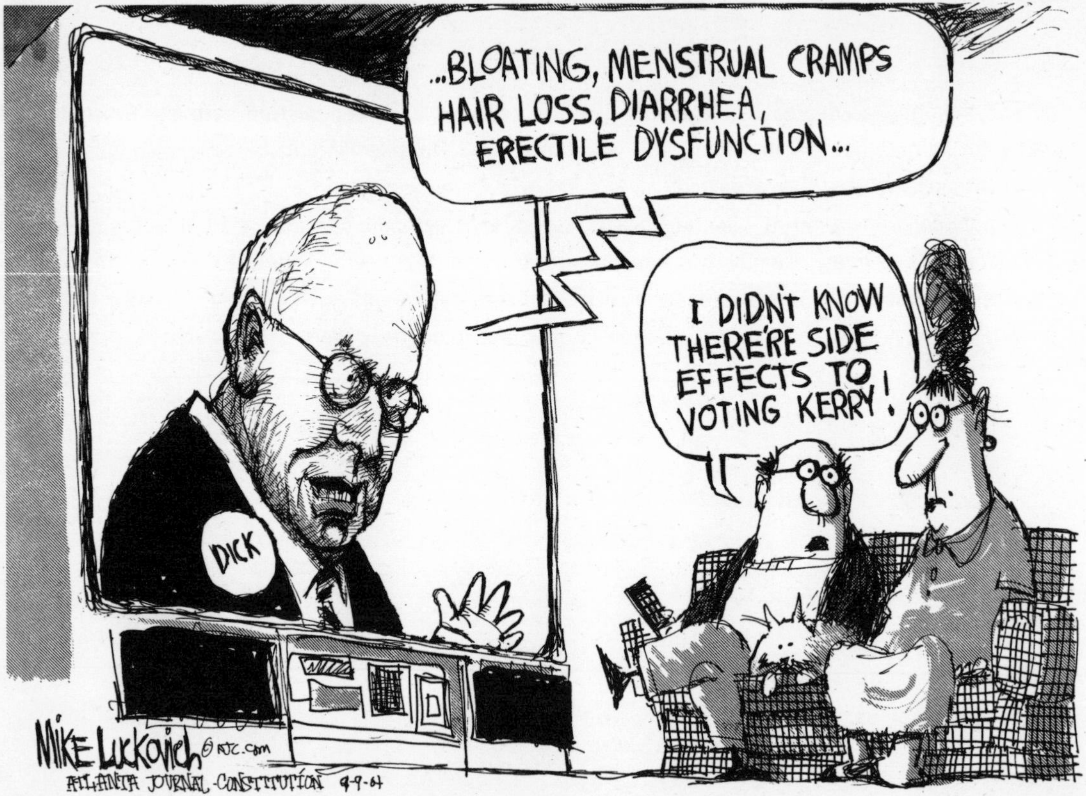
...BLOATING, MENSTRUAL CRAMPS HAIR LOSS, DIARRHEA, ERECTILE DYSFUNCTION...
DICK
I DIDN'T KNOW THERE'RE SIDE EFFECTS TO VOTING KERRY!
MIKE LUCKOVICH © AJC.com
ATLANTA JOURNAL-CONSTITUTION 9-9-04

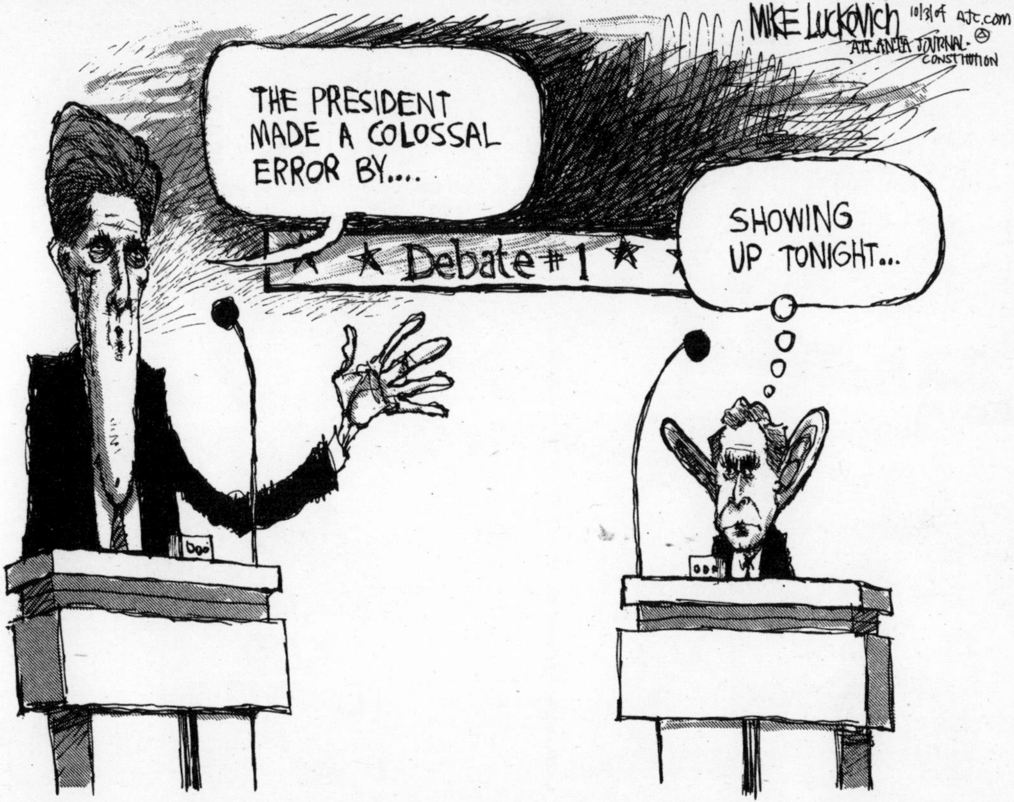
MIKE LUCKOVICH 10/1/04 ajc.com
ATLANTA JOURNAL-CONSTITUTION
THE PRESIDENT MADE A COLOSSAL ERROR BY....
Debate #1
SHOWING UP TONIGHT...

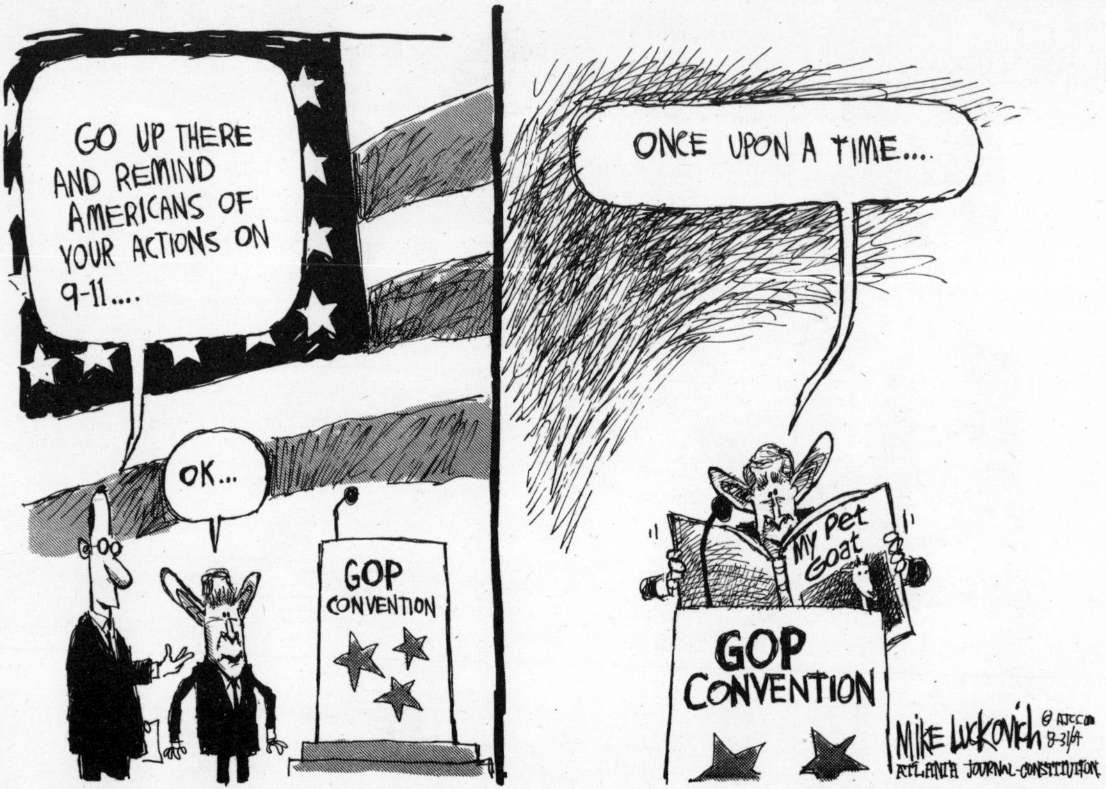
GO UP THERE AND REMIND AMERICANS OF YOUR ACTIONS ON 9-11....
OK...
GOP CONVENTION
ONCE UPON A TIME....
My Pet Goat
GOP CONVENTION
MIKE LUCKOVICH
ATLANTA JOURNAL-CONSTITUTION

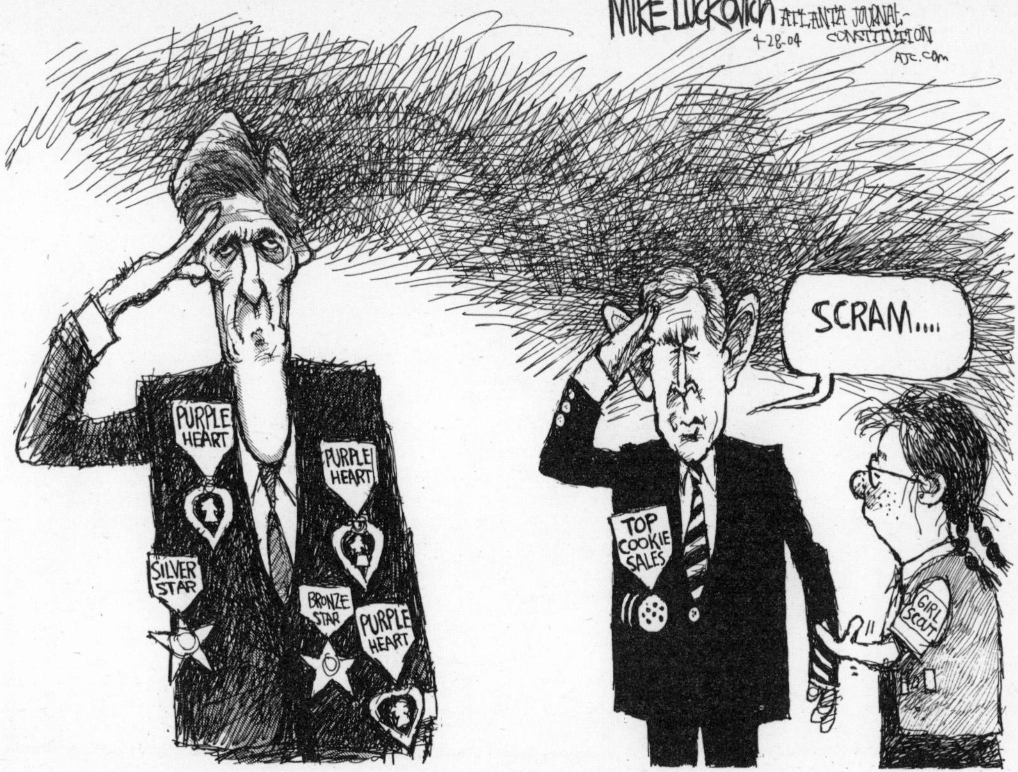
MIKE LUCKOVICH ATLANTA JOURNAL-CONSTITUTION
4-28-04
AJC.com
PURPLE HEART
PURPLE HEART
SILVER STAR
BRONZE STAR
PURPLE HEART
TOP COOKIE SALES
SCRAM....
GIRL SCOUT

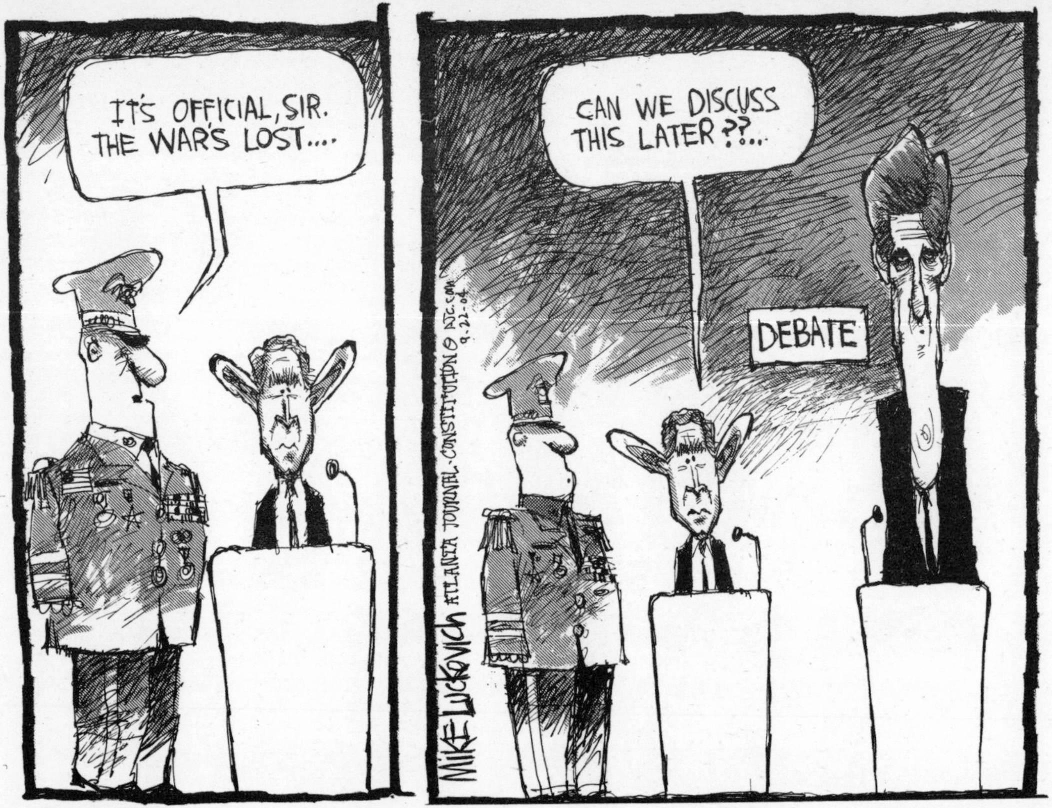
IT'S OFFICIAL, SIR. THE WAR'S LOST....
CAN WE DISCUSS THIS LATER??...
DEBATE
MIKE LUCKOVICH ATLANTA JOURNAL-CONSTITUTION © AJC.COM 9-22-04

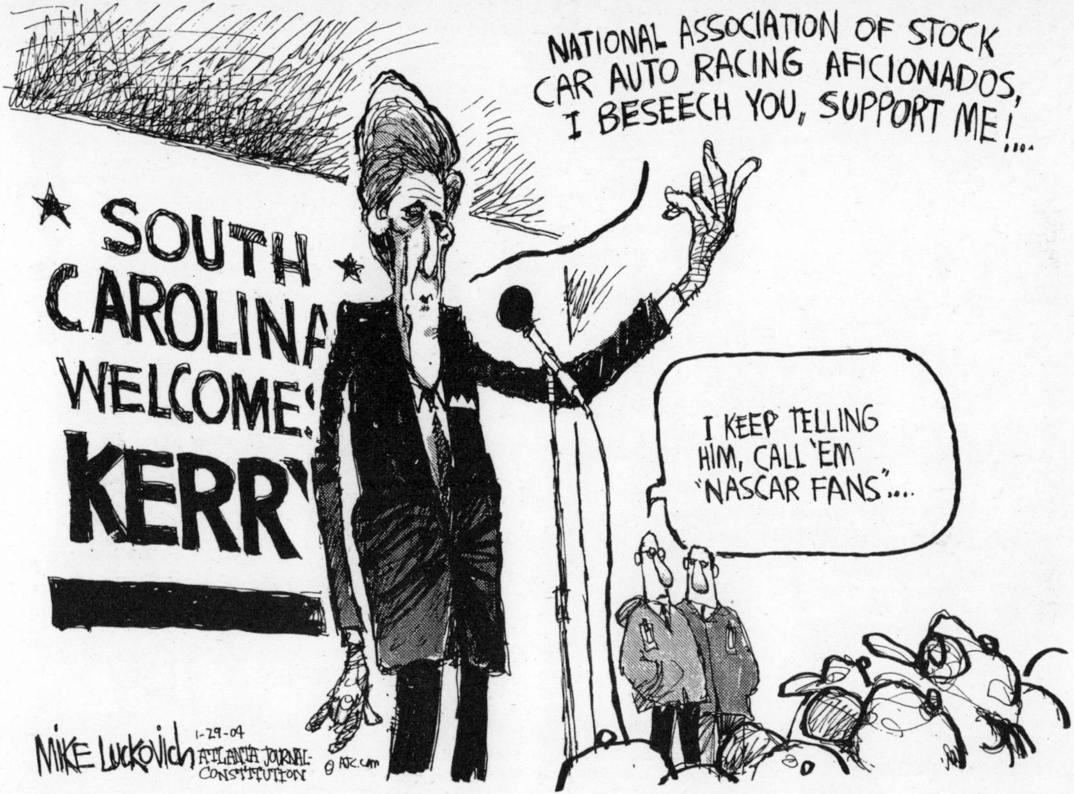
NATIONAL ASSOCIATION OF STOCK CAR AUTO RACING AFICIONADOS, I BESEECH YOU, SUPPORT ME!...
SOUTH CAROLINA WELCOMES KERRY
I KEEP TELLING HIM, CALL 'EM "NASCAR FANS"....
MIKE LUCKOVICH 1-29-04 ATLANTA JOURNAL-CONSTITUTION © AJC.com

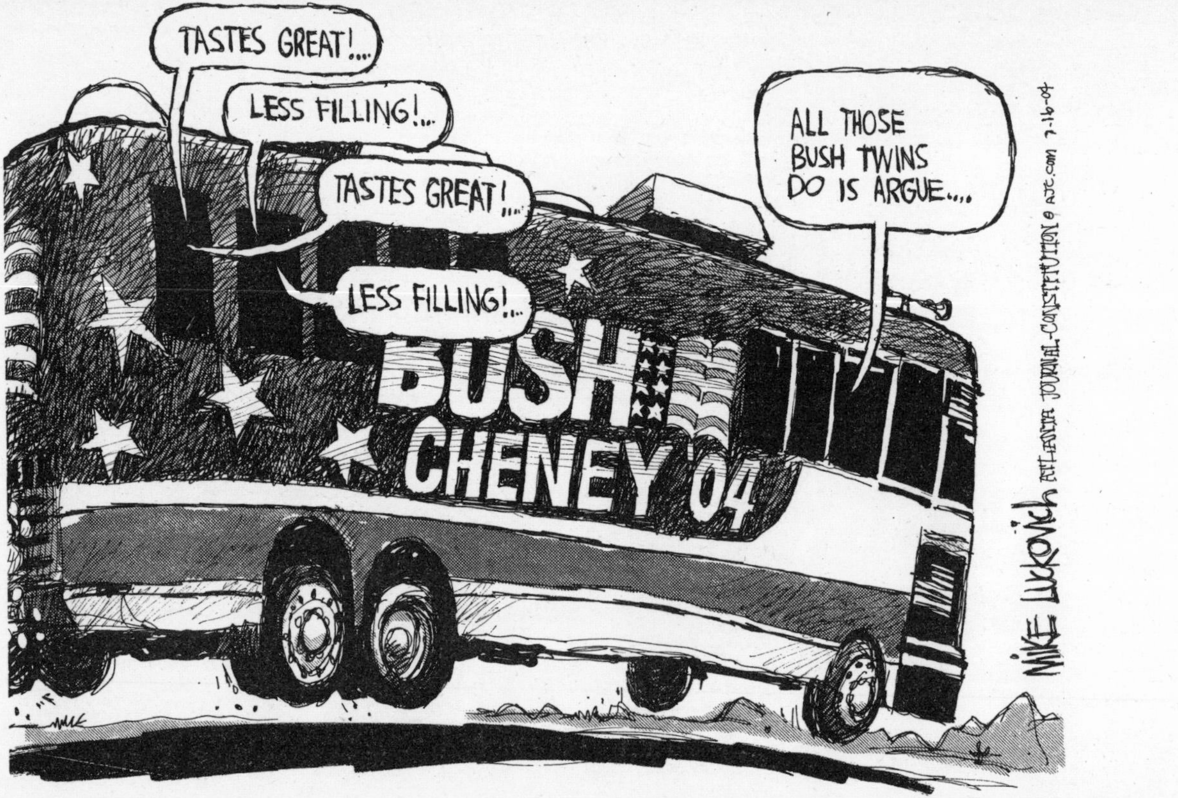
TASTES GREAT!....
LESS FILLING!...
TASTES GREAT!....
LESS FILLING!...
ALL THOSE BUSH TWINS DO IS ARGUE.....
BUSH
CHENEY '04
MIKE LUCKOVICH
ATLANTA JOURNAL-CONSTITUTION © AJC.com 2-16-04

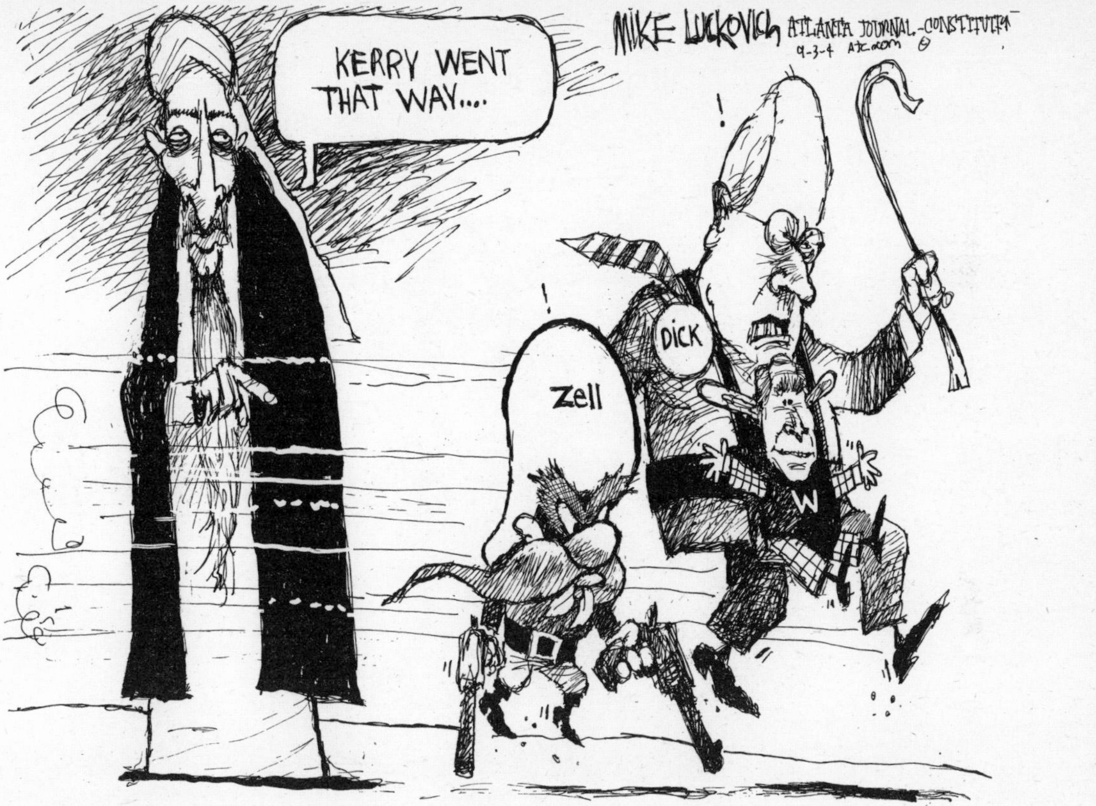
MIKE LUCKOVICH ATLANTA JOURNAL-CONSTITUTION
9-3-4 AJC.com
KERRY WENT THAT WAY....
ZELL
DICK
W

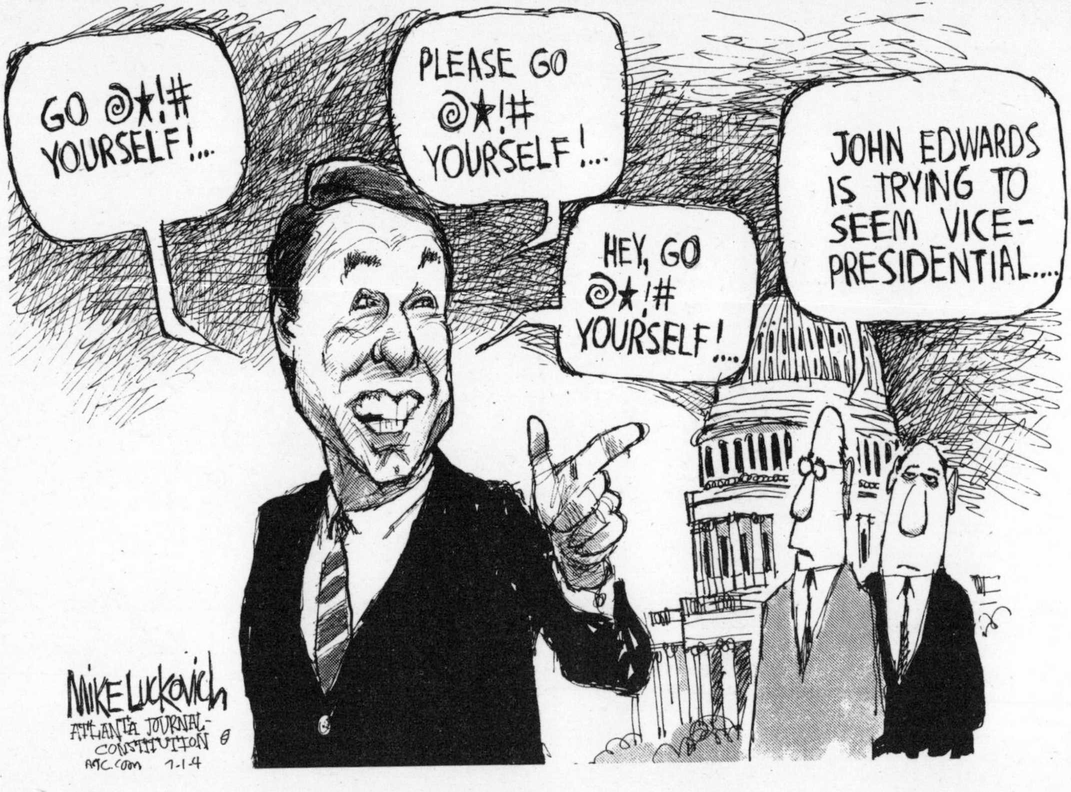
GO @★!# YOURSELF!...
PLEASE GO @★!# YOURSELF!...
HEY, GO @★!# YOURSELF!...
JOHN EDWARDS IS TRYING TO SEEM VICE-PRESIDENTIAL....
MIKE LUCKOVICH
ATLANTA JOURNAL-CONSTITUTION
AJC.com 7-1-4

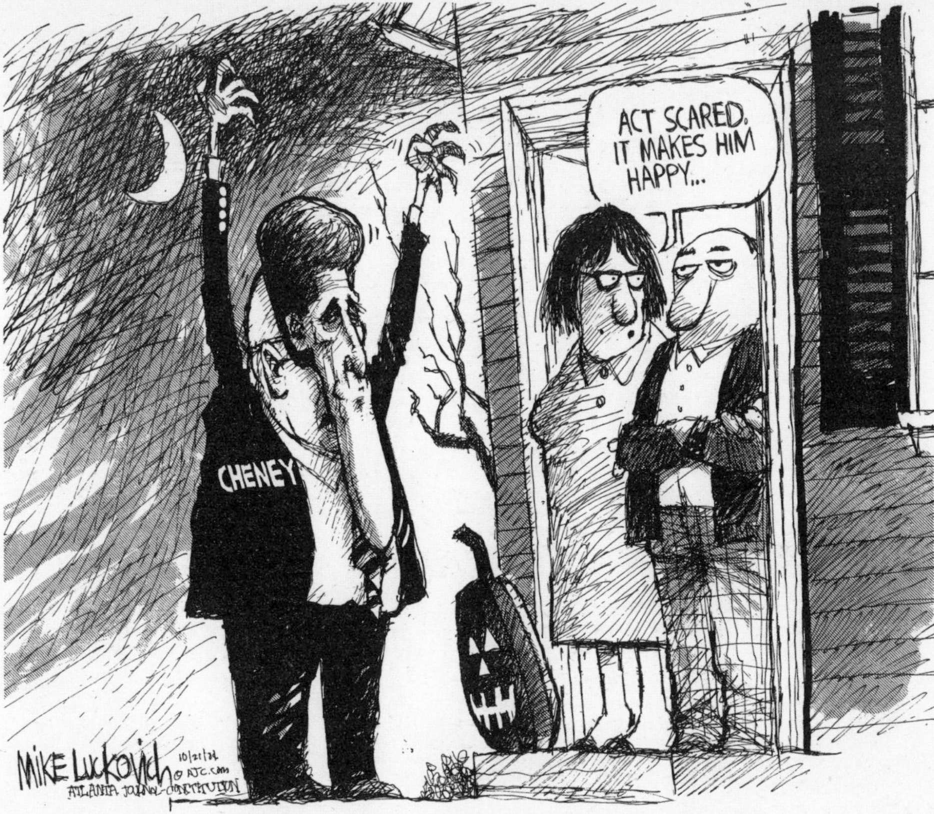
CHENEY
ACT SCARED.
IT MAKES HIM
HAPPY...
MIKE LUCKOVICH
ATLANTA JOURNAL-CONSTITUTION

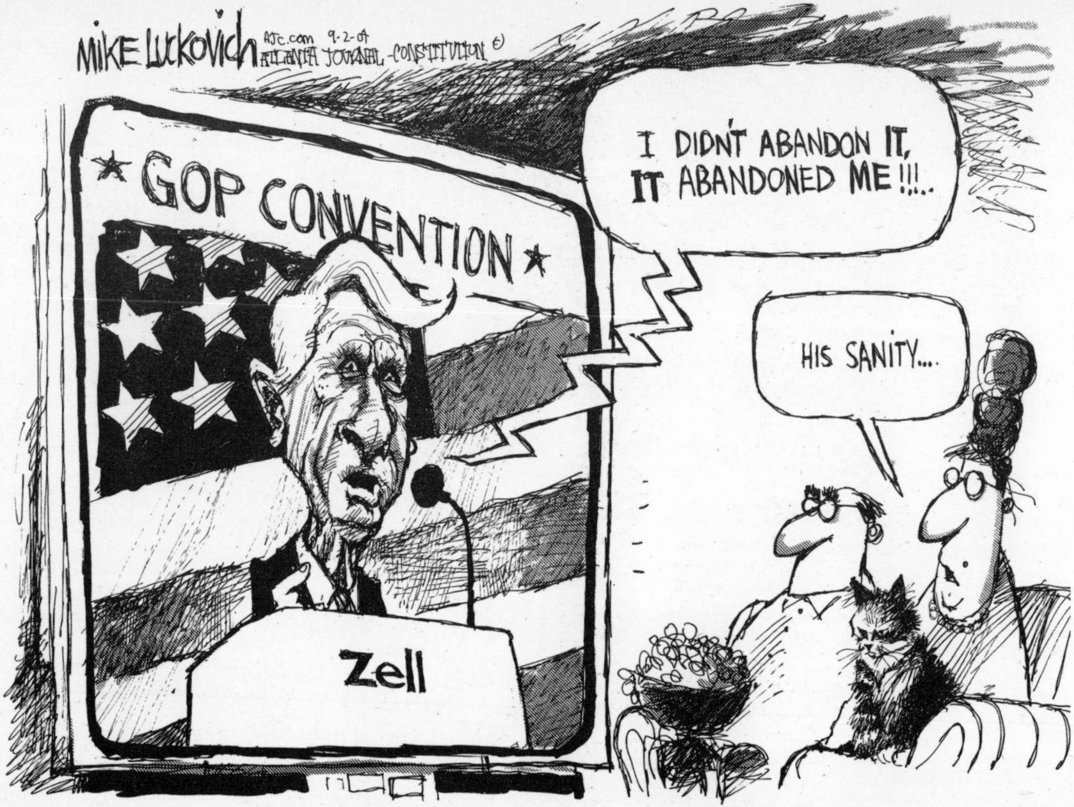
MIKE LUCKOVICH AJC.com 9-2-04 ATLANTA JOURNAL-CONSTITUTION
★GOP CONVENTION★
I DIDN'T ABANDON IT, IT ABANDONED ME!!!...
HIS SANITY....
Zell

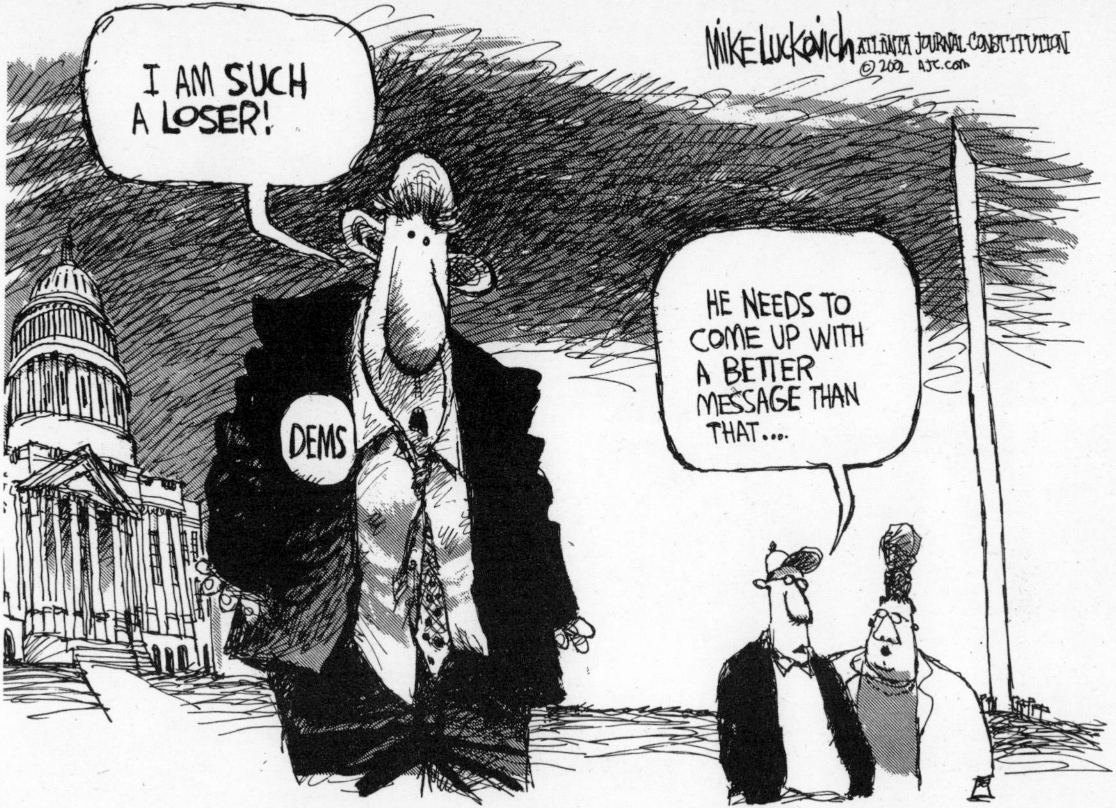
MIKE LUCKOVICH ATLANTA JOURNAL-CONSTITUTION
© 2002 AJC.com
I AM SUCH A LOSER!
DEMS
HE NEEDS TO COME UP WITH A BETTER MESSAGE THAN THAT....

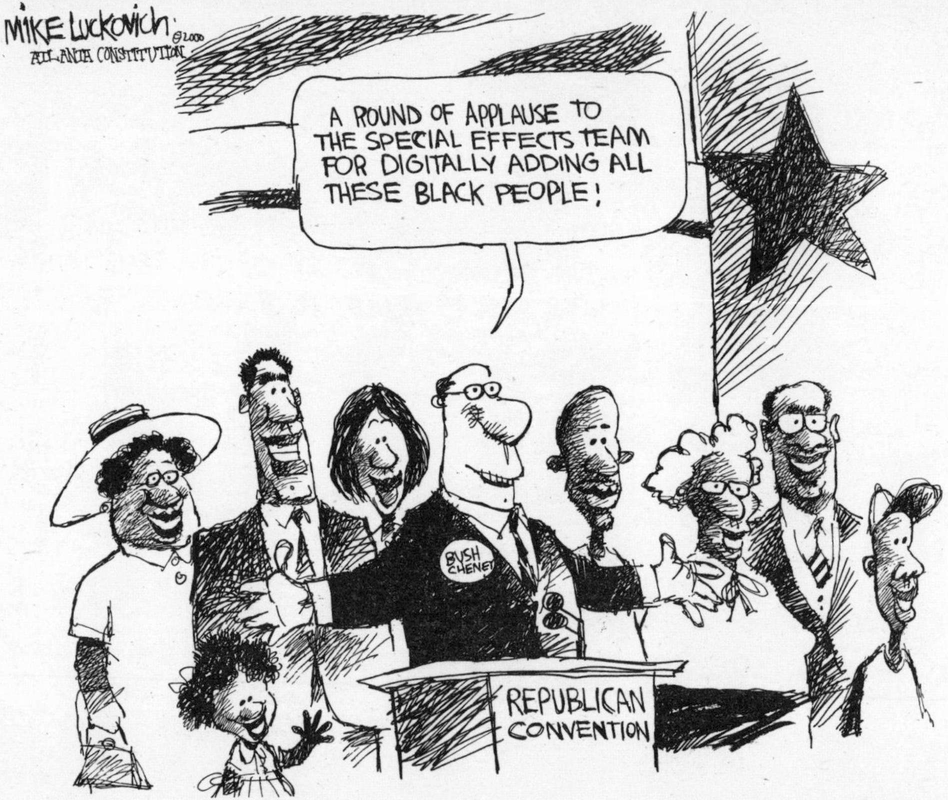
MIKE LUCKOVICH ©2000 ATLANTA CONSTITUTION
A ROUND OF APPLAUSE TO THE SPECIAL EFFECTS TEAM FOR DIGITALLY ADDING ALL THESE BLACK PEOPLE!
BUSH CHENEY
REPUBLICAN CONVENTION

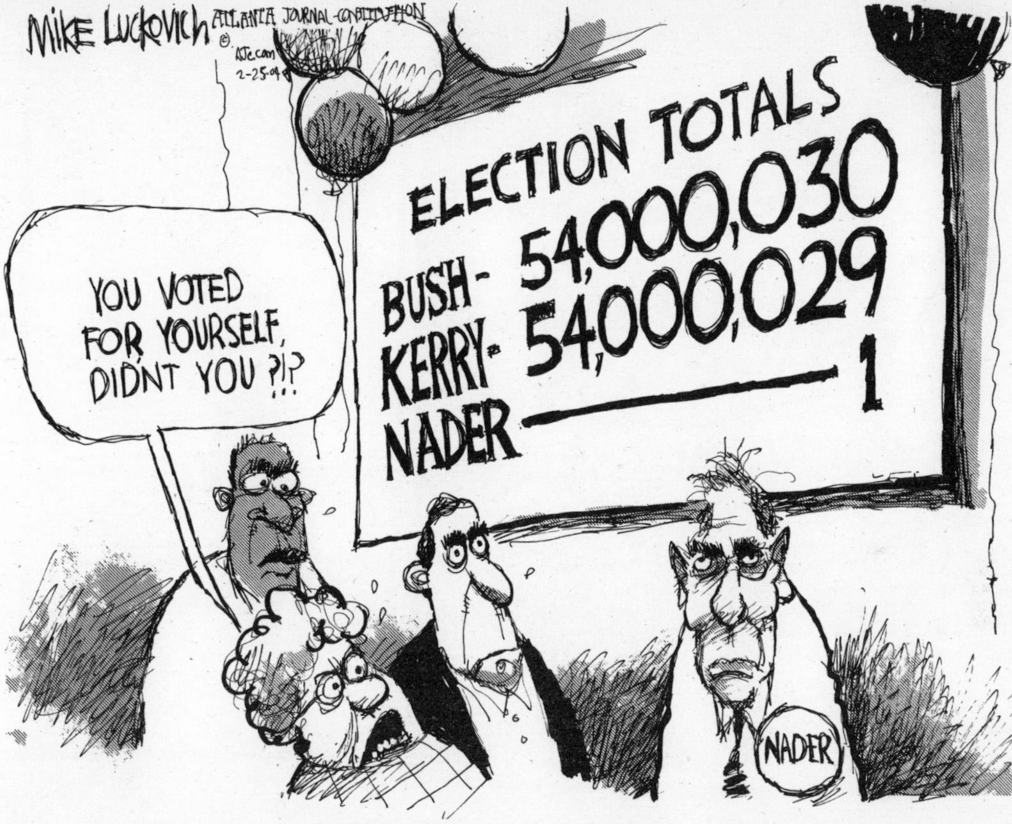

Mike Luckovich
ATLANTA JOURNAL-CONSTITUTION
ELECTION TOTALS
BUSH- 54,000,030
KERRY- 54,000,029
NADER 1
YOU VOTED FOR YOURSELF, DIDN'T YOU ?!?
NADER

THE PASSION
IT'S REIGNITED CONTROVERSY OVER WHO KILLED CHRIST...
JOHN KERRY.
RNC
MIKE LUCKOVICH ATLANTA JOURNAL-CONSTITUTION AJC.COM 2-15-04

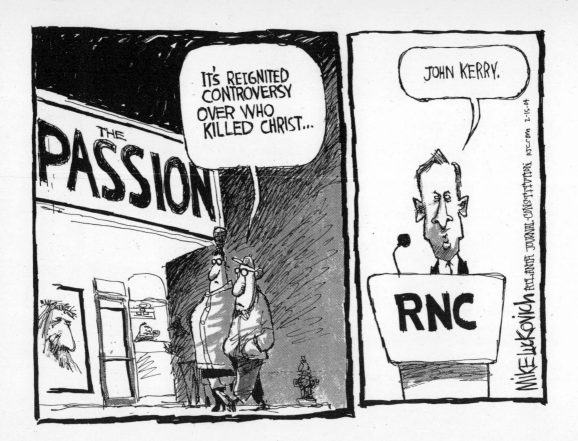

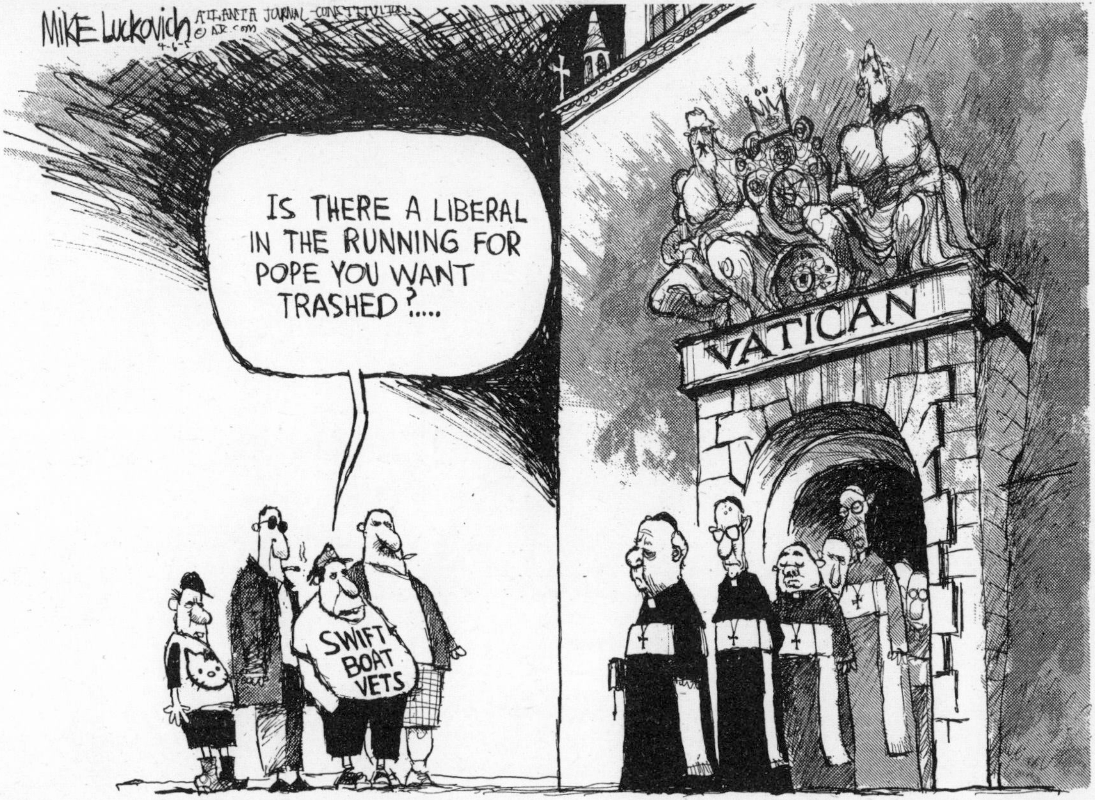
MIKE LUCKOVICH
IS THERE A LIBERAL IN THE RUNNING FOR POPE YOU WANT TRASHED?.....
VATICAN
SWIFT BOAT VETS

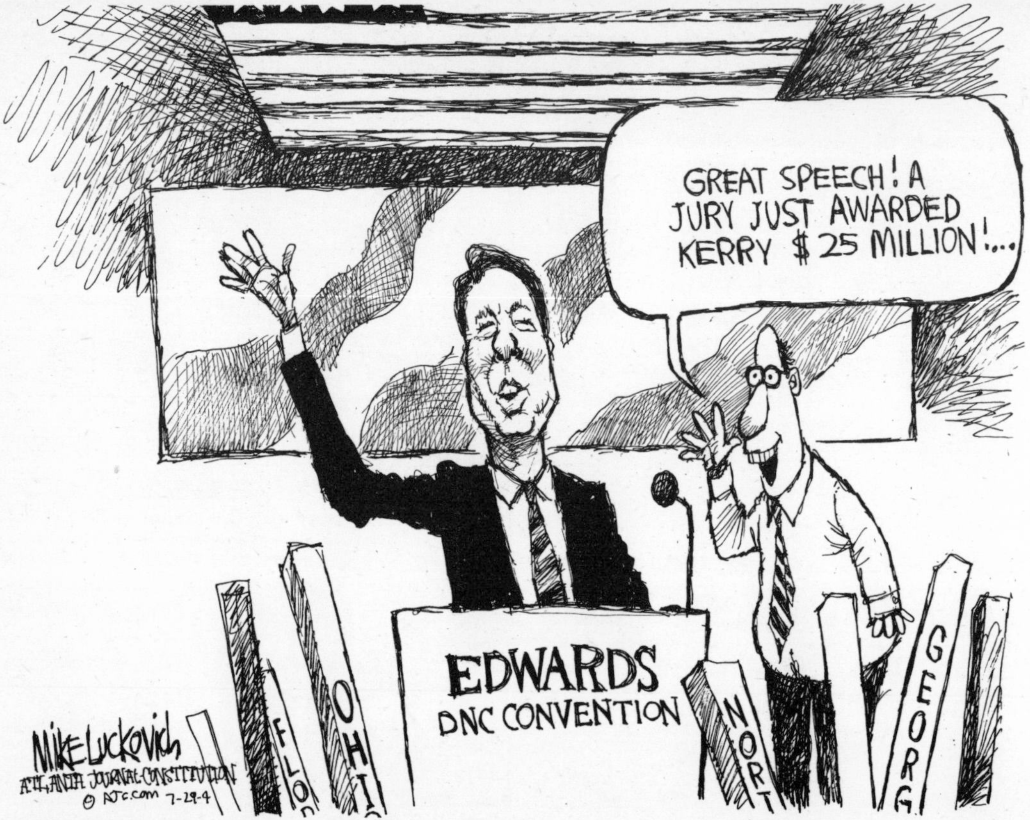
GREAT SPEECH! A JURY JUST AWARDED KERRY $25 MILLION!...
EDWARDS
DNC CONVENTION
OHIO
FLOR
NORT
GEORG
Mike Luckovich
Atlanta Journal-Constitution
© AJC.com 7-29-4

The Republicans

Thanks to the Republicans, DC is awash in corruption. And not just small-time corruption. This is organized, massive, make-the-Mafia-jealous type corruption. Besides aiding and abetting Bush in violating the Constitution and giving tax cuts to rich people, they don't do much. But as elections approach, they dust off their favorites — gay marriage and flag-burning bans. These have sure-fire appeal to their remaining core supporters, known affectionately by both Republicans and Democrats as "the idiots."

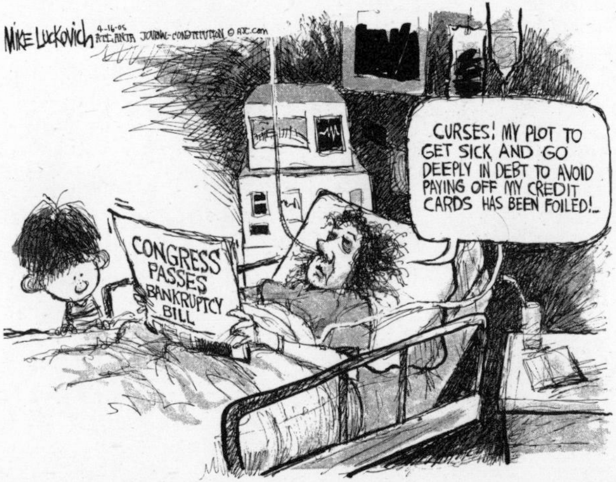
MIKE LUCKOVICH
CONGRESS PASSES BANKRUPTCY BILL
CURSES! MY PLOT TO GET SICK AND GO DEEPLY IN DEBT TO AVOID PAYING OFF MY CREDIT CARDS HAS BEEN FOILED!

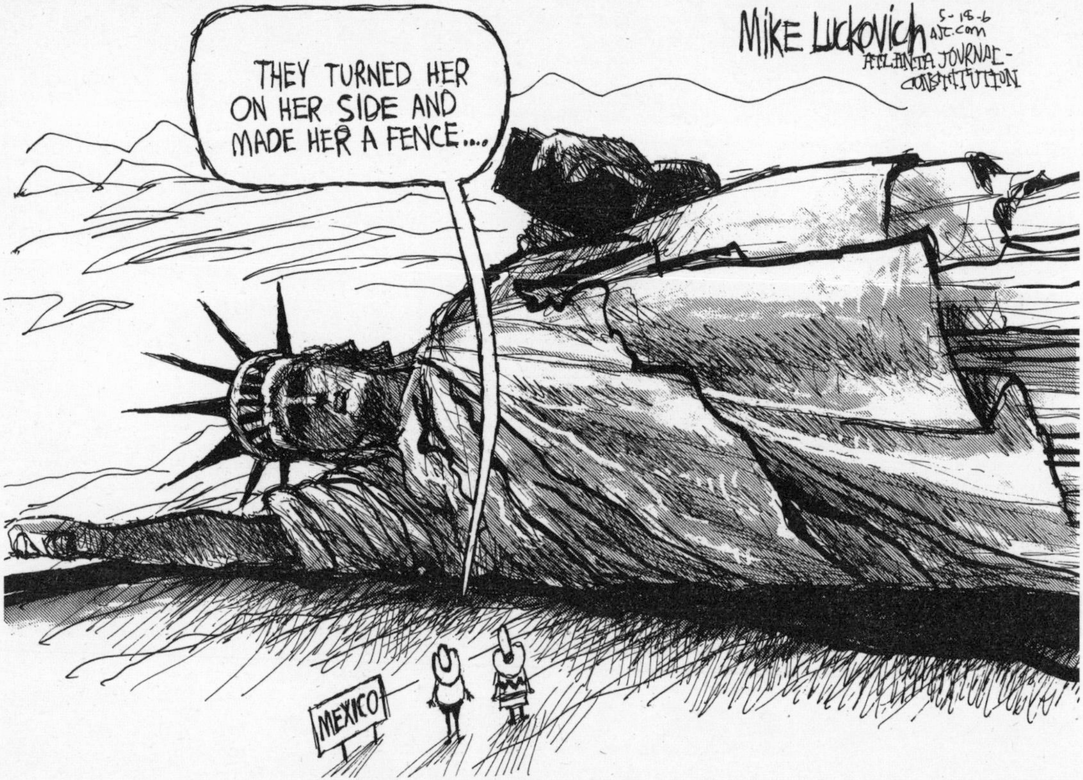
THEY TURNED HER ON HER SIDE AND MADE HER A FENCE....
MIKE LUCKOVICH 5-18-6 ajc.com ATLANTA JOURNAL-CONSTITUTION
MEXICO

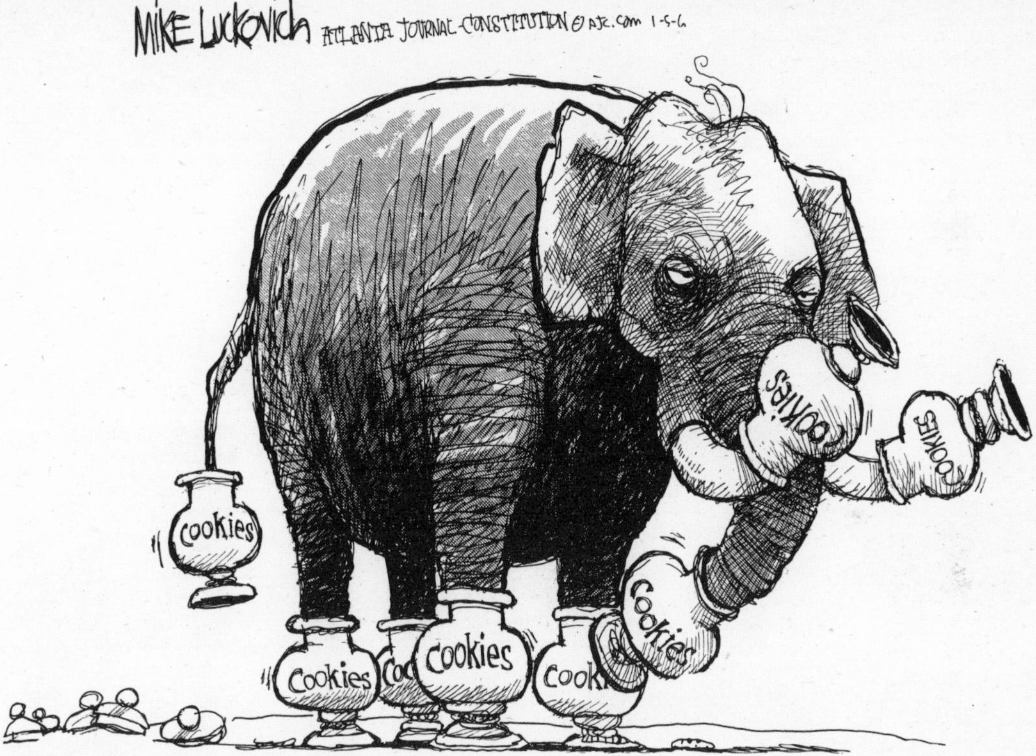
MIKE LUCKOVICH ATLANTA JOURNAL-CONSTITUTION © ajc.com 1-5-6
Cookies
Cookies
Cookies
Cookies
Cookies
Cookies
Cookies

LINEUP

6

5

4

3

GOP
SCANDALS

MIKE LUCKOVICH © AJC.com 9-30-5
ATLANTA JOURNAL-CONSTITUTION

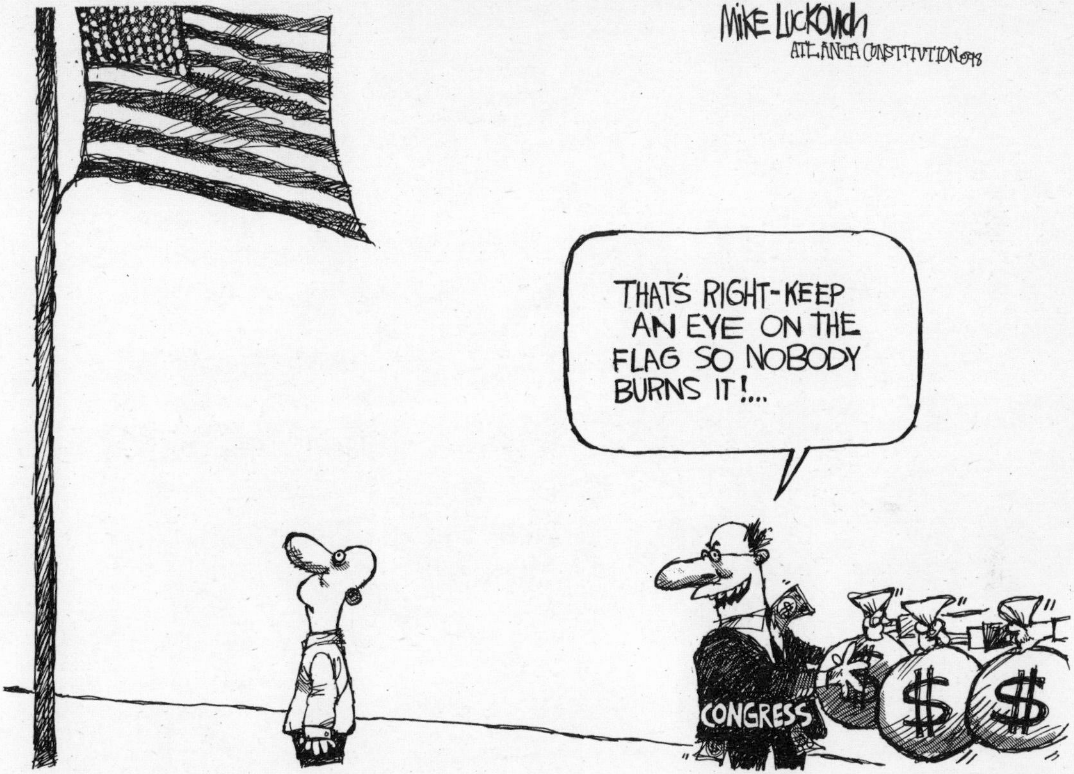
MIKE LUCKOVICH
ATLANTA CONSTITUTION
THAT'S RIGHT - KEEP AN EYE ON THE FLAG SO NOBODY BURNS IT!...
CONGRESS
$
$

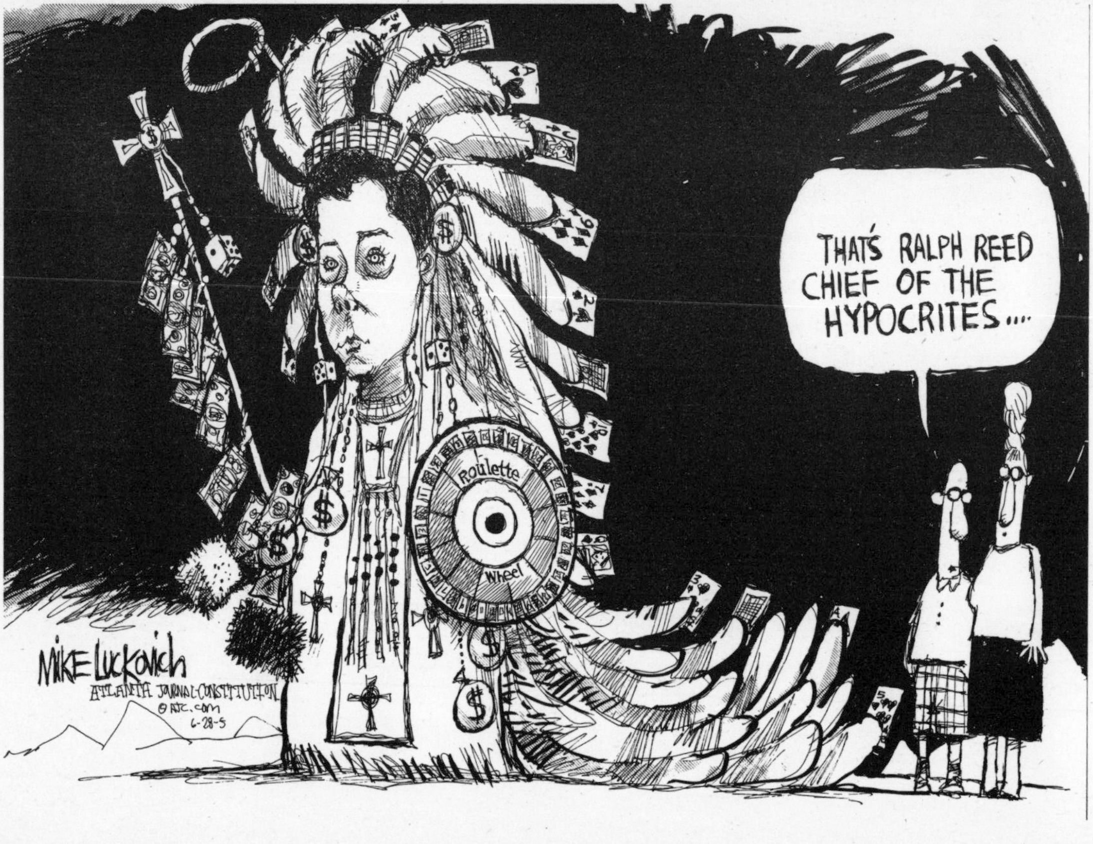
THAT'S RALPH REED CHIEF OF THE HYPOCRITES....
Roulette
Wheel
MIKE LUCKOVICH
ATLANTA JOURNAL-CONSTITUTION
©AJC.com
6-28-5

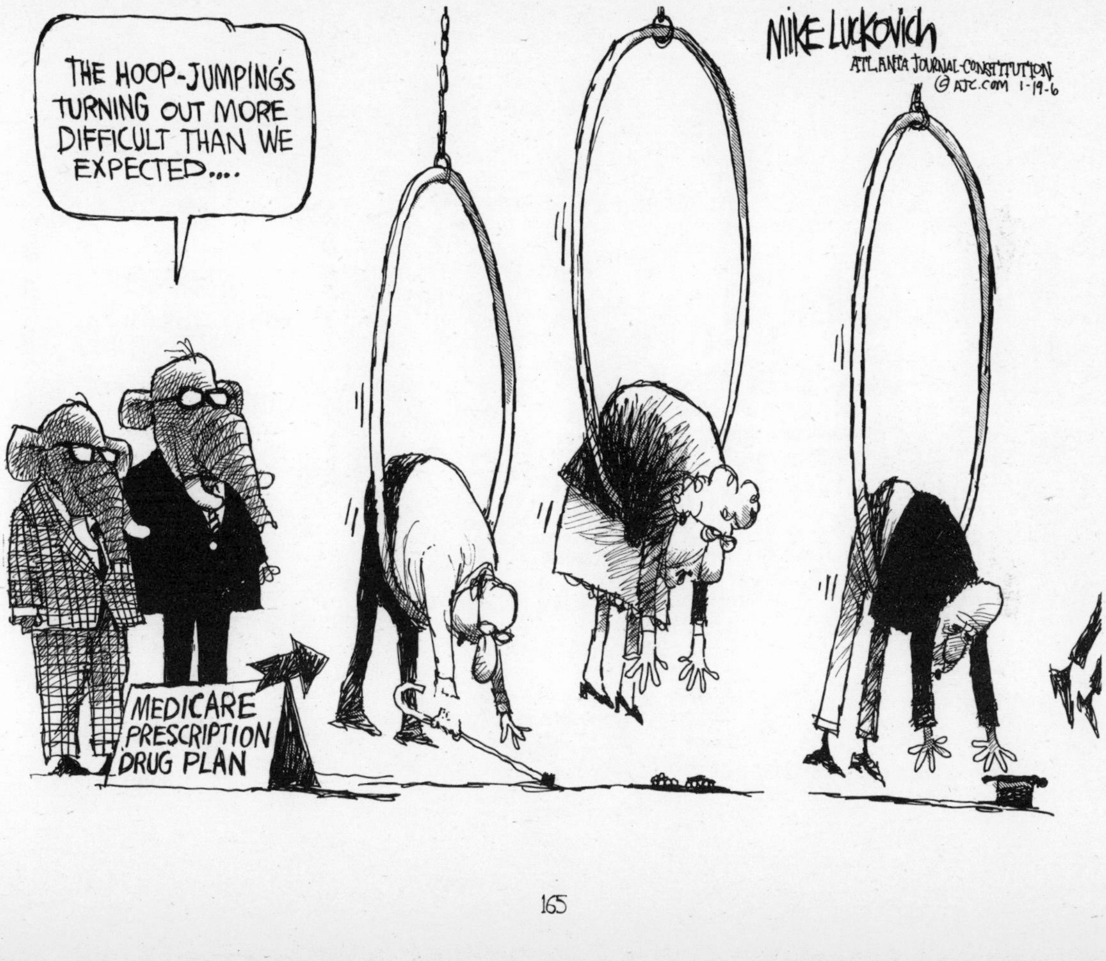
THE HOOP-JUMPING'S TURNING OUT MORE DIFFICULT THAN WE EXPECTED....
MEDICARE PRESCRIPTION DRUG PLAN
MIKE LUCKOVICH
ATLANTA JOURNAL-CONSTITUTION
© AJC.COM 1-19-6

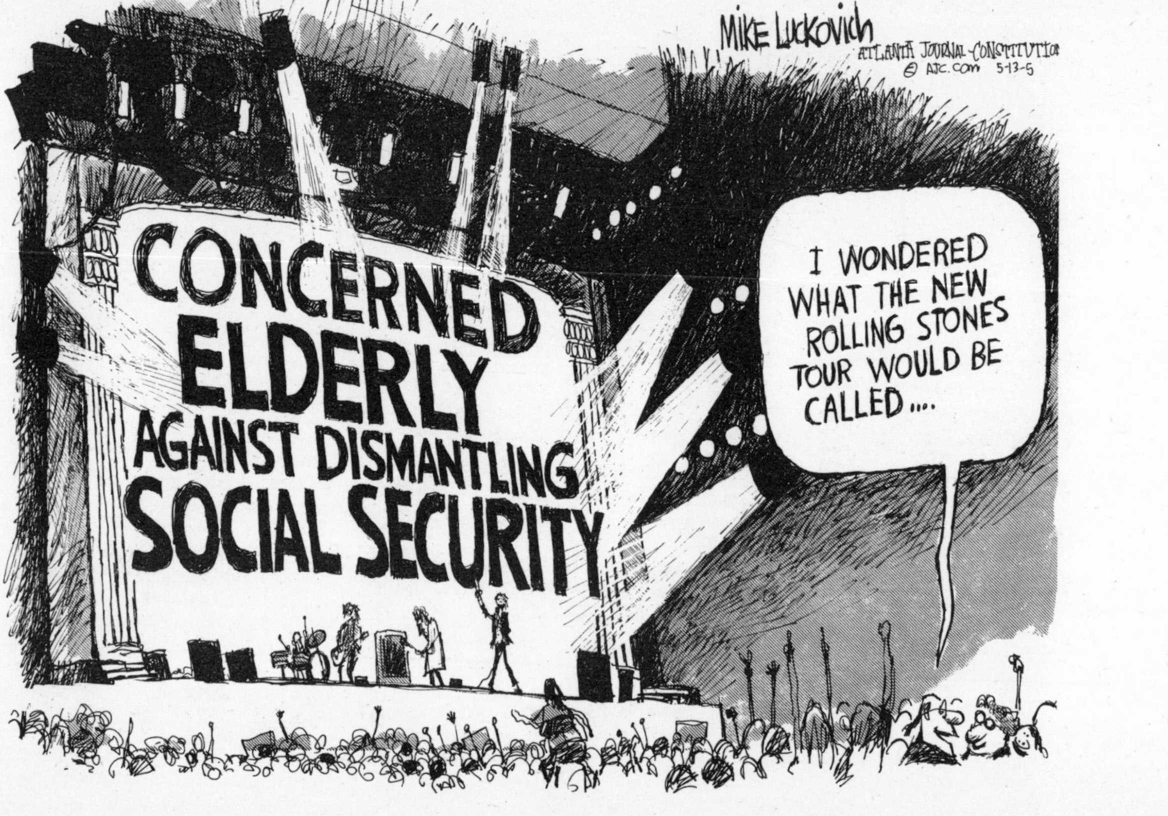
MIKE LUCKOVICH
ATLANTA JOURNAL-CONSTITUTION
© AJC.COM 5-13-5
CONCERNED ELDERLY AGAINST DISMANTLING SOCIAL SECURITY
I WONDERED WHAT THE NEW ROLLING STONES TOUR WOULD BE CALLED....

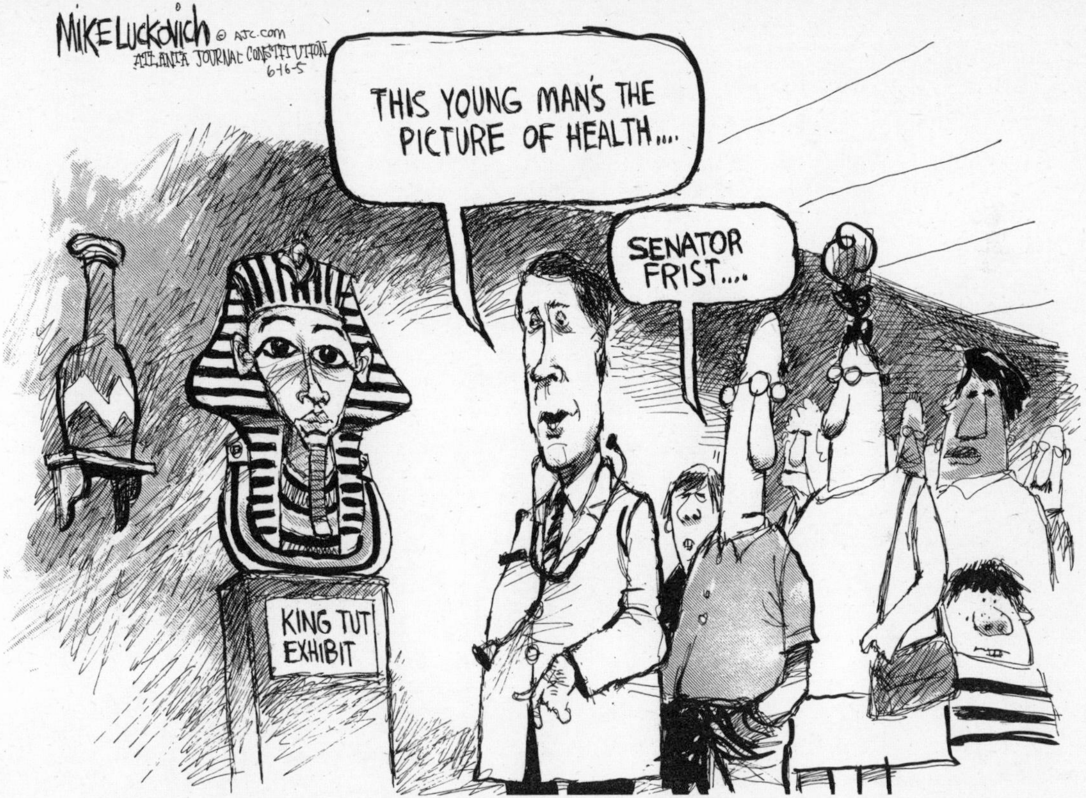
MIKE LUCKOVICH © AJC.com
ATLANTA JOURNAL CONSTITUTION
THIS YOUNG MAN'S THE PICTURE OF HEALTH....
SENATOR FRIST....
KING TUT EXHIBIT

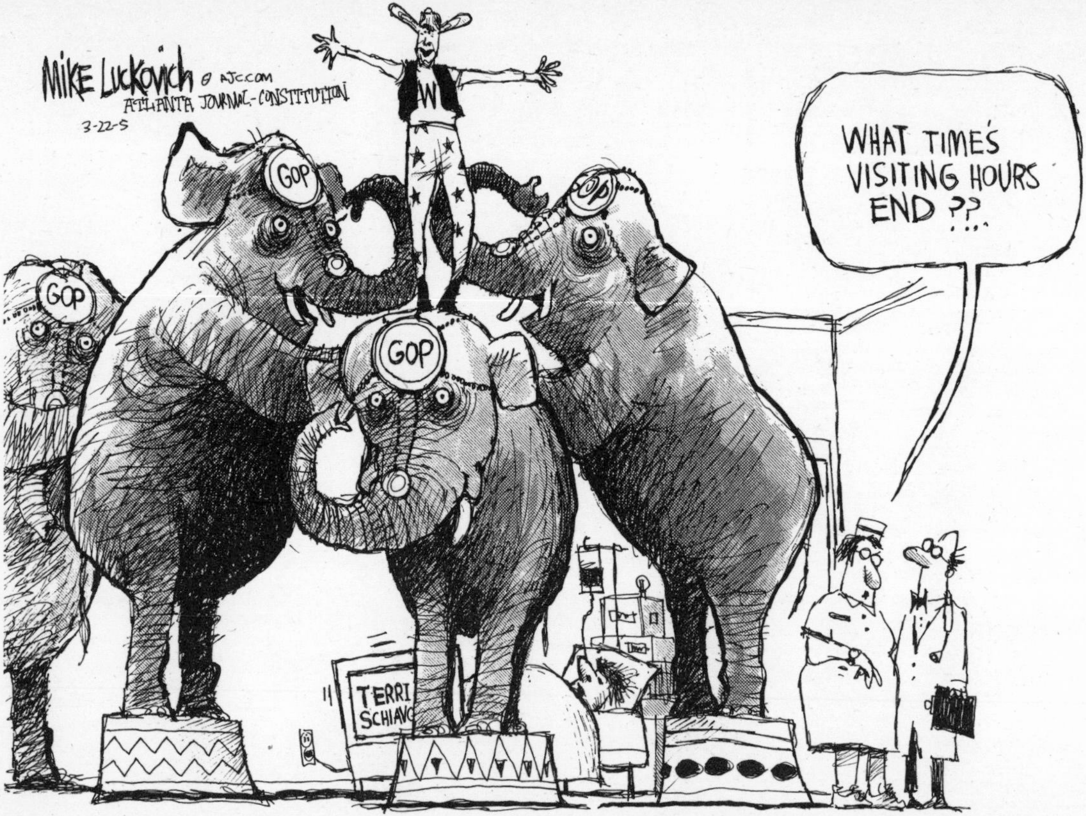
MIKE LUCKOVICH © AJC.COM
ATLANTA JOURNAL-CONSTITUTION
3-22-5
W
GOP
GOP
GOP
GOP
TERRI SCHIAVO
WHAT TIME'S VISITING HOURS END ??

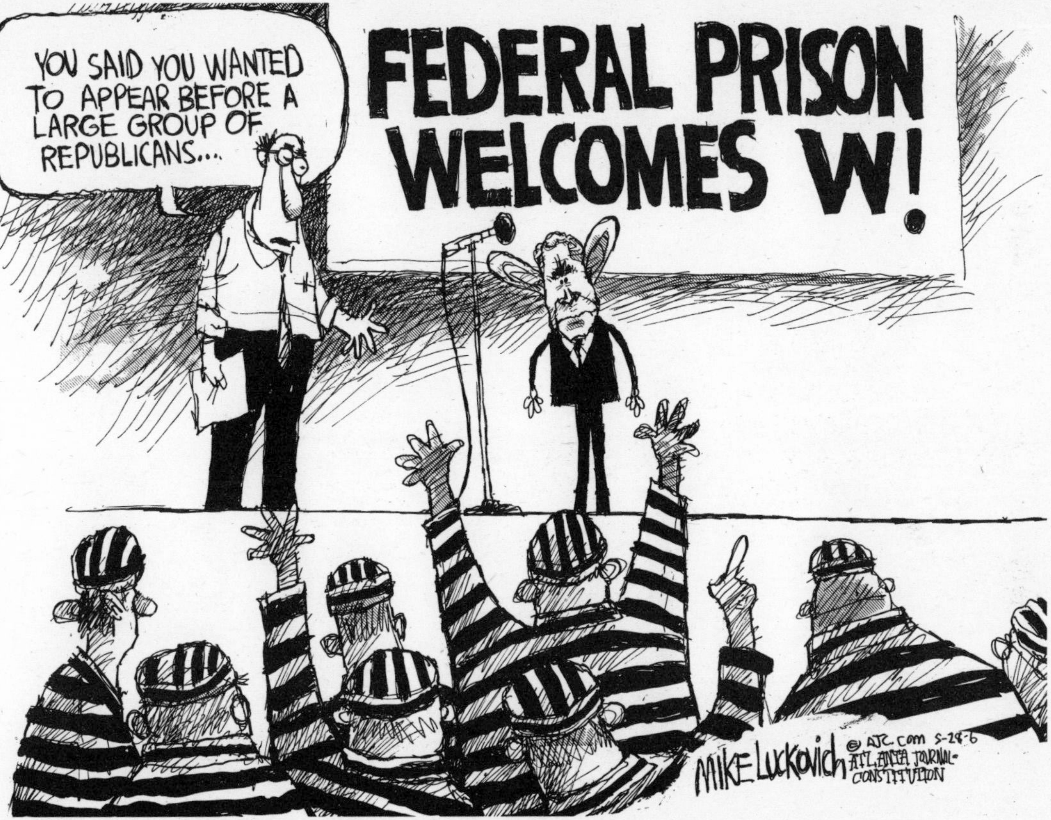
YOU SAID YOU WANTED TO APPEAR BEFORE A LARGE GROUP OF REPUBLICANS...
FEDERAL PRISON WELCOMES W!
MIKE LUCKOVICH
© AJC.com 5-28-6 ATLANTA JOURNAL-CONSTITUTION

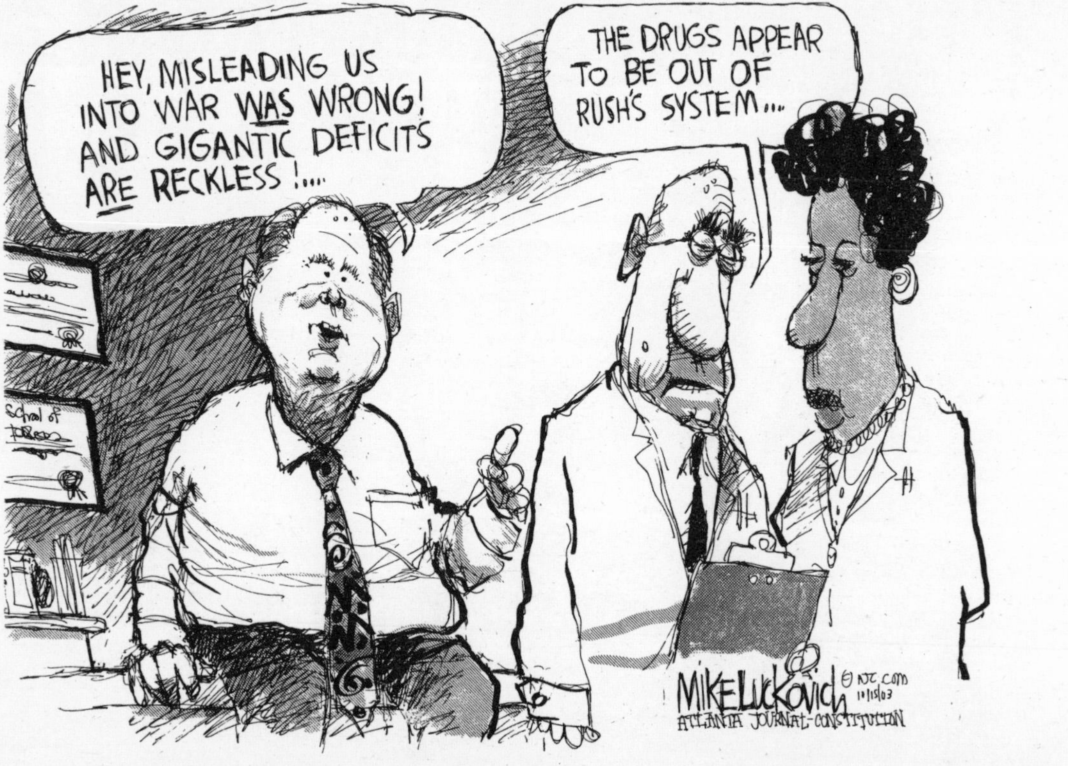
HEY, MISLEADING US INTO WAR WAS WRONG! AND GIGANTIC DEFICITS ARE RECKLESS!....
THE DRUGS APPEAR TO BE OUT OF RUSH'S SYSTEM....
MIKE LUCKOVICH
ATLANTA JOURNAL-CONSTITUTION

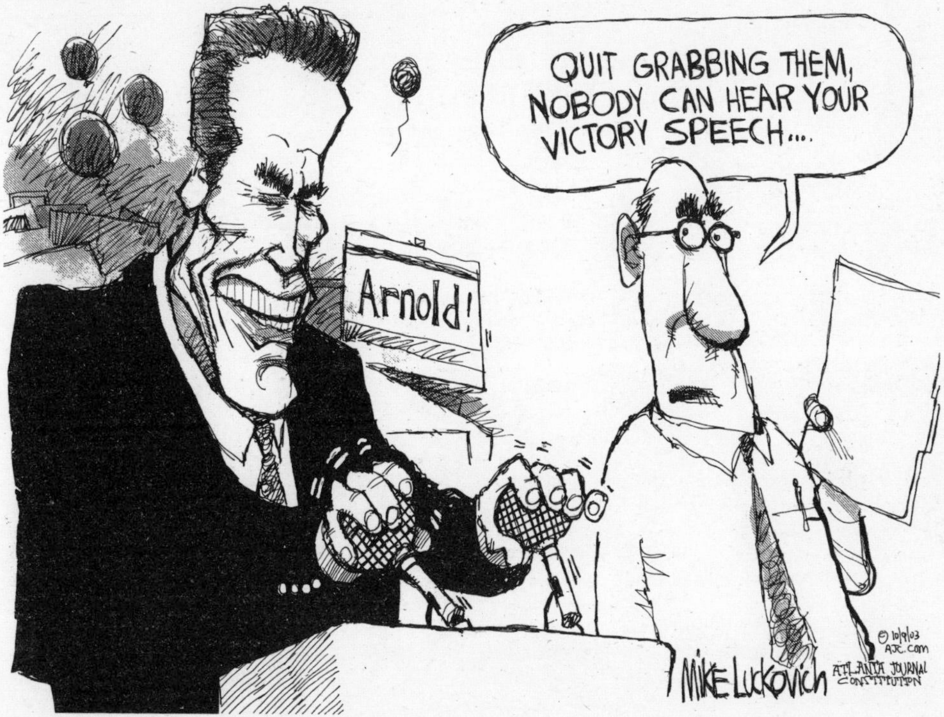
QUIT GRABBING THEM, NOBODY CAN HEAR YOUR VICTORY SPEECH....
Arnold!
© 10/9/03 AJC.com
MIKE LUCKOVICH
ATLANTA JOURNAL CONSTITUTION

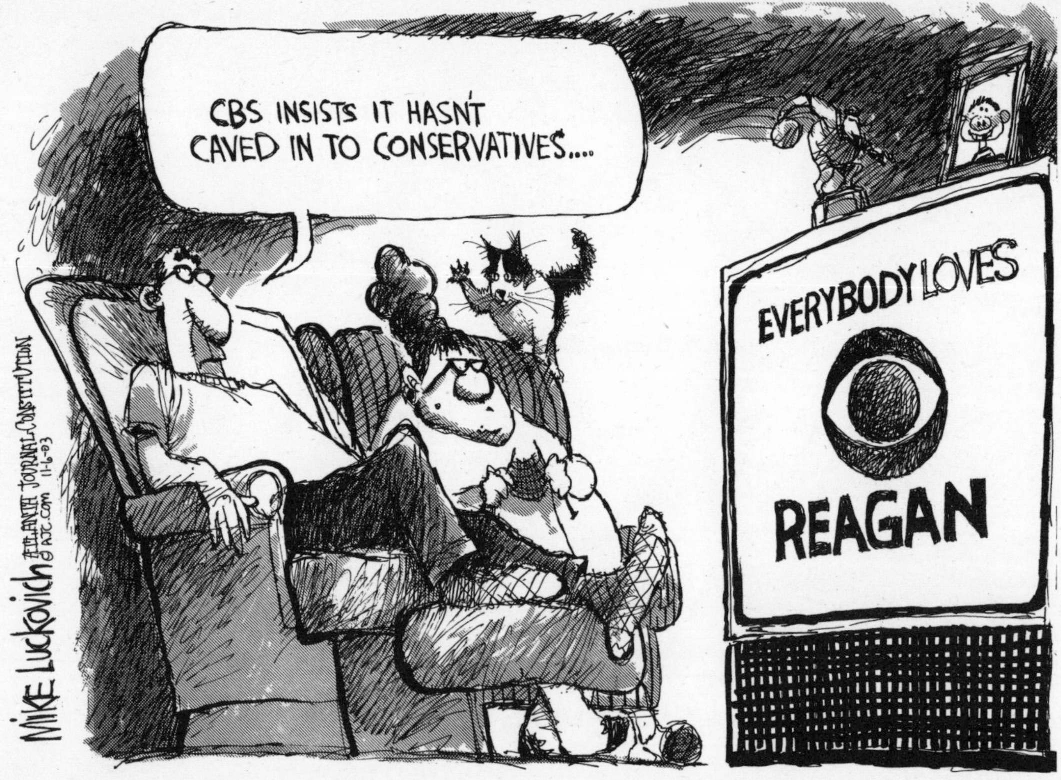
CBS INSISTS IT HASN'T CAVED IN TO CONSERVATIVES....
EVERYBODY LOVES
REAGAN
Mike Luckovich
ATLANTA JOURNAL-CONSTITUTION
©AJC.com 11-6-03

A White House Dinner

Stephen Colbert's barbed harpoons got all the attention at the 2006 White House Correspondents' Association Dinner. But that was inside the banquet hall.

Outside, in the corridors of the Washington Hilton, two men named Mike stalked George Clooney, watched Henry Kissinger's back and, well, if there was excessive alcohol consumption, it came much later.

Mikes Luckovich and Peters, editorial cartoonists for *The Atlanta Journal-Constitution* and the *Dayton Daily News*, respectively, arrived early for the big *Newsweek* cocktail party before the dinner. Both were carrying the tools of their favorite prank: a phone cord borrowed from their hotel phones and dark glasses. Luckovich takes up the story:

George Clooney came in with his father, so I talked to him briefly. George Clooney was like the main celebrity at the dinner, so the room quickly filled up with people, various media, politicians, and others that I didn't recognize. It was getting hot, so Mike and I left the cocktail party and went outside.

People were still coming in, so Mike and I put our dark glasses on and put the phone cords in our ears and then snaked them behind and into our jackets. And we stood outside and pretended we were security.

We were on each side of the door, and we kept having to remind each other not to smile. The party was winding down and the dinner was getting close to starting. When George Clooney and his father left, Mike and I got right in behind them and pretended we were their security. We still had our dark glasses and the phone cords in our ears.

So we were going down the hallway toward the dinner, and Clooney and his father and numerous hangers-on turned into this curtained room. Mike and I went in, but the real security kicked us out after about 10 seconds.

People heading toward the dinner all saw George Clooney go into this room, so there was a mass of people outside this curtained area, so Mike and I stood outside the opening and pretended that we were security and continued to remain unsmiling. We were waiting for Clooney to come out; we were going to follow him again. But Henry Kissinger walked out. He said to Mike and me, "Can you take me to the security area?" (You had to go through a metal detector to get to the dinner.)

So we said, "Certainly, sir." So we became Henry Kissinger's security. It was just the two of us, right behind Kissinger, right at his back. He's walking down this hallway to get to the metal detector to go into the banquet hall, and a crowd surrounded him and began taking his picture. So after a few seconds, I yelled out, "No more photos!" in a very authoritative voice, and everyone stopped taking photos.

Here's this goof — I'm wearing tortoise-shell sunglasses and a phone cord out my ear, and they're thinking, "OK, that's his security." So we continued to walk and we got up to the metal detector, and Kissinger went through it and proceeded into the banquet hall. We let Henry go and then went on to the next thing. We pretended we were security at the metal detector — telling people they had to take their shoes off and stuff like that.

Nobody did, believe it or not.

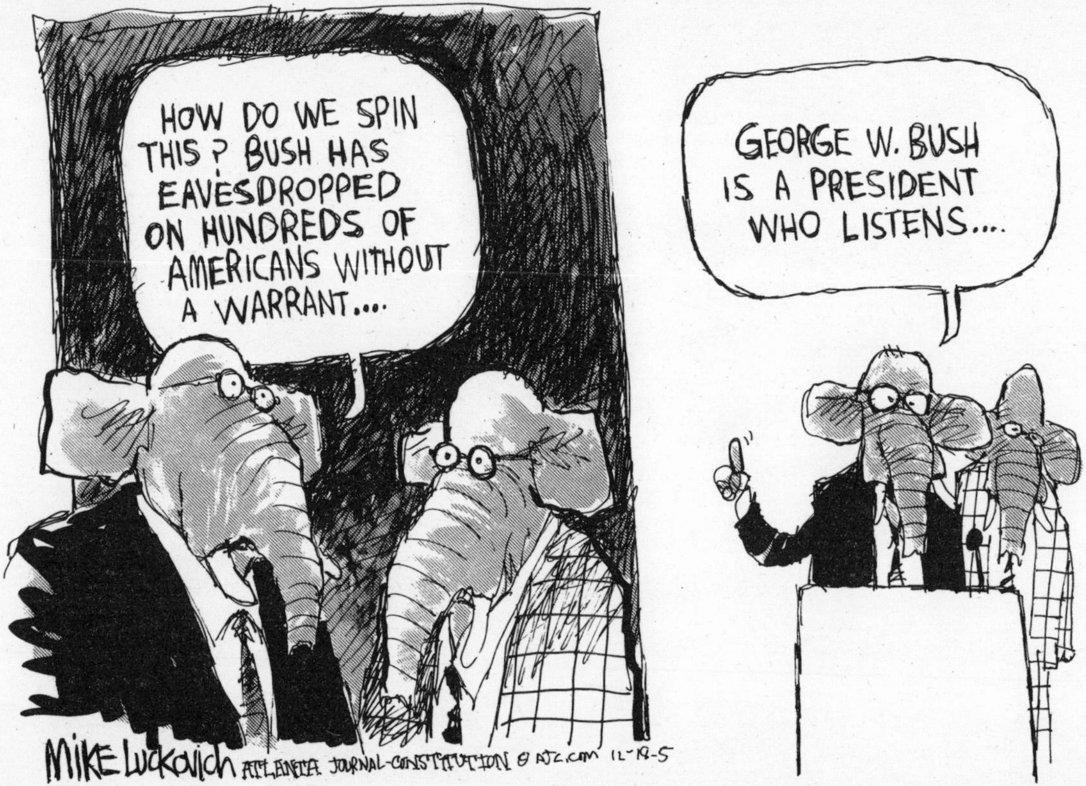
HOW DO WE SPIN THIS? BUSH HAS EAVESDROPPED ON HUNDREDS OF AMERICANS WITHOUT A WARRANT....
GEORGE W. BUSH IS A PRESIDENT WHO LISTENS....
MIKE LUCKOVICH ATLANTA JOURNAL-CONSTITUTION © AJC.COM 12-18-5

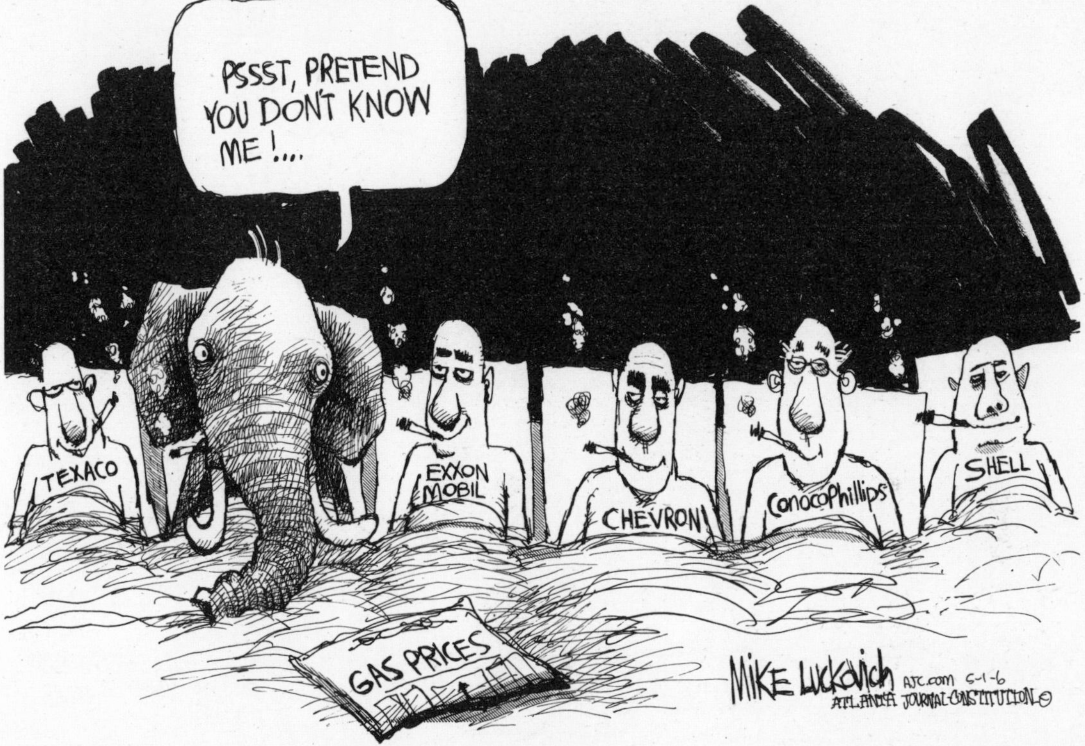
PSSST, PRETEND YOU DON'T KNOW ME!....
TEXACO
EXXON MOBIL
CHEVRON
ConocoPhillips
SHELL
GAS PRICES
MIKE LUCKOVICH AJC.com 5-1-6
ATLANTA JOURNAL-CONSTITUTION ©

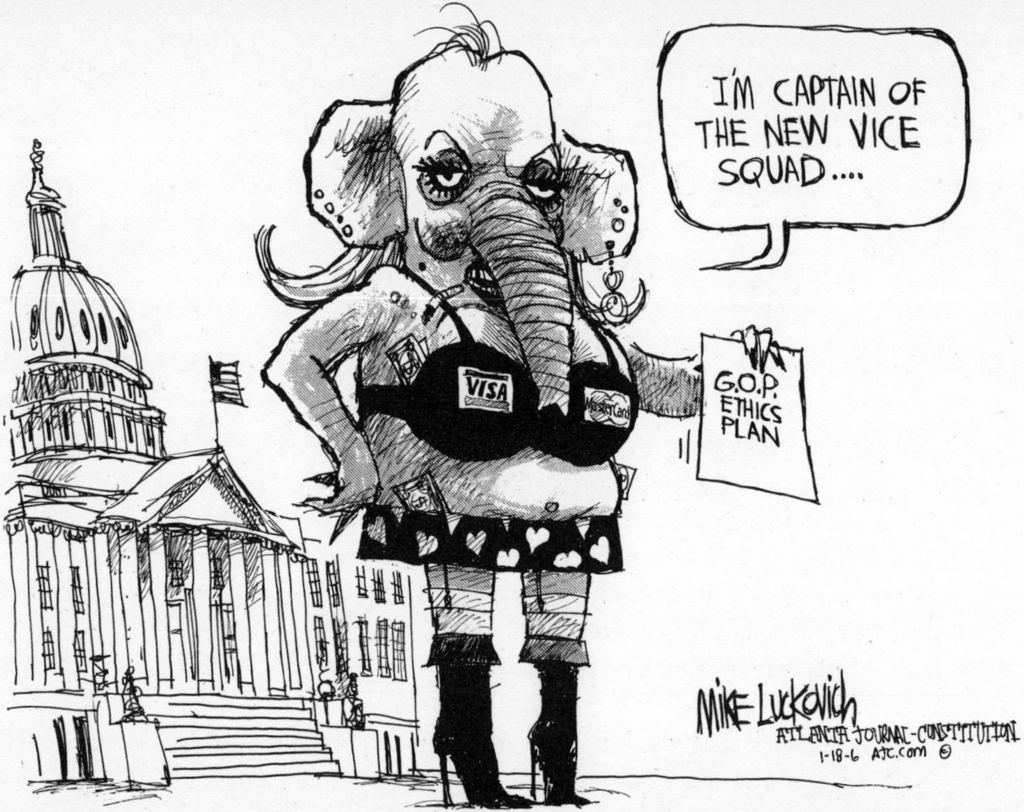
I'M CAPTAIN OF THE NEW VICE SQUAD....
VISA
MasterCard
G.O.P. ETHICS PLAN
MIKE LUCKOVICH
ATLANTA JOURNAL-CONSTITUTION
1-18-6 AJC.com ©

Dick Army

Cartoonists mainly work from their offices; however, our editors occasionally let us out, like during political conventions. In 2000, I attended both the Democratic and Republican conventions. At the Republican convention, I hung out with five other editorial cartoonists, plus Dave Barry the humor columnist. We attended various parties and political events trying to come up with subjects for cartoons and columns. We went to one important party the Republicans were having. We just showed up out front and — because Dave Barry is so well known — were able to talk our way in.

The party was pretty boring, but we noticed in the middle of the room, a raised rectangular catwalk about ten feet long, two feet high, and three feet wide. In the corner of the room we also saw a bright orange traffic cone, so Dave Barry, the rest of the cartoonists and I took the traffic cone and got up on the box and, with drinks in hand, began telling people walking by that this was the VIP area and that they weren't allowed up here. We all thought that was really funny for about twenty minutes, but then it started to get old, so I went out onto the dance floor and found the then House Majority Leader, Dick Armey, and told him to follow me to the VIP area. He climbed up with me and the other cartoonists onto the VIP box.

Dave Barry was returning from the restroom and as he got back on the box, I said, "Dave, look, it's Dick Armey!" Dave didn't have his glasses on so he got right up to Dick's face and he said, "Are you really Dick Armey?" Dick replied, "Yeah, and if there was a dick army, Barney Frank would join it." Barney Frank being the openly gay congressman from Massachusetts. We were all kind of shocked he had said that but we didn't really think about it because we were all kind of acting sophomoric up on that silly box. Throughout the night, we entertained other politicians and celebrities up on the box, such as Representative Asa Hutchinson, Jack Valenti, head of the motion picture industry, and conservative columnist David Horowitz.

The next day, I walked into the *Atlanta Journal-Constitution* workspace at the convention and was recounting the previous night's events to my editor and top reporters, when I got to the part about Dick Armey making the Barney Frank joke. Everyone got quiet. They ended up writing a story about it. With Dick Armey's previous comments about Barney Frank, it became a big story, because the Republicans were trying to make everyone think that they were a very inclusive party when it came to minorities and women.

Dick Armey should never have made those comments to us. Although we were goofballs up on a little black box that we called the VIP area, we're still loosely regarded as journalists. However, because of the situation, I did feel a little conflicted about the whole thing coming out.

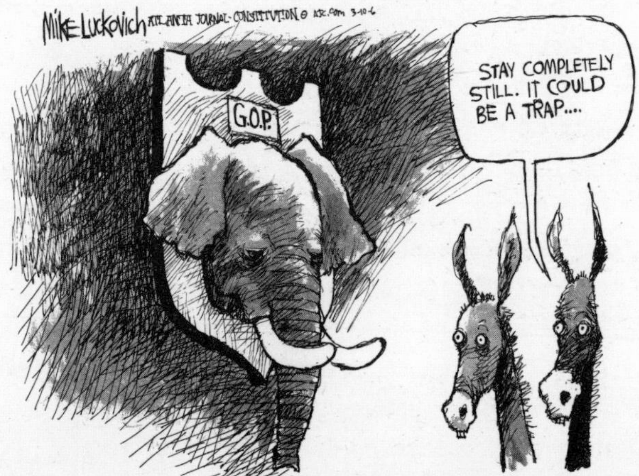
MIKE LUCKOVICH ATLANTA JOURNAL-CONSTITUTION
G.O.P.
STAY COMPLETELY STILL. IT COULD BE A TRAP....

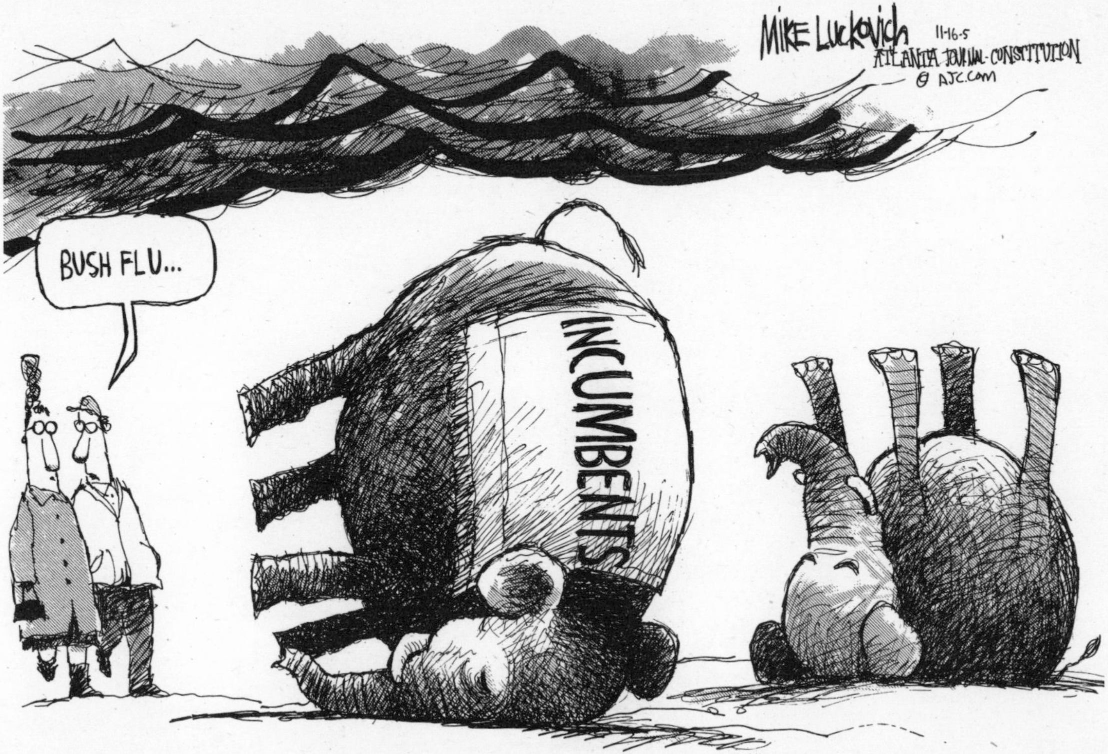
MIKE LUCKOVICH 11-16-5
ATLANTA JOURNAL-CONSTITUTION
© AJC.COM
BUSH FLU...
INCUMBENTS

THANKS FOR EVERY-
THING, DADDY!!...

CORRUPTION

TOM
DELAY

Mike Luckovich @AJC.com
ATLANTA JOURNAL-CONSTITUTION
4-5-6

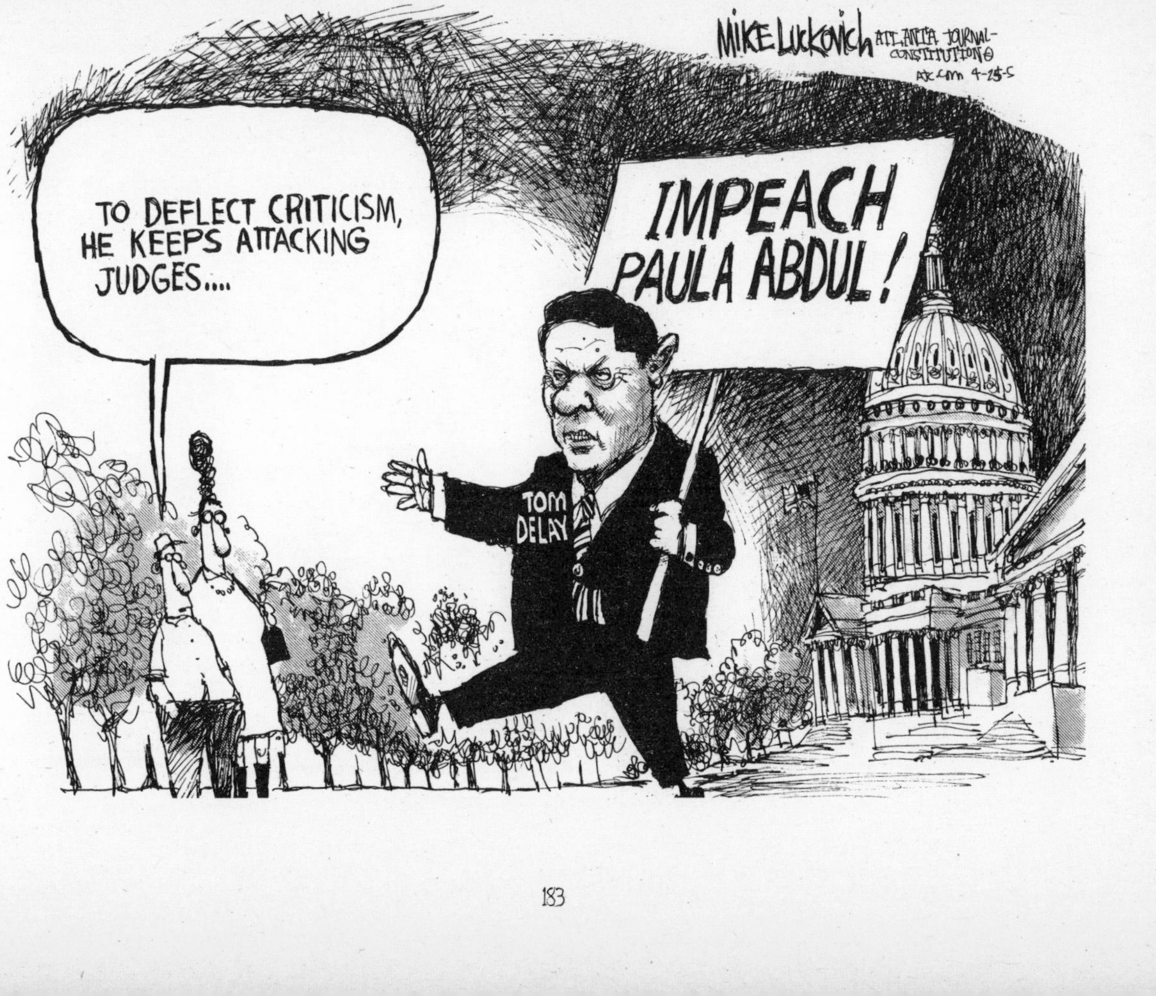
MIKE LUCKOVICH ATLANTA JOURNAL-CONSTITUTION
TO DEFLECT CRITICISM, HE KEEPS ATTACKING JUDGES....
IMPEACH PAULA ABDUL!
TOM DELAY

FULFILLING SUCH A REQUEST REQUIRES A SUBSTANTIAL CONTRIBUTION...
TOM DELAY
MIKE LUCKOVICH ATLANTA JOURNAL-CONSTITUTION © AJC.COM 10-21-5
JUST GIVE HIM YOUR FINGERPRINTS....
BOOKING
LAWYER
DELAY
INK
POLICE

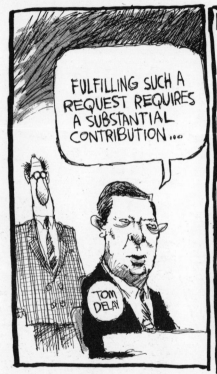

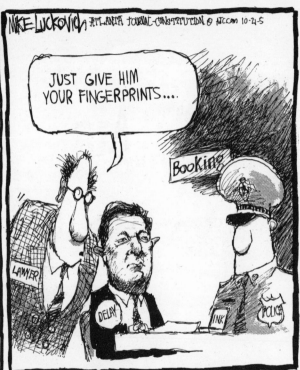

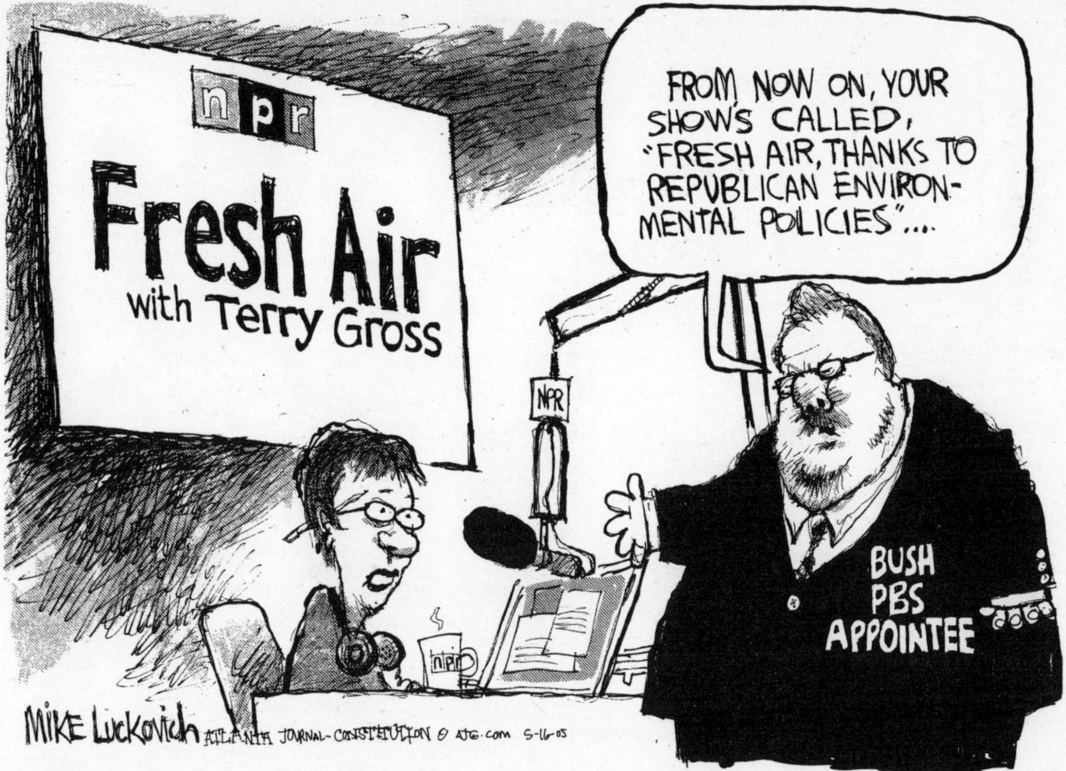
npr
Fresh Air
with Terry Gross
FROM NOW ON, YOUR SHOW'S CALLED, "FRESH AIR, THANKS TO REPUBLICAN ENVIRON-MENTAL POLICIES"...
NPR
npr
BUSH PBS APPOINTEE
MIKE LUCKOVICH ATLANTA JOURNAL-CONSTITUTION © AJC.com 5-16-05

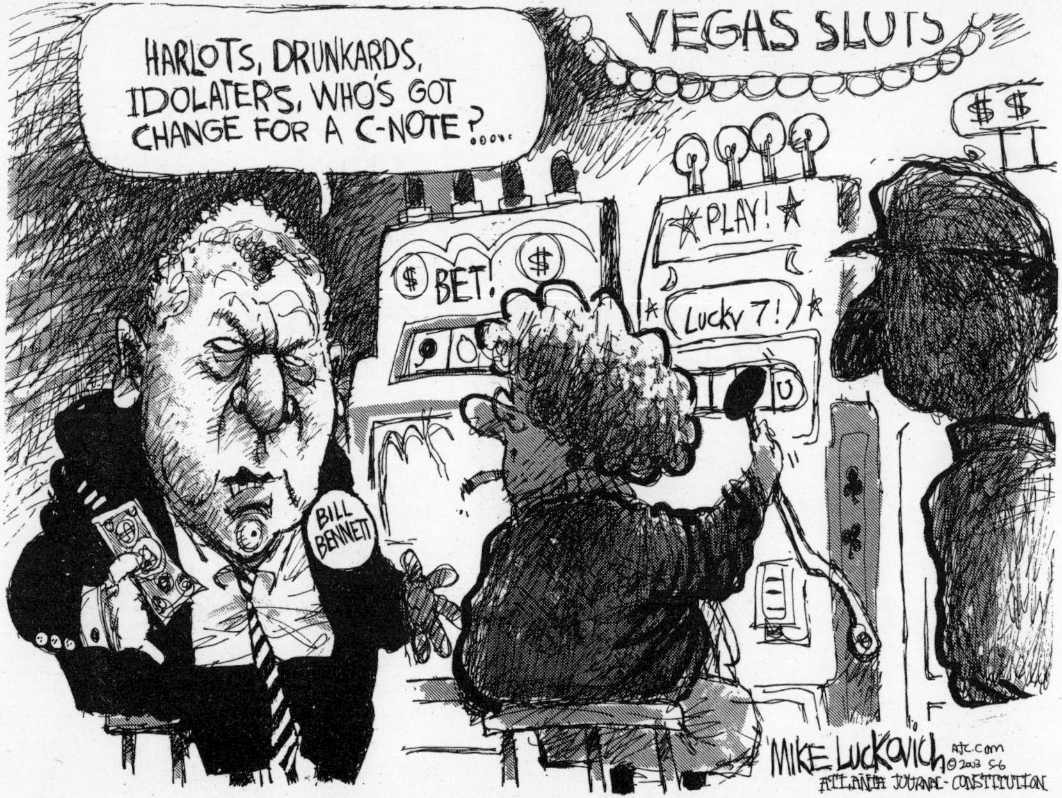
HARLOTS, DRUNKARDS, IDOLATERS, WHO'S GOT CHANGE FOR A C-NOTE?....
VEGAS SLUTS
$$
BET!
PLAY!
Lucky 7!
BILL BENNETT
MIKE LUCKOVICH
AJC.com
©2003
ATLANTA JOURNAL-CONSTITUTION

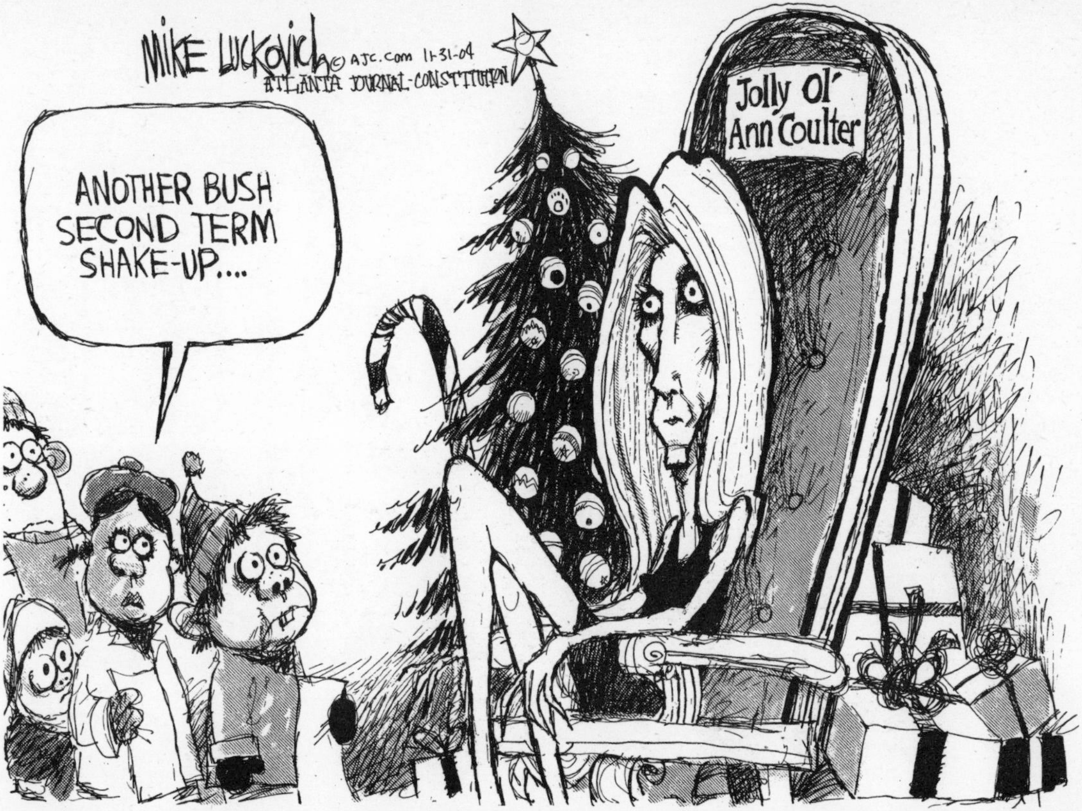
MIKE LUCKOVICH © AJC.com 11-31-04
ATLANTA JOURNAL-CONSTITUTION
ANOTHER BUSH SECOND TERM SHAKE-UP....
Jolly Ol' Ann Coulter

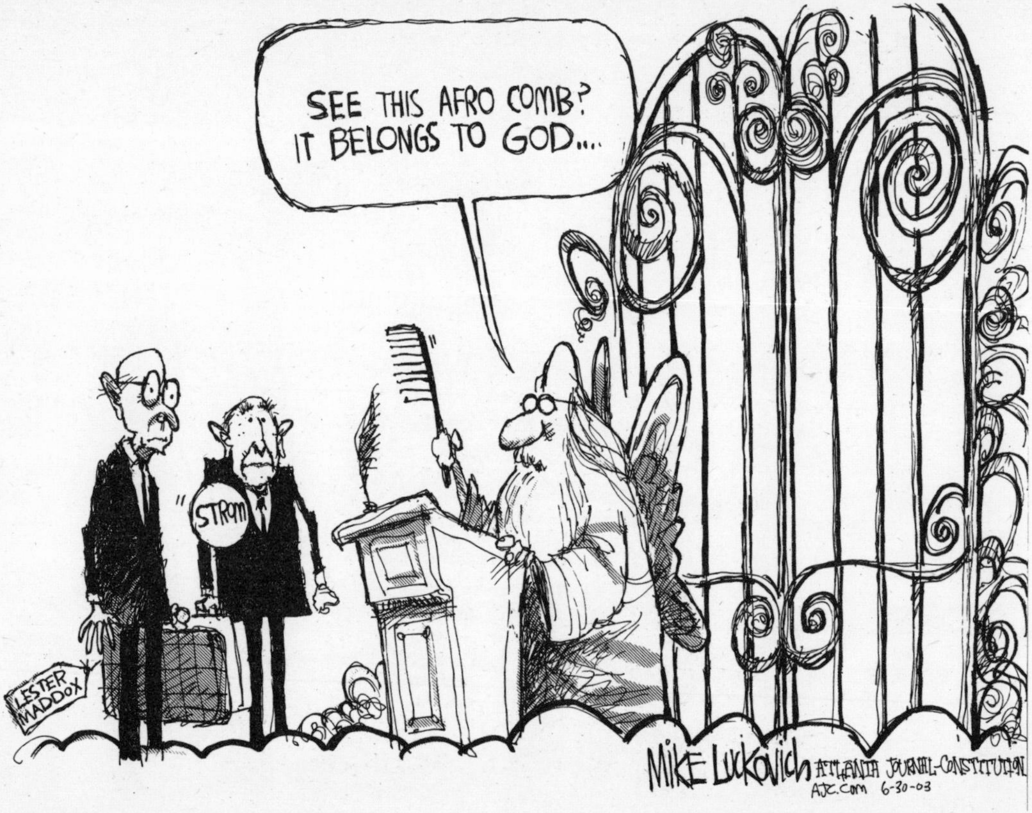
SEE THIS AFRO COMB?
IT BELONGS TO GOD...
STROM
LESTER MADDOX
MIKE LUCKOVICH ATLANTA JOURNAL-CONSTITUTION
AJC.com 6-30-03

Supreme Court

In 2000, they voted him into office. The Supreme Court is Bush's favorite red state.

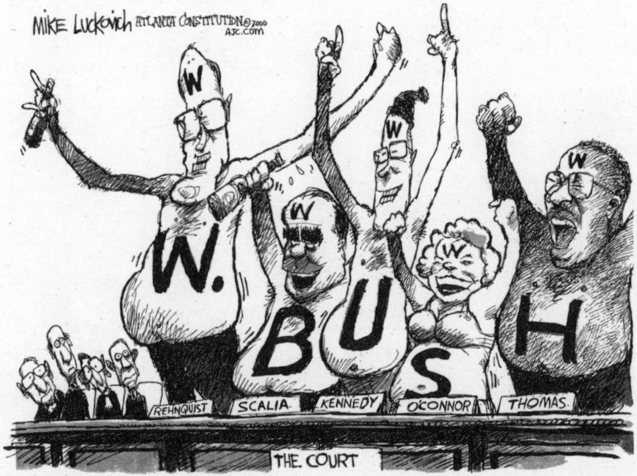
MIKE LUCKOVICH ATLANTA CONSTITUTION ©2000 AJC.COM
W
W
W
W
W
W.
BU
S
H
REHNQUIST
SCALIA
KENNEDY
O'CONNOR
THOMAS
THE COURT

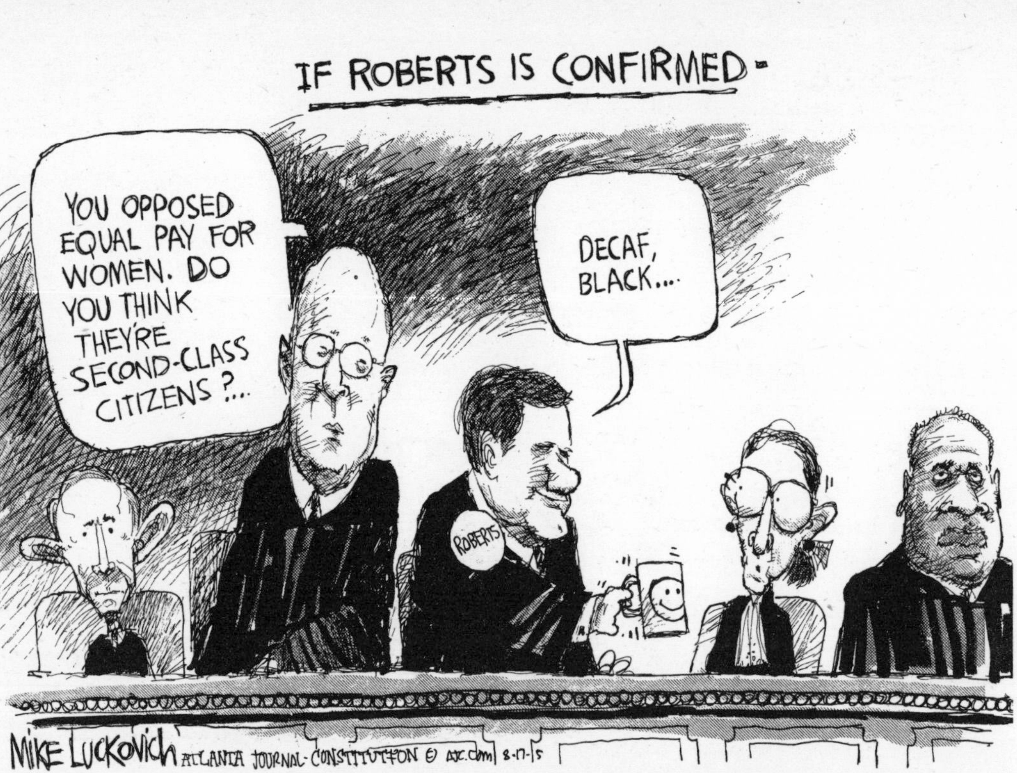
IF ROBERTS IS CONFIRMED-
YOU OPPOSED EQUAL PAY FOR WOMEN. DO YOU THINK THEY'RE SECOND-CLASS CITIZENS?...
DECAF, BLACK....
ROBERTS
MIKE LUCKOVICH ATLANTA JOURNAL-CONSTITUTION © AJC.com 8-17-5

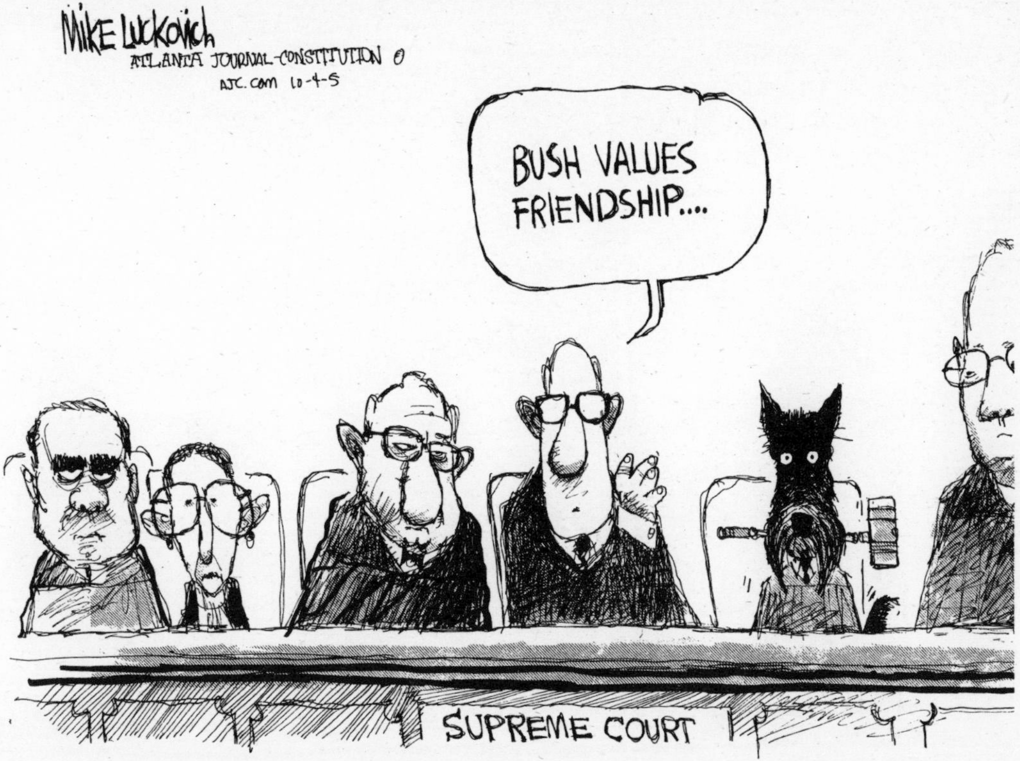
MIKE LUCKOVICH
ATLANTA JOURNAL-CONSTITUTION
AJC.com 10-4-5
BUSH VALUES FRIENDSHIP....
SUPREME COURT

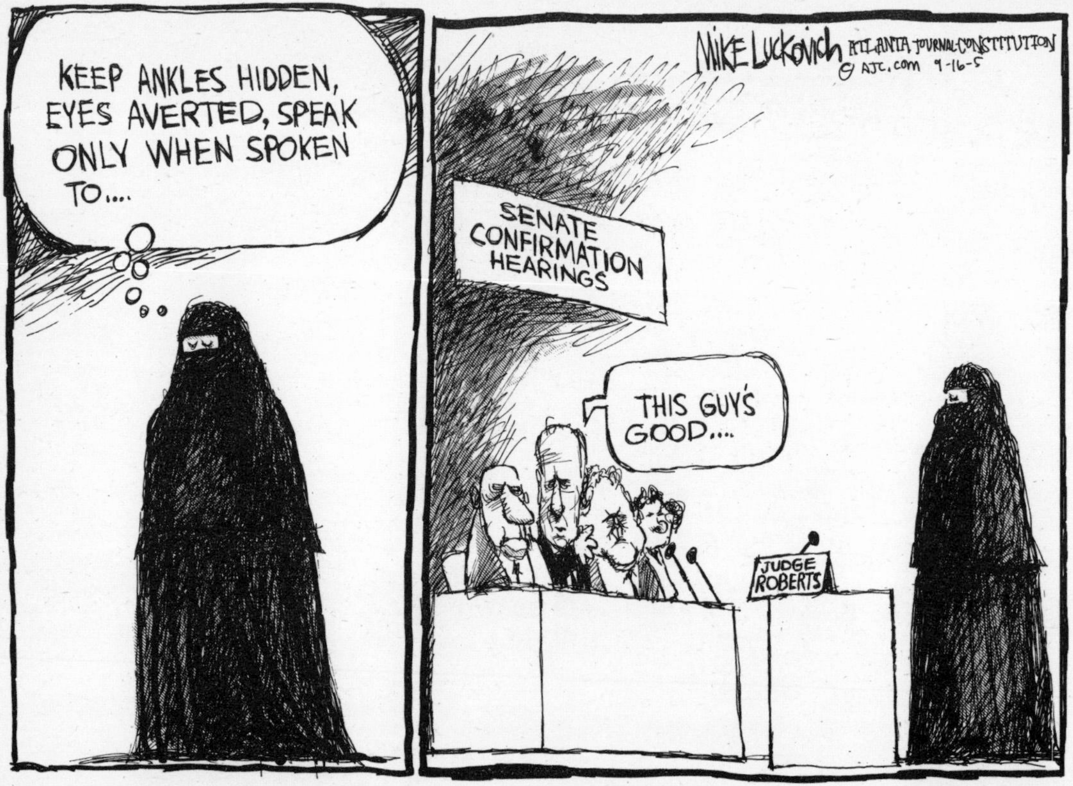
KEEP ANKLES HIDDEN, EYES AVERTED, SPEAK ONLY WHEN SPOKEN TO....
MIKE LUCKOVICH ATLANTA JOURNAL-CONSTITUTION
© AJC.com 9-16-5
SENATE CONFIRMATION HEARINGS
THIS GUY'S GOOD....
JUDGE ROBERTS

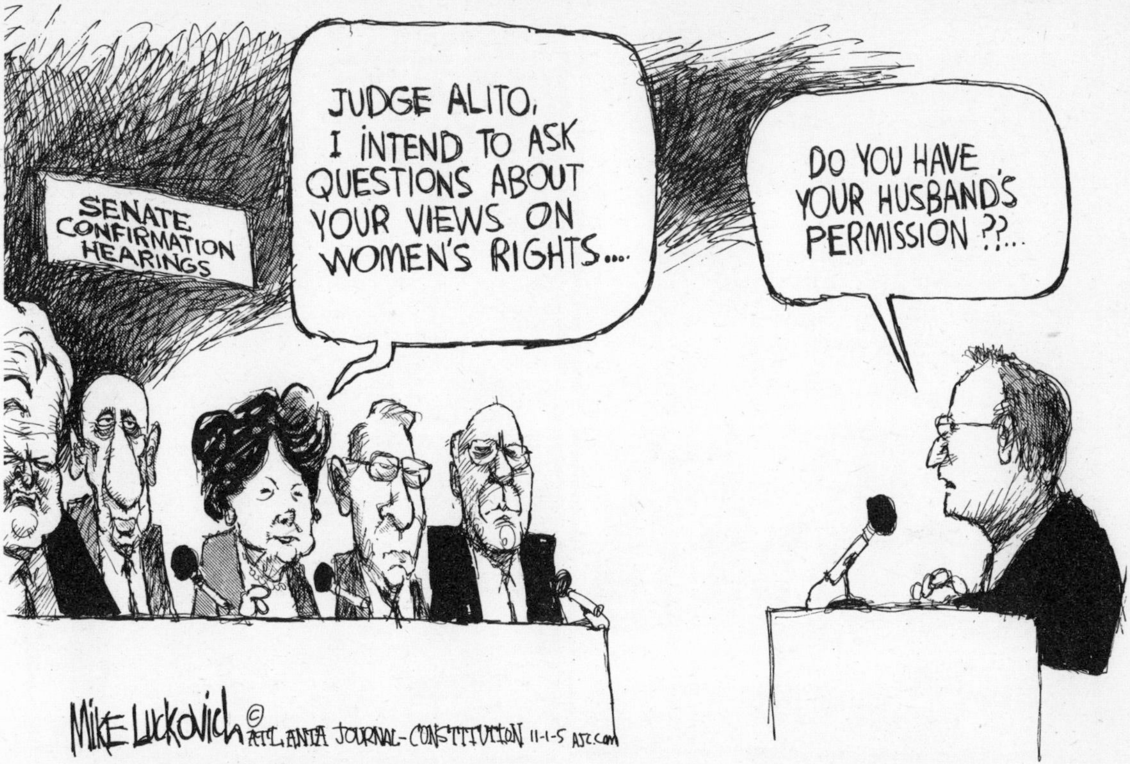
SENATE CONFIRMATION HEARINGS
JUDGE ALITO, I INTEND TO ASK QUESTIONS ABOUT YOUR VIEWS ON WOMEN'S RIGHTS....
DO YOU HAVE YOUR HUSBAND'S PERMISSION ??...
MIKE LUCKOVICH © ATLANTA JOURNAL-CONSTITUTION 11-1-5 AJC.com

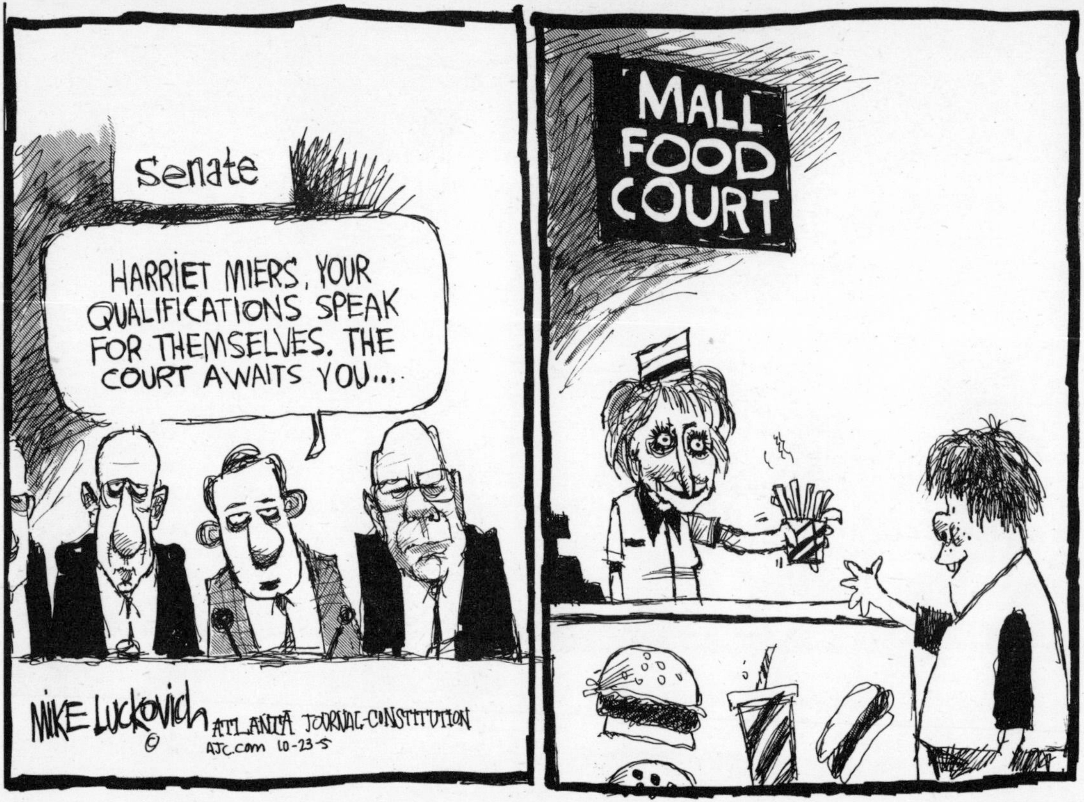
Senate
HARRIET MIERS, YOUR QUALIFICATIONS SPEAK FOR THEMSELVES. THE COURT AWAITS YOU...
MIKE LUCKOVICH © ATLANTA JOURNAL-CONSTITUTION AJC.com 10-23-5
MALL FOOD COURT

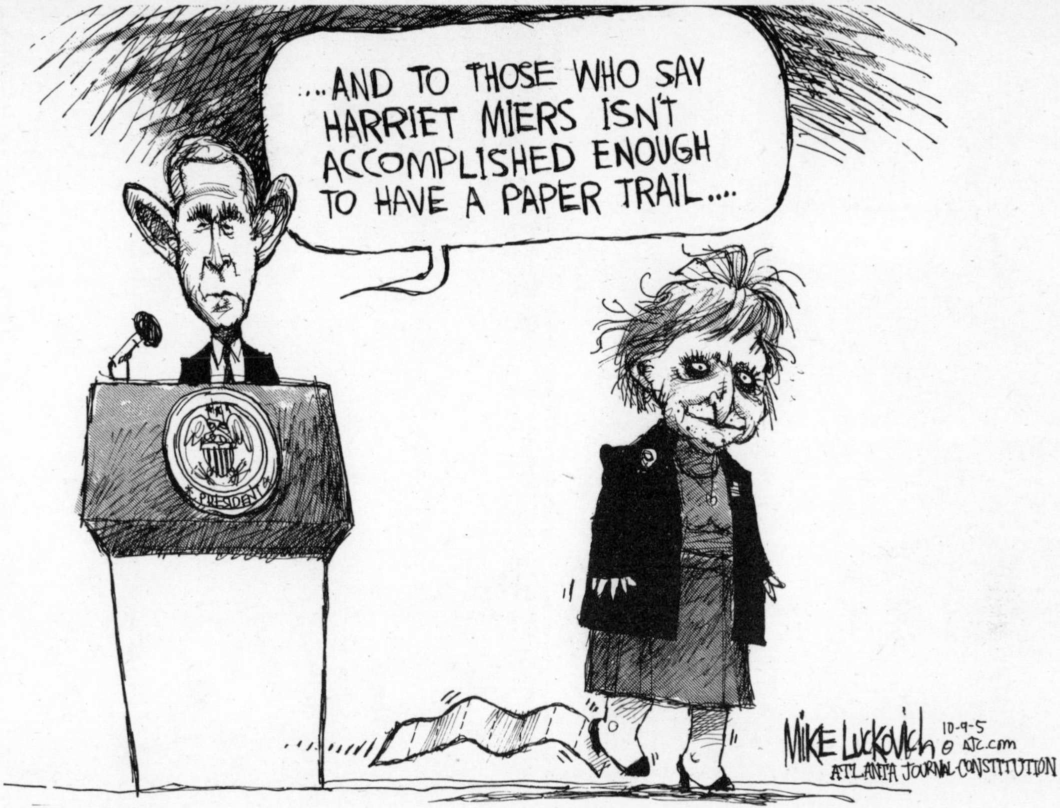
...AND TO THOSE WHO SAY HARRIET MIERS ISN'T ACCOMPLISHED ENOUGH TO HAVE A PAPER TRAIL....
PRESIDENT
MIKE LUCKOVICH 10-9-5 © AJC.com
ATLANTA JOURNAL-CONSTITUTION

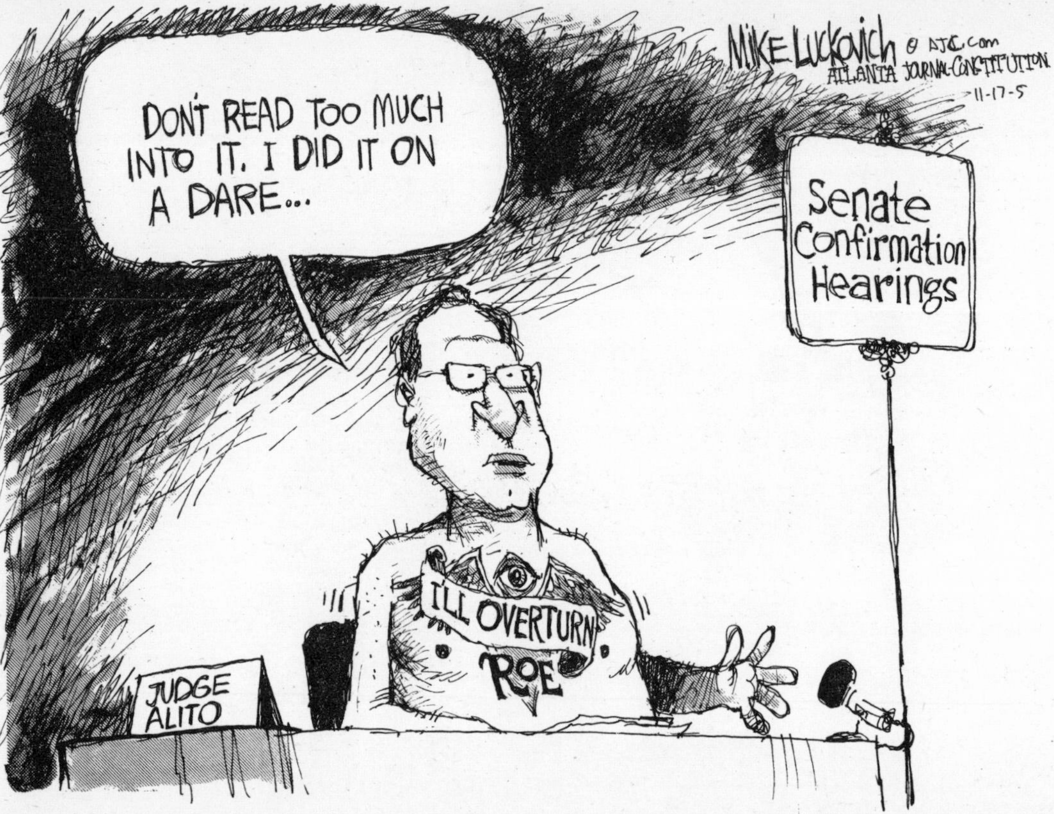
MIKE LUCKOVICH © AJC.com
ATLANTA JOURNAL-CONSTITUTION
11-17-5
DON'T READ TOO MUCH INTO IT. I DID IT ON A DARE...
Senate Confirmation Hearings
I'LL OVERTURN ROE
JUDGE ALITO

Religion

When leaders wear their religion on their sleeves, I worry. Especially if they think God is working through them. Both Bush and Bin Laden think they're on God's side. I'm guessing they're both wrong.

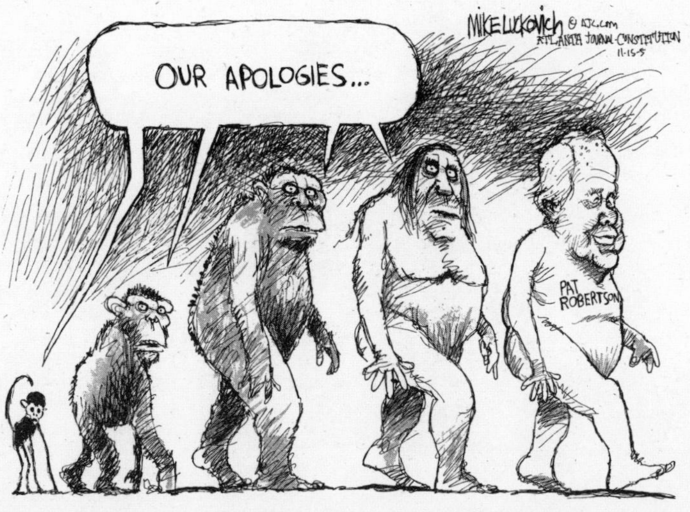
OUR APOLOGIES...
PAT ROBERTSON
MIKE LUCKOVICH

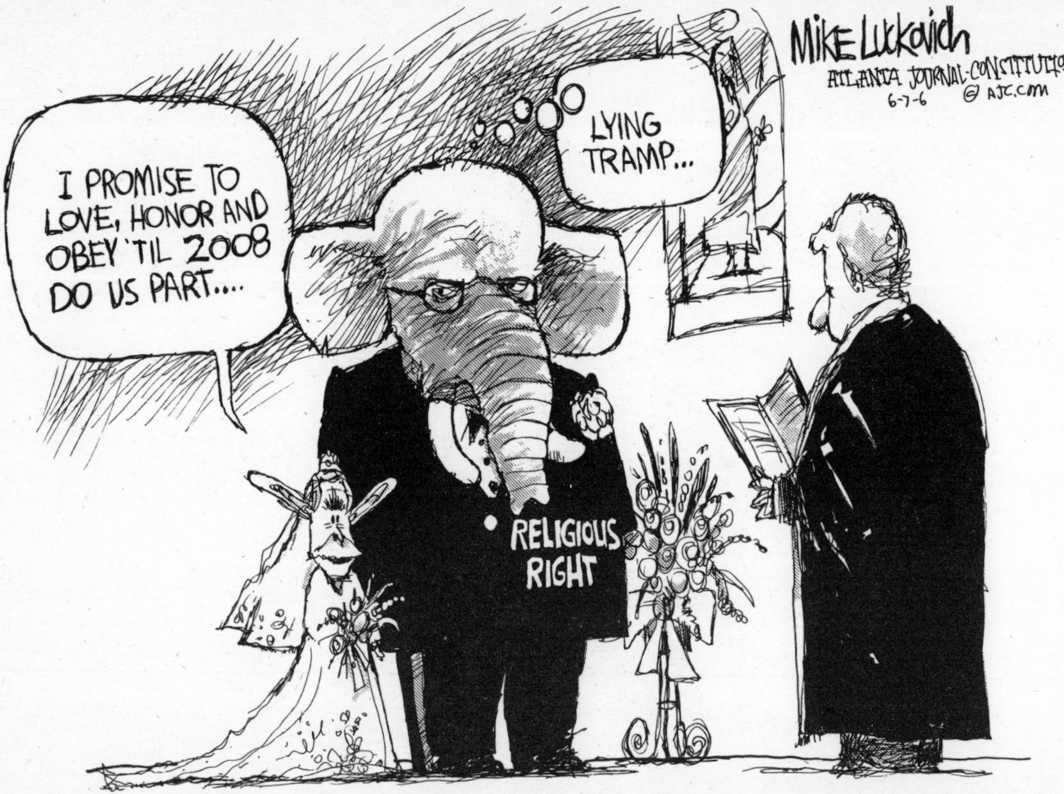
I PROMISE TO LOVE, HONOR AND OBEY 'TIL 2008 DO US PART....
LYING TRAMP...
RELIGIOUS RIGHT
MIKE LUCKOVICH
ATLANTA JOURNAL-CONSTITUTION
6-7-6 © AJC.COM

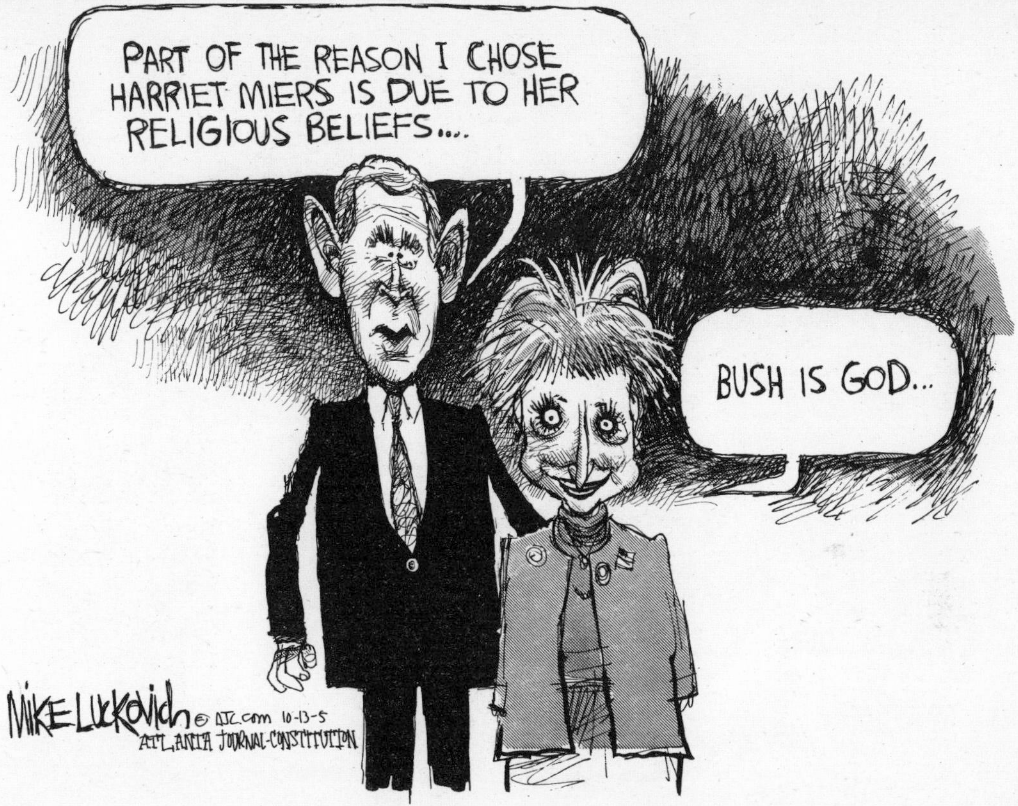
PART OF THE REASON I CHOSE HARRIET MIERS IS DUE TO HER RELIGIOUS BELIEFS....
BUSH IS GOD...
MIKE LUCKOVICH © AJC.com 10-13-5
ATLANTA JOURNAL-CONSTITUTION

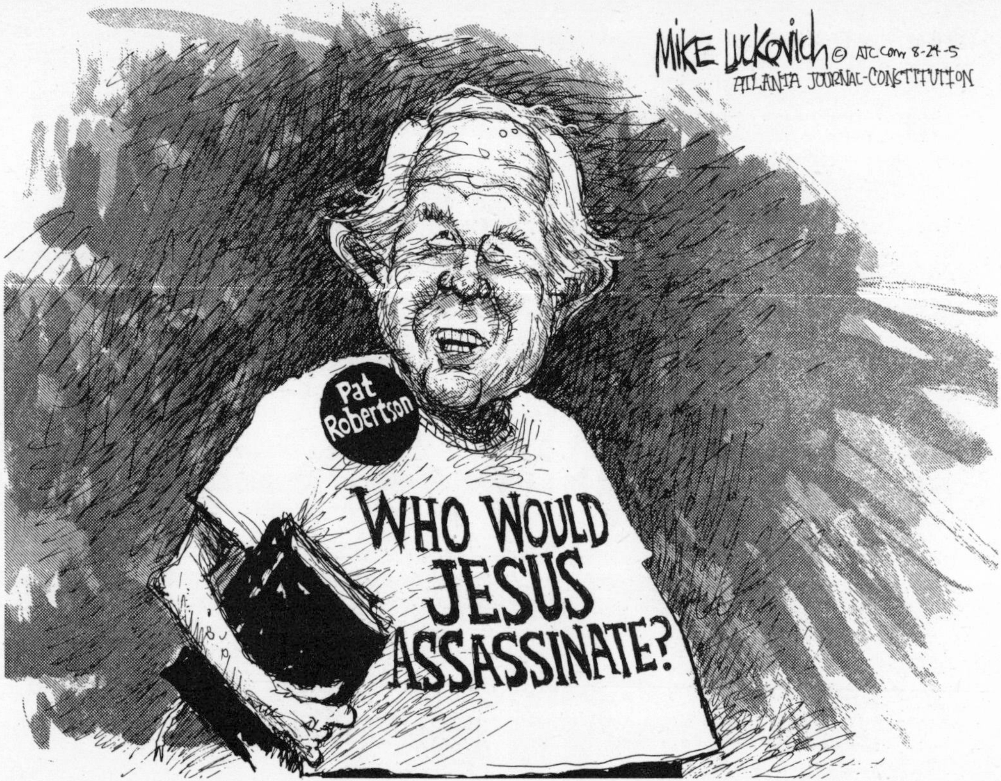
MIKE LUCKOVICH © AJC.com 8-24-5
ATLANTA JOURNAL-CONSTITUTION
Pat Robertson
WHO WOULD JESUS ASSASSINATE?

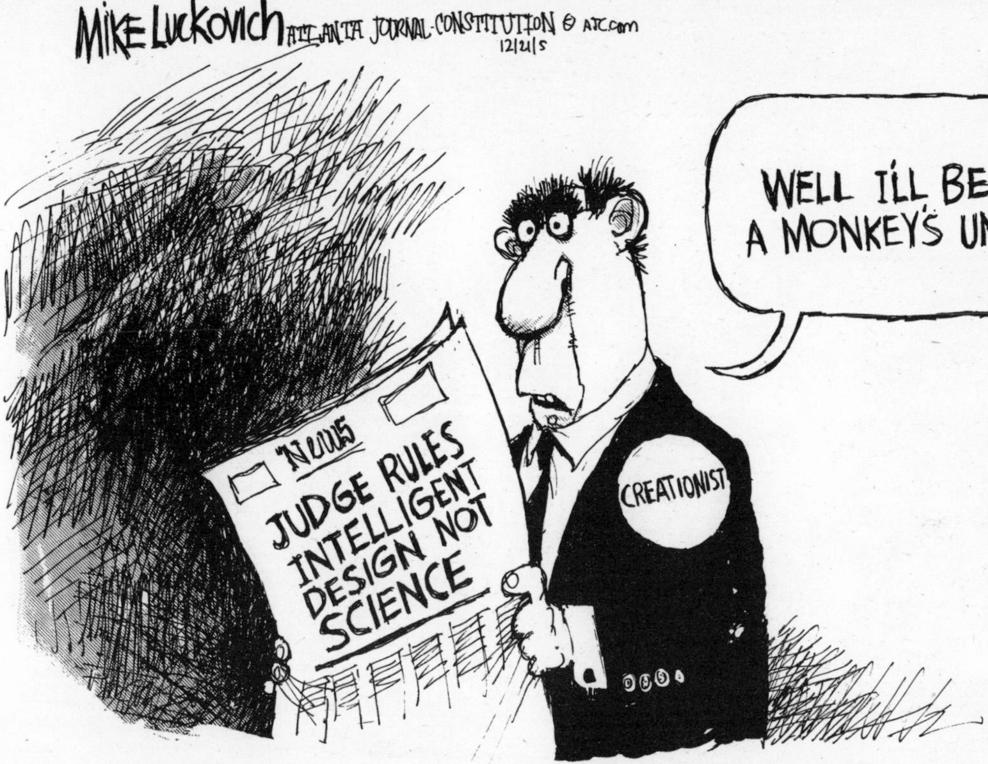
MIKE LUCKOVICH ATLANTA JOURNAL-CONSTITUTION © AJC.com
12/21/5
WELL I'LL BE A MONKEY'S UNCLE!
NEWS
JUDGE RULES INTELLIGENT DESIGN NOT SCIENCE
CREATIONIST

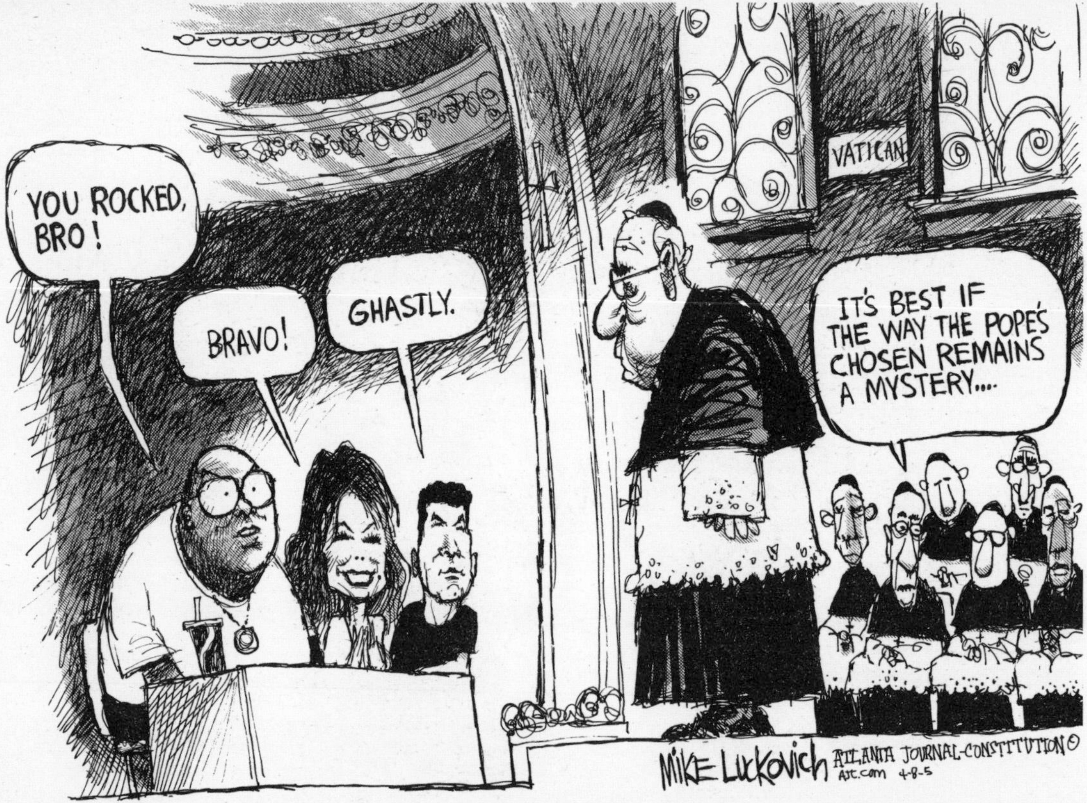
YOU ROCKED, BRO!
BRAVO!
GHASTLY.
VATICAN
IT'S BEST IF THE WAY THE POPE'S CHOSEN REMAINS A MYSTERY....
MIKE LUCKOVICH ATLANTA JOURNAL-CONSTITUTION ©
AJC.com 4-8-5

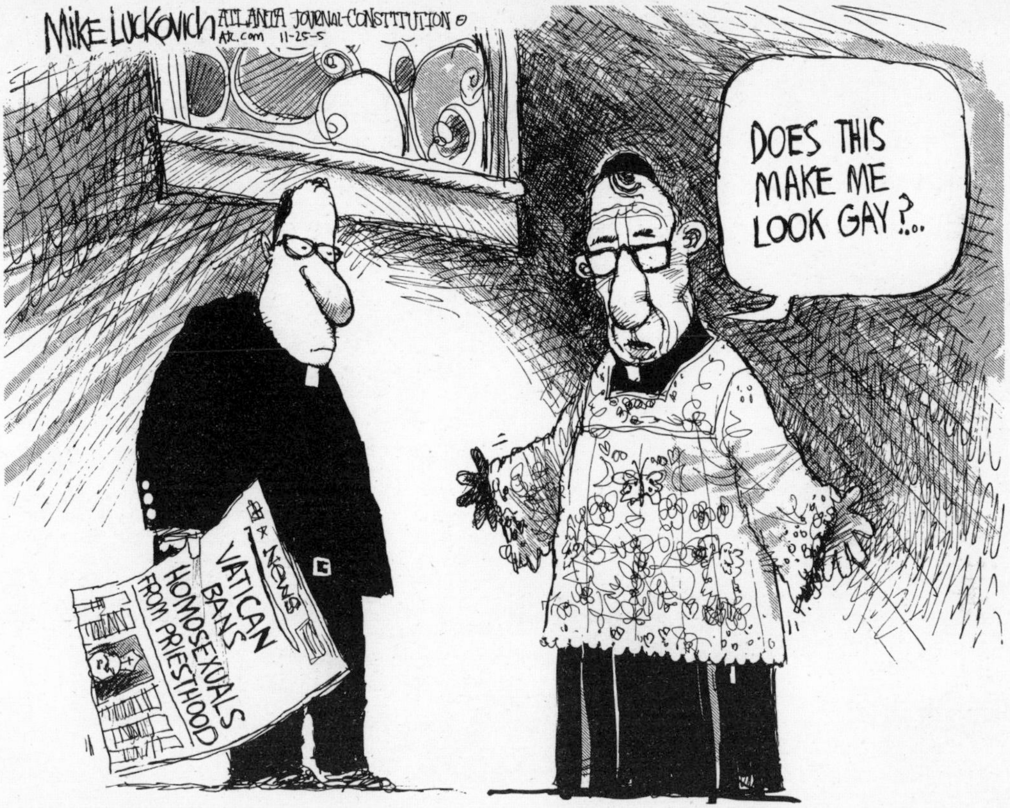
MIKE LUCKOVICH ATLANTA JOURNAL-CONSTITUTION ©
AJC.com 11-25-5
DOES THIS MAKE ME LOOK GAY?...
NEWS
VATICAN BANS HOMOSEXUALS FROM PRIESTHOOD

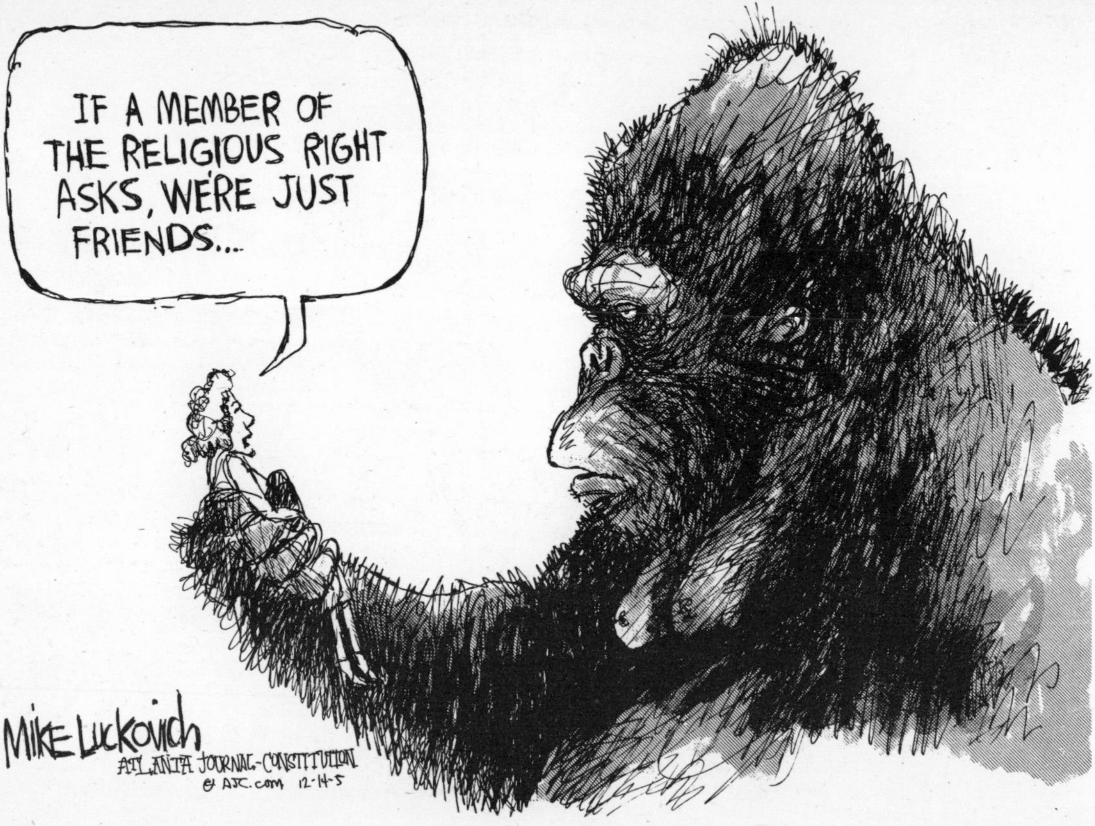
IF A MEMBER OF THE RELIGIOUS RIGHT ASKS, WE'RE JUST FRIENDS....
MIKE LUCKOVICH
ATLANTA JOURNAL-CONSTITUTION
@ AJC.com 12-14-5

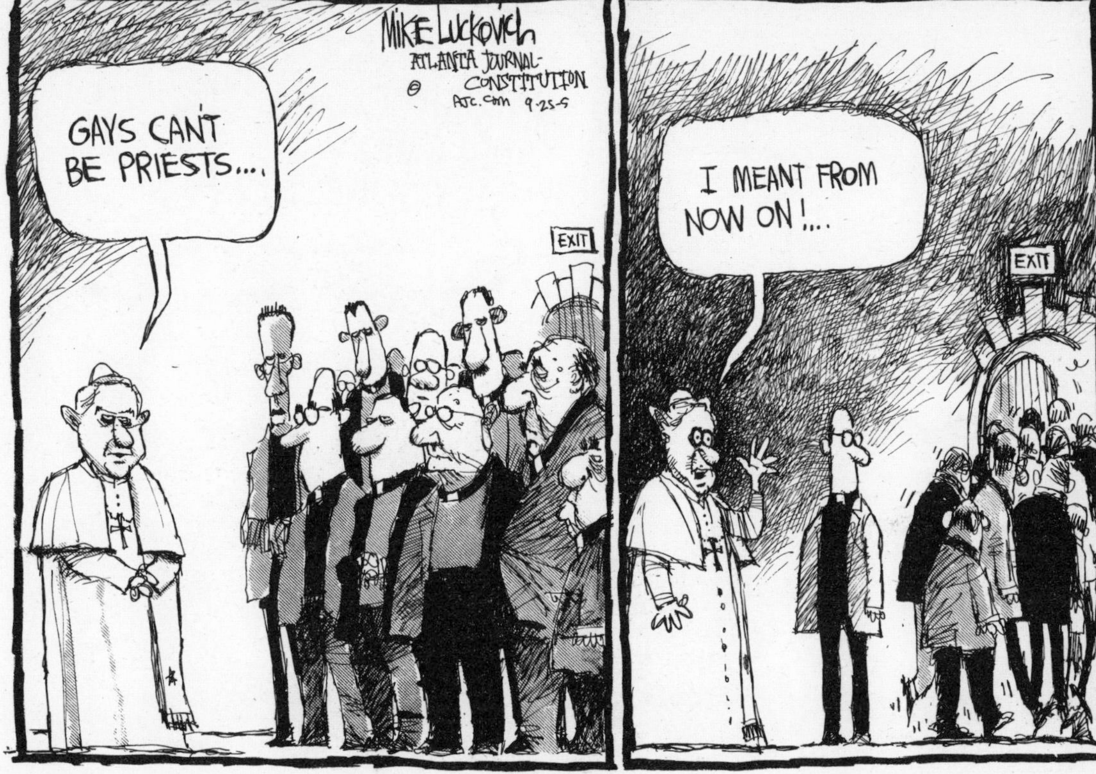
GAYS CAN'T BE PRIESTS....
MIKE LUCKOVICH
ATLANTA JOURNAL-CONSTITUTION
©
AJC.com 9-25-5
EXIT
I MEANT FROM NOW ON!...
EXIT

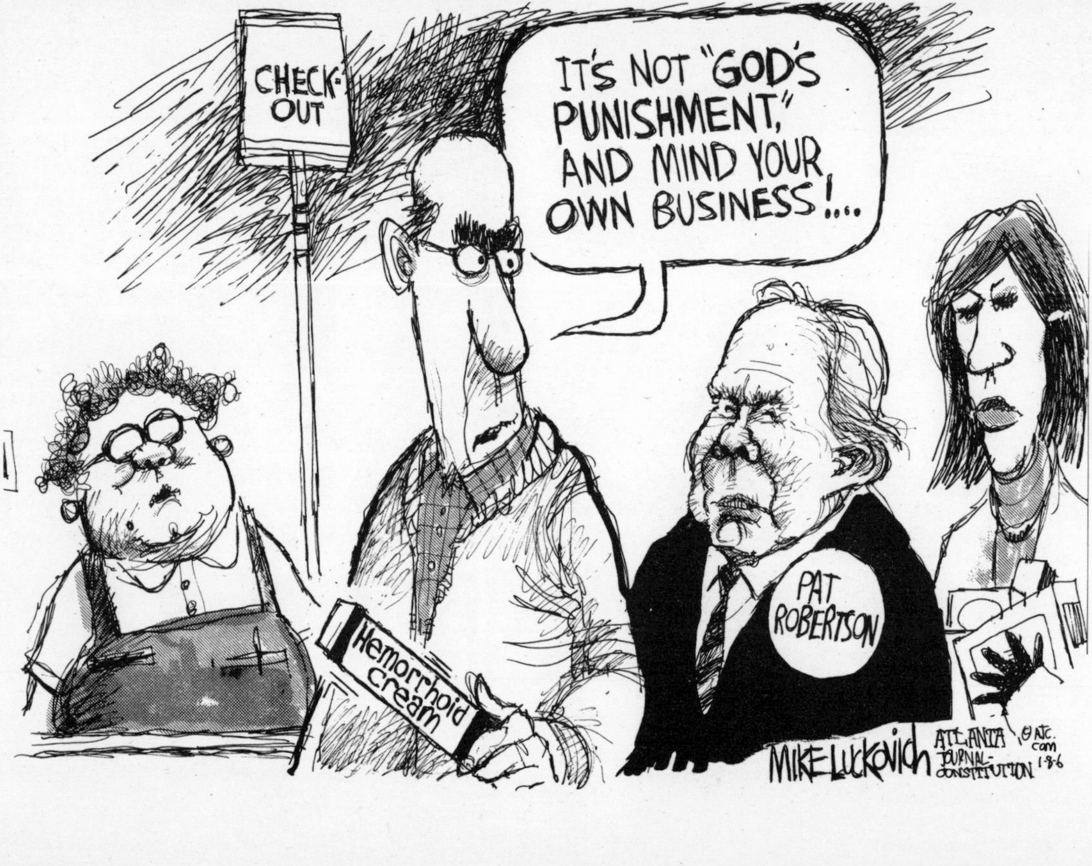
CHECK-OUT
IT'S NOT "GOD'S PUNISHMENT," AND MIND YOUR OWN BUSINESS!....
Hemorrhoid cream
PAT ROBERTSON
MIKE LUCKOVICH
ATLANTA JOURNAL-CONSTITUTION

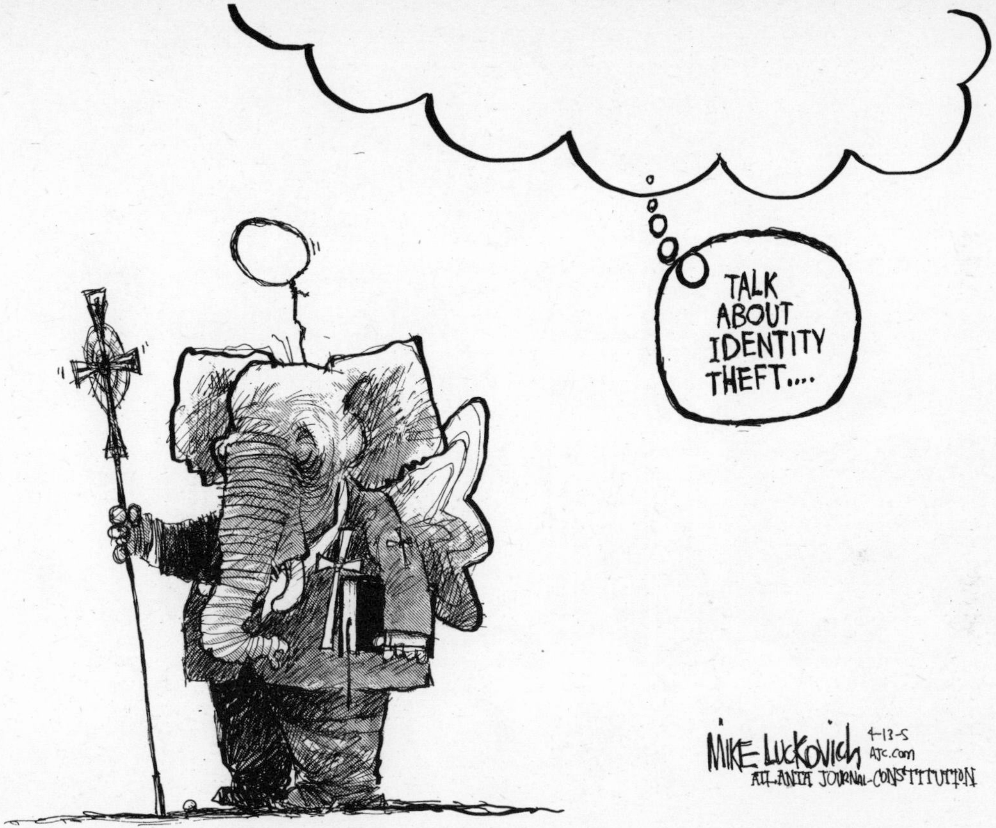
TALK ABOUT IDENTITY THEFT....
MIKE LUCKOVICH 4-13-5 AJC.com
ATLANTA JOURNAL-CONSTITUTION

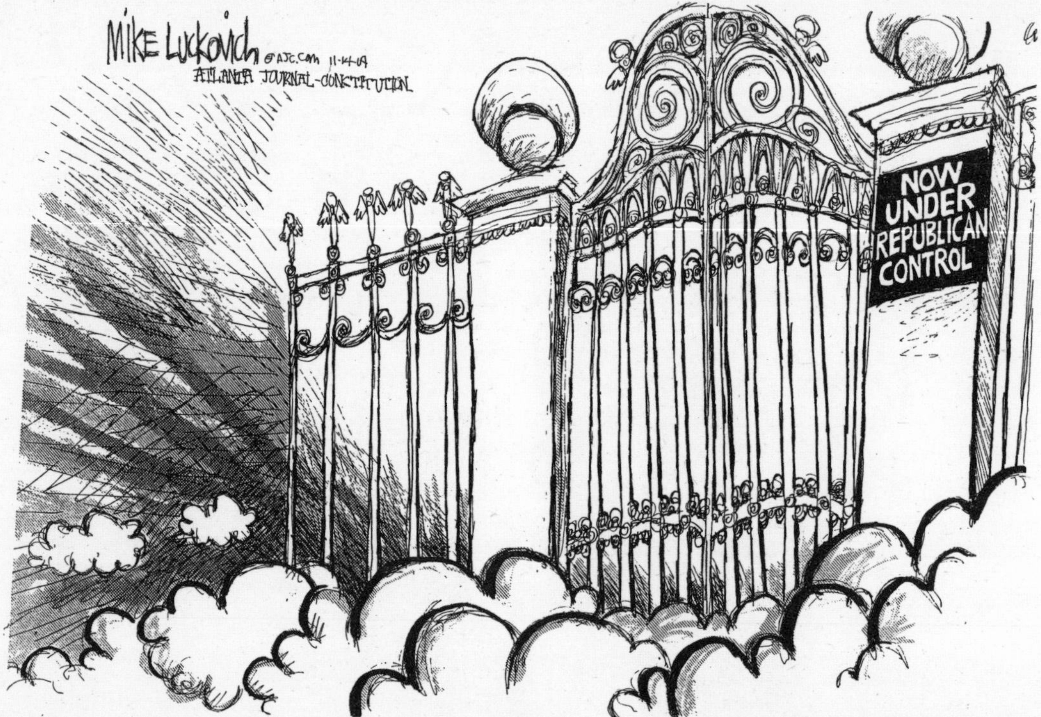
MIKE LUCKOVICH
@AJC.COM 11-14-04
ATLANTA JOURNAL-CONSTITUTION
NOW UNDER REPUBLICAN CONTROL

Clinton

I miss having Clinton as president. The Monica scandal was a gift to cartoonists. When it was unfolding, I was outraged at Bill for sullying the Oval Office. However, after witnessing Bush's ethical behavior, a president having sex and lying about it seems quaint. I prefer presidents who lie about private stuff that doesn't result in anybody getting killed.

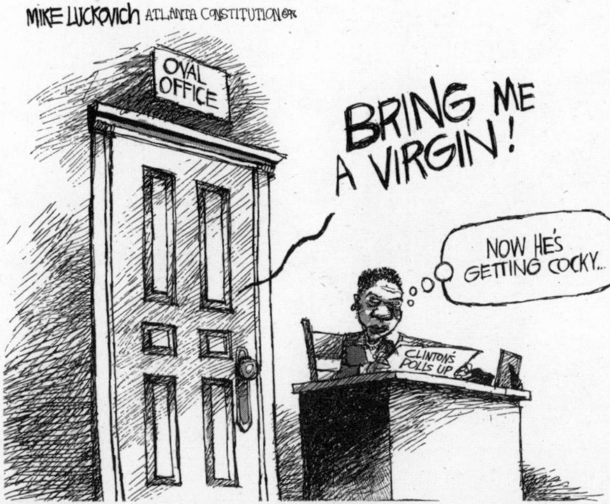

MIKE LUCKOVICH ATLANTA CONSTITUTION
OVAL OFFICE
BRING ME A VIRGIN!
NOW HE'S GETTING COCKY...
CLINTON'S POLLS UP

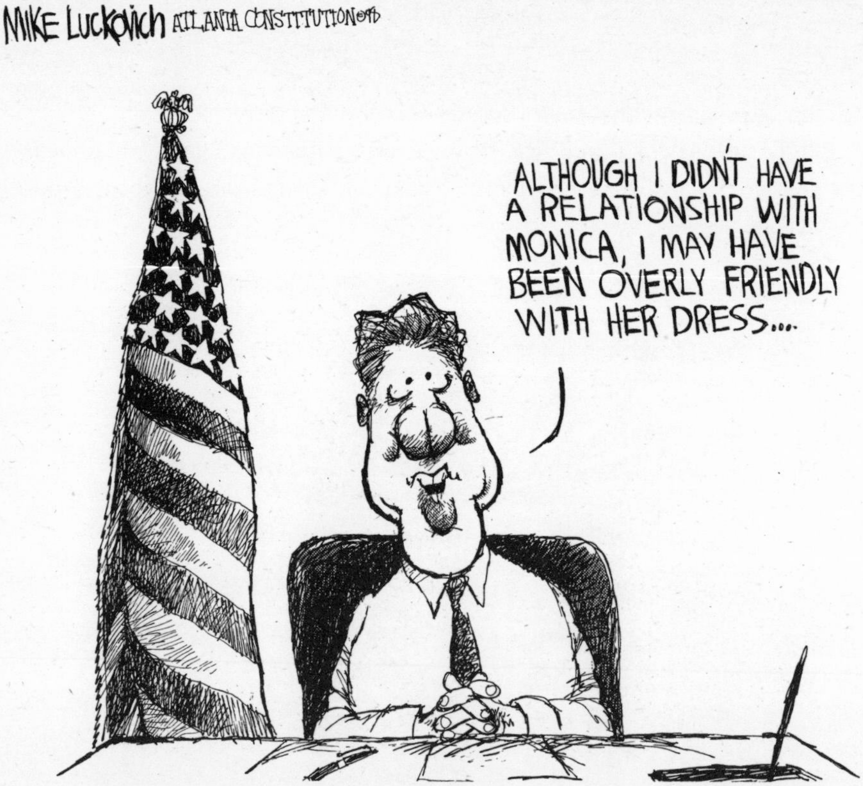
MIKE LUCKOVICH ATLANTA CONSTITUTION ©98
ALTHOUGH I DIDN'T HAVE A RELATIONSHIP WITH MONICA, I MAY HAVE BEEN OVERLY FRIENDLY WITH HER DRESS....

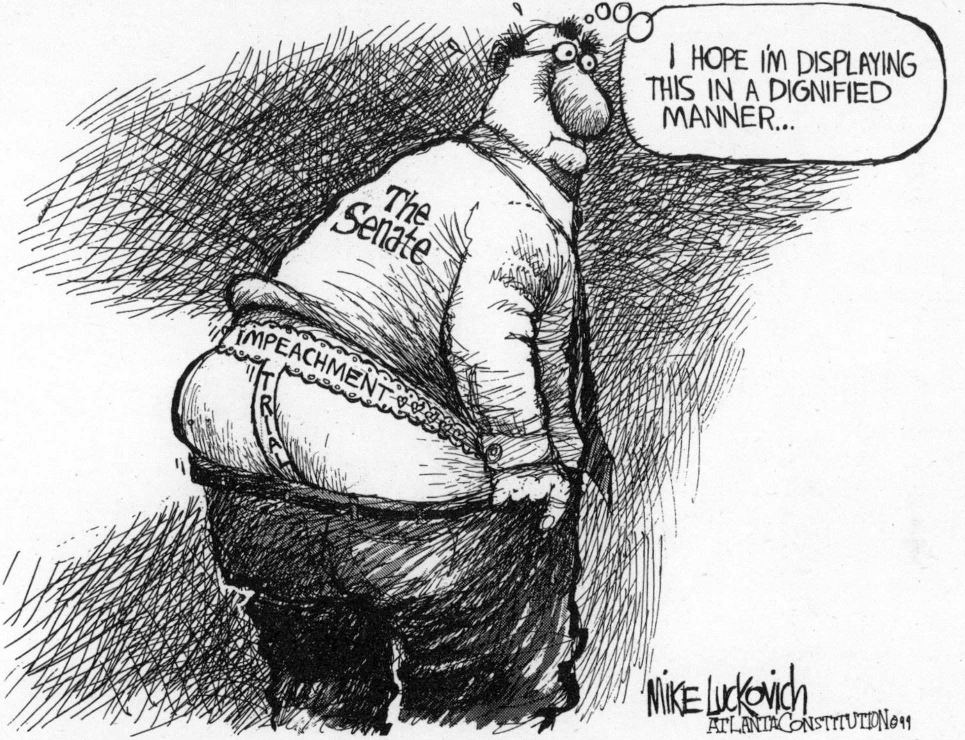
I HOPE I'M DISPLAYING THIS IN A DIGNIFIED MANNER...
The Senate
IMPEACHMENT
TRIAL
MIKE LUCKOVICH
ATLANTA CONSTITUTION©99

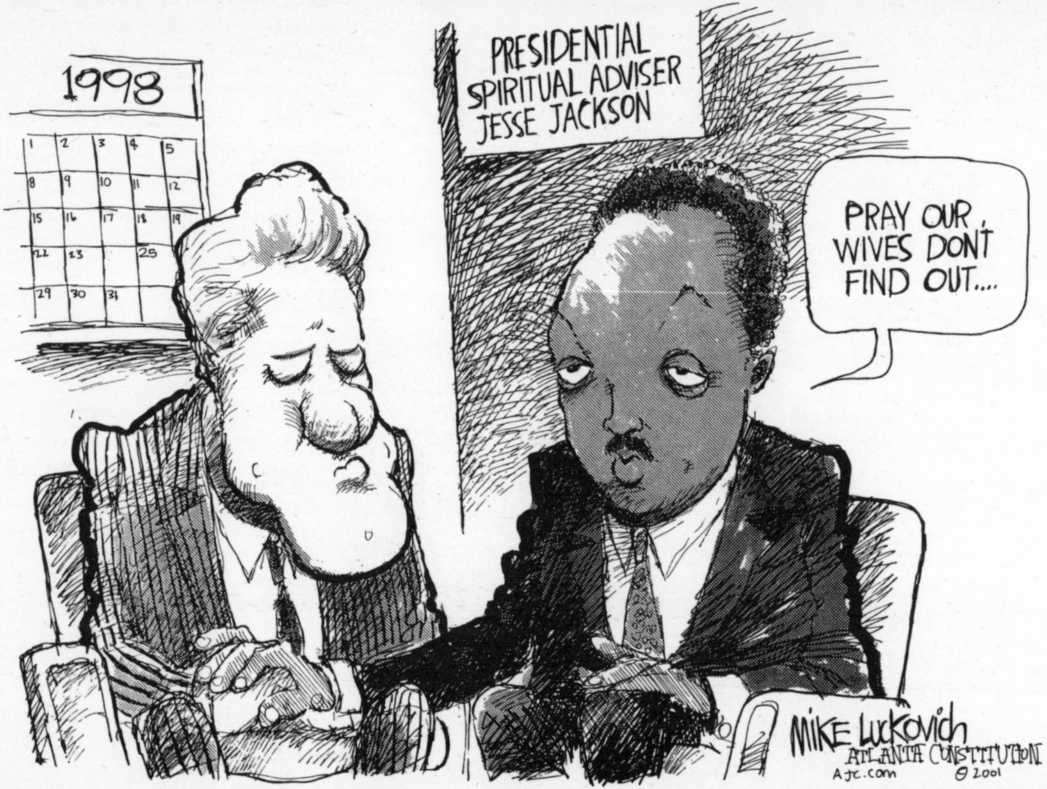
1998
PRESIDENTIAL
SPIRITUAL ADVISER
JESSE JACKSON
PRAY OUR, WIVES DON'T FIND OUT....
MIKE LUCKOVICH
ATLANTA CONSTITUTION
Ajc.com
© 2001

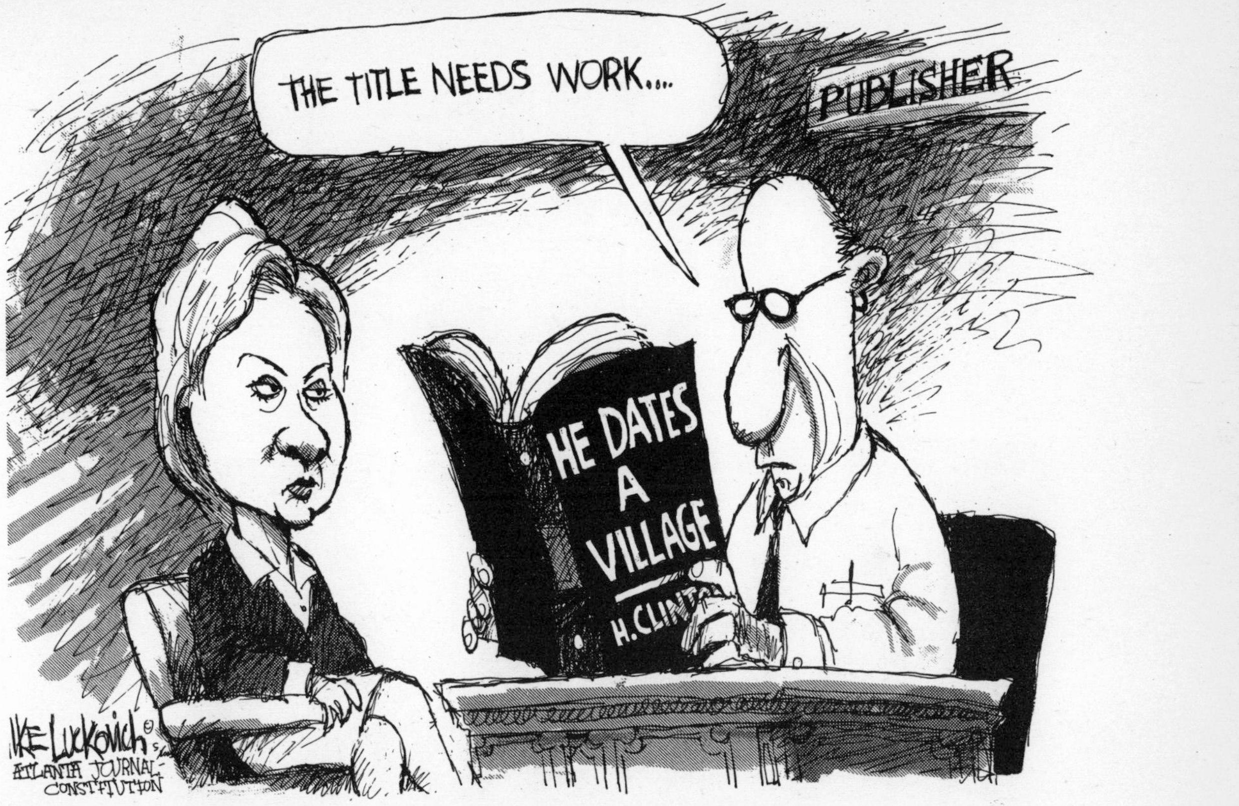
THE TITLE NEEDS WORK....
PUBLISHER
HE DATES A VILLAGE
H. CLINT
IKE LUCKOVICH
ATLANTA JOURNAL-CONSTITUTION

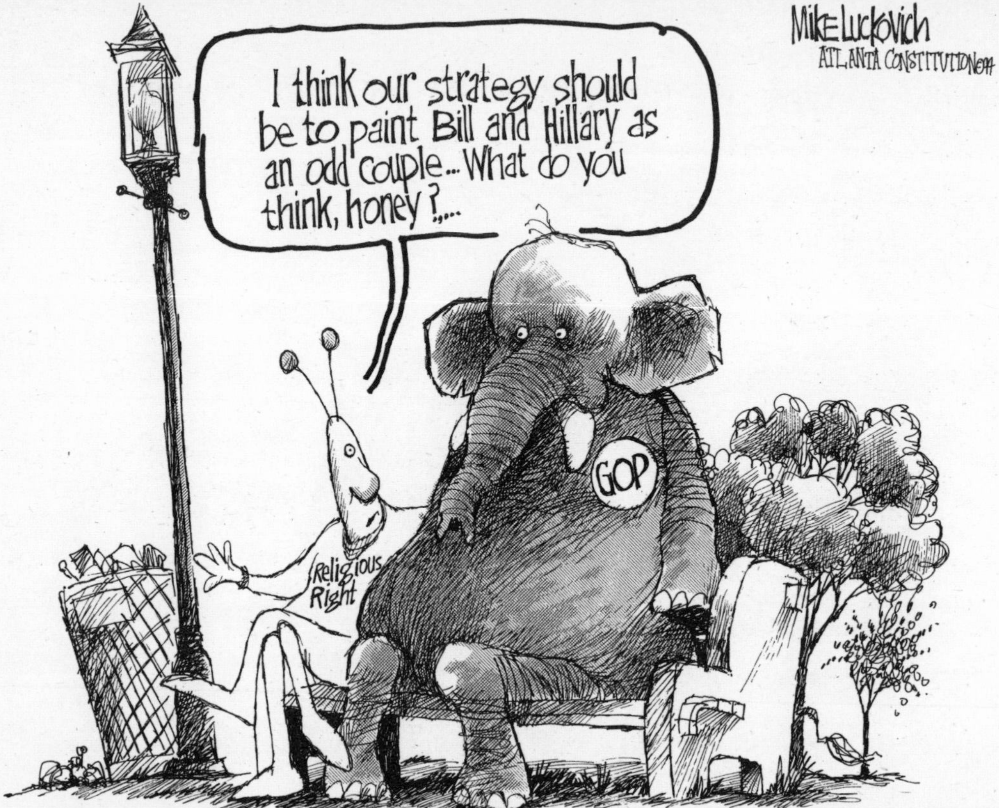
I think our strategy should be to paint Bill and Hillary as an odd couple... What do you think, honey?...
GOP
Religious Right
Mike Luckovich
ATLANTA CONSTITUTION

INVESTIGATION OF THE CLINTONS: $ 52 MILLION
THE JOY OF TORMENTING BILL AND HILLARY FOR SIX YEARS: PRICELESS

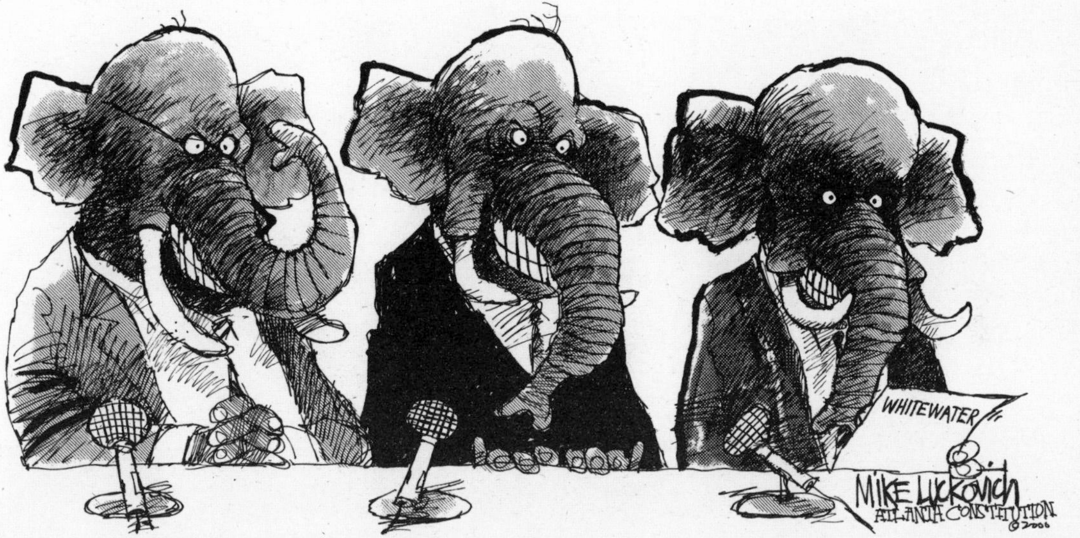
WHITEWATER
MIKE LUCKOVICH
ATLANTA CONSTITUTION
©2000

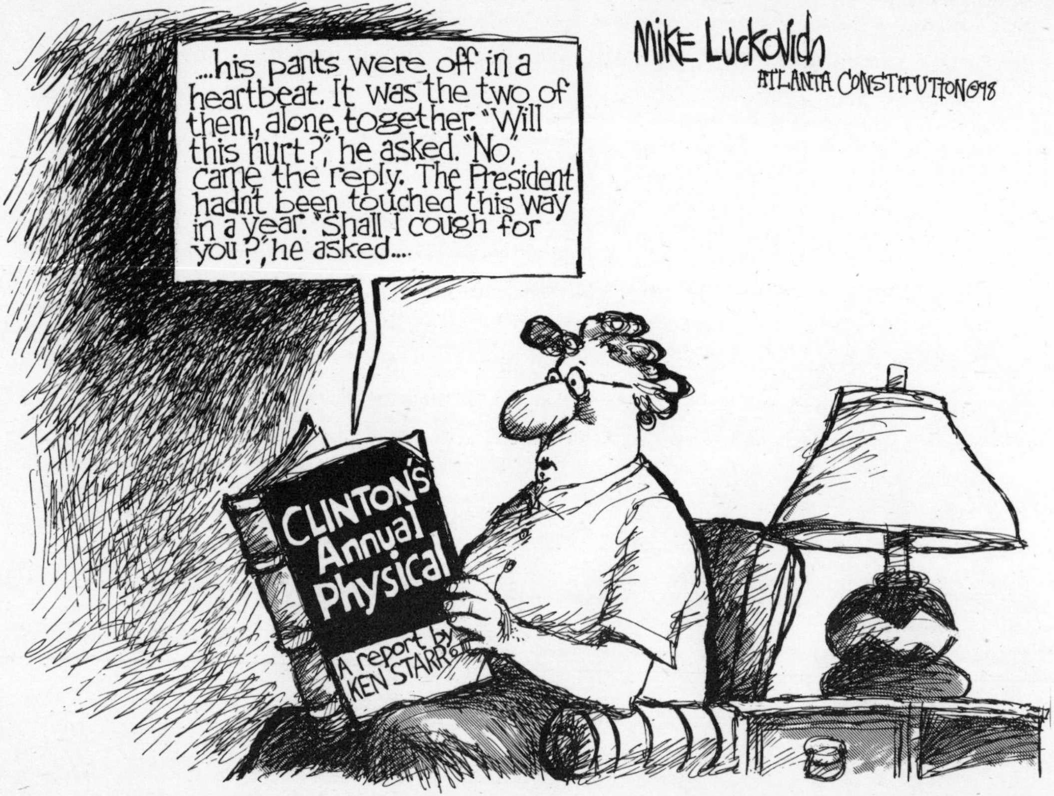
...his pants were off in a heartbeat. It was the two of them, alone, together. "Will this hurt?," he asked. "No," came the reply. The President hadn't been touched this way in a year. "Shall I cough for you?," he asked....
CLINTON'S Annual Physical
A report by KEN STARR
MIKE LUCKOVICH
ATLANTA CONSTITUTION ©98

My Day on Air Bill

I Feel Bill's Plane

Using my considerable influence, I have secured a place aboard Air Force One after only two years of begging. Fourteen seats on the plane rotate regularly throughout the press corps that travels with the president. Some journalists have been making these campaign jaunts with various presidents for a decade or more.

The White House isn't sure what to do with me. They've never had a cartoonist aboard before.

But Tuesday, here I am at Andrews Air Force Base outside Washington, sitting in the plane and waiting for an 8:30 a.m. departure to Kansas City and then St. Louis.

I have the same feeling I had when sneaking into movies as a kid. I sit in the back, periodically stroking my lush leather seat. A *Newsweek* photographer sitting next to me tells me I can pick anything from a large menu by requesting it on the phone next to my seat. "Something weird," I thought, figuring it would be funny to have *Rumble in the Bronx*, a Jackie Chan martial arts movie playing on Air Force One. I get my movie.

Twenty minutes into the flight a presidential aide interrupts Jackie and invites me to the front of the plane. I step into a good-sized office with a large wooden desk, with President Clinton behind it. I'm in the airborne equivalent of the Oval Office.

So what do I say?

I tell him about *Rumble in the Bronx*.

"Oh, yeah. A Jackie Chan movie. Did you know he has a new one out?"

"No," I admit. I'm amazed that this guy who could probably recite the federal statutes for drainage-ditch placement knows about Jackie Chan movies too.

I am nervous — not only because I am meeting the president but also because I want to give him a just-published book of my editorial cartoons. The cartoon on the cover shows an aide in the White House telling Clinton, "More bad news. The bloody glove fits Hillary."

Handing over the book, I tell him I hope he has a good sense of humor. But when he looks at the cover, he laughs — roars really.

Whew!

Then I ask for a favor: "Mr. President, would you consider doing a drawing of yourself? Ronald Reagan did a caricature of himself and look what happened to him — he got a second term."

Clinton smiles but makes no promises.

Then Germany Chancellor Helmut Kohl calls. Clinton, not me.

An aide starts to boot me out, but Clinton says, "He can stay."

So I stay, sketching Clinton, with his half glasses perched on his nose, as he chats with Kohl. I don't dare stop sketching, because I'm afraid I'll get kicked out. Finally, I have to leave because the plane is landing. Clinton, still on the phone, gestures for me to show him what I was drawing and laughs at the caption: "So Helmut, tell me about Der Wienerschnitzel."

Back in my seat in the rear bowels of the plane, I realize I didn't say goodbye.

Grounded in Kansas City

Once we land, the president and the press corps travel in a motorcade. In the front of the motorcade are city cops on motorcycles. Then two presidential limos so that no one knows which one the president is in.

Then a big black Suburban, known as the battle wagon. Inside is CAT, or Counter Attack Team, muscle-bound guys dressed in black with flak jackets loaded up with impressive automatic weapons. They look like Rambo's carpool.

Then come a string of limos and vans with dignitaries (Lord knows who), followed by more vans carrying us — the all-important members of the press.

As we snake along in the motorcade, people stand outside of homes and businesses waving and cheering. Young and old, rich and poor. All just to see a cartoonist!

Downtime with the Press

Throughout my day on the campaign trail, the press seems, well, mostly bored. Day after day, they hear the same speeches, same jokes, see the same president who they swear will shake every hand in every crowd if an aide doesn't stop him. We spend what they call downtime, waiting for the president while he's in private meetings.

Anyway, after sitting around for hours, the motorcade goes back on the road, then back to Air Force One. Suddenly, news breaks out.

Clinton throws a hastily arranged press conference on the tarmac: the United Nations has approved the Nuclear Test Ban Treaty. Everybody wakes up.

The First Cartoonist

Then we're back on the plane and I'm thinking about that caricature I want from the president, and thinking about all the world leaders Clinton's going to want to talk to about the Test Ban Treaty. And then the photographer next to me punches me and says, "He's here."

And he is. Up at the front of the press seating, smiling and motioning for me. In his hand, a drawing.

I get up from my seat and at that exact moment the plane takes off. I'm twenty feet from the president, but I can't get to him because I'm fighting the force of takeoff. I'm pulling myself forward on the seats in front of me and yelling, "I'm on my way, Mr. President!"

Clinton turns away from me and begins to surf into the acceleration — his body forward, kind of suspending himself with his arms out like he's flying.

I do that too.

When the plane levels off, Clinton hands me a drawing. Of him. A caricature fresh from the presidential pen. I look at it and say — you know, to the leader of the free world — "Sir, it's obvious now to me why you're trying hard to keep your day job." And he's laughing and explaining the cartoon to me, but I'm shocked it's happening and laughing so hard not much gets through to me. The whole press corps is taking pictures, laughing and having a good time too.

Then suddenly he's gone and I'm back in my seat, completely worn out with a big smile on my face.

And a caricature of the president to take home.

Aboard Air Force One

HOW DID I EVER GET TALKED INTO THIS! MAYBE LUCKOVICH SHOULD BE PRESIDENT. ... [GOP ↓]
HEY, MIKE NOW I FEEL MY PAIN! I'M NOT GOOD AT THIS —
BC 9/10/96

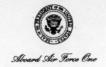

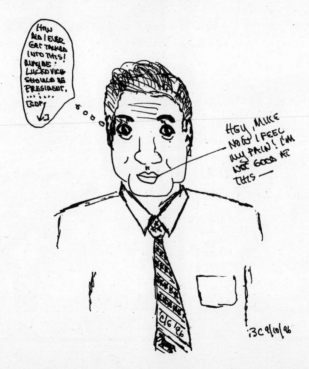

JUNK FOOD CAUGHT UP WITH ME. I WON'T BE ABLE TO CAMPAIGN FOR YOU....
BILL
Mayor McCheese
MIKE LUCKOVICH
ATLANTA JOURNAL- CONSTITUTION
© AJC.com

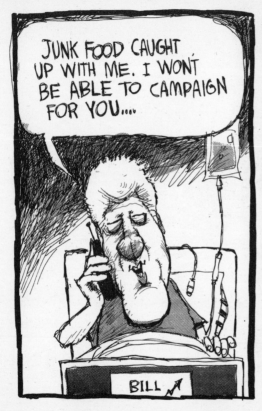

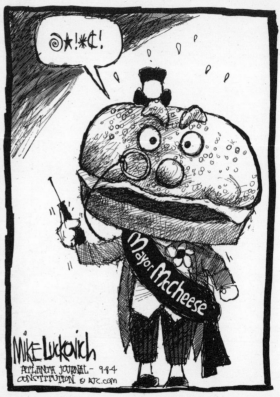

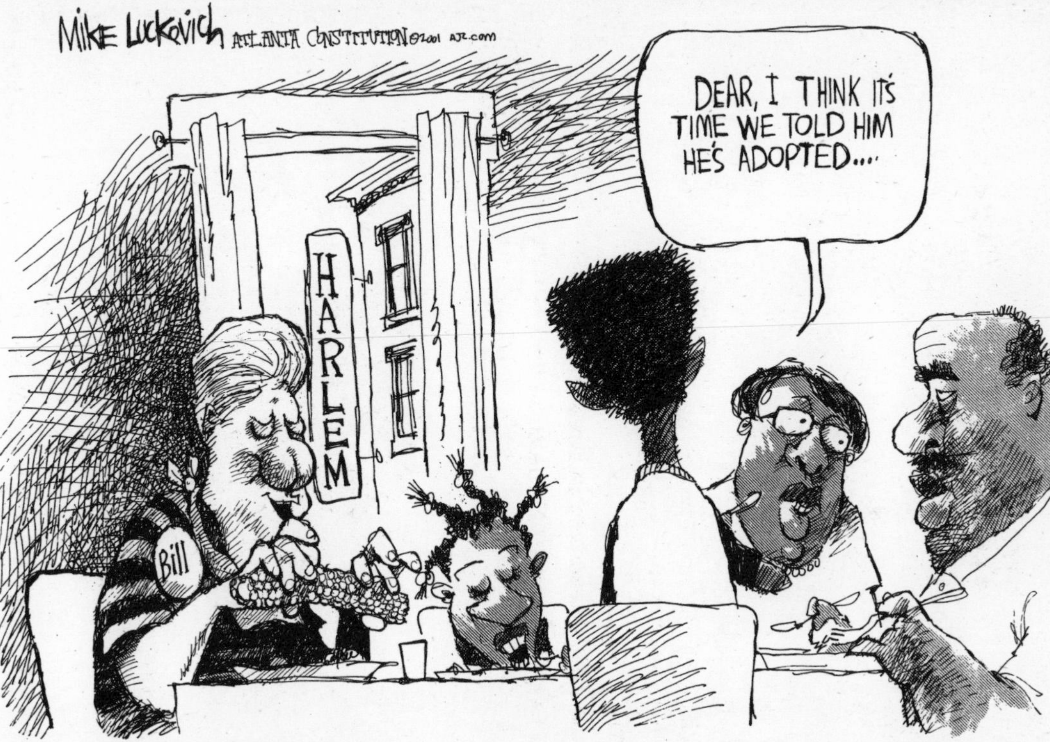
MIKE LUCKOVICH ATLANTA CONSTITUTION ©2001 AJC.com
DEAR, I THINK IT'S TIME WE TOLD HIM HE'S ADOPTED....
HARLEM
Bill

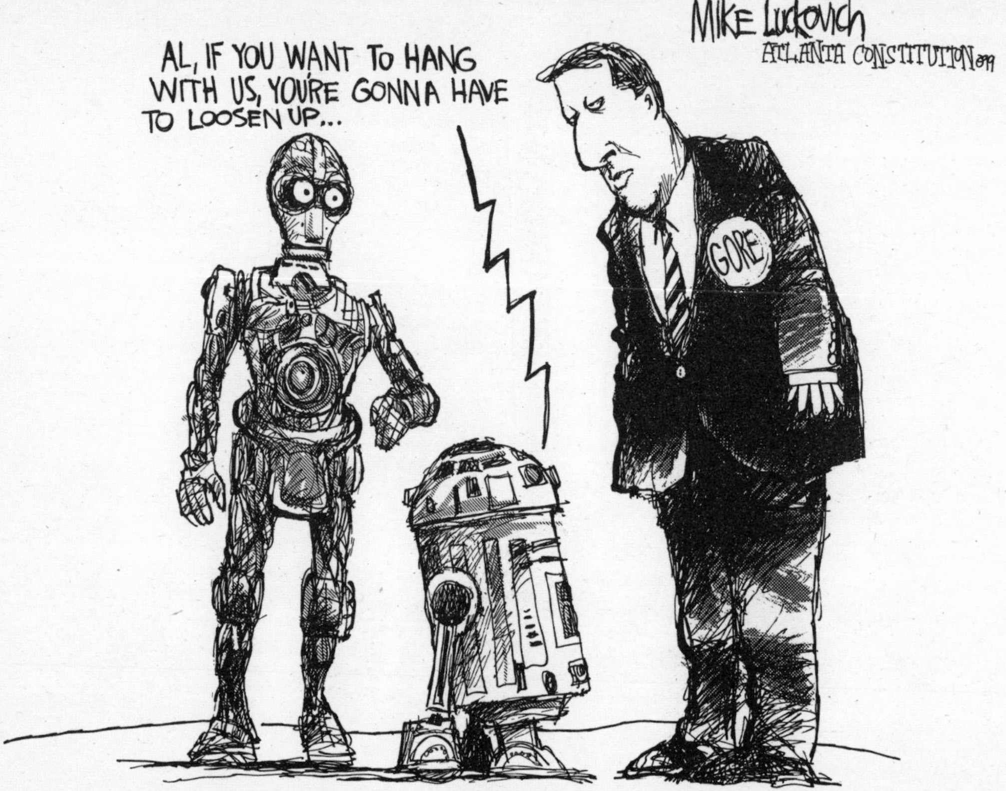
AL, IF YOU WANT TO HANG WITH US, YOU'RE GONNA HAVE TO LOOSEN UP...
GORE
MIKE LUCKOVICH
ATLANTA CONSTITUTION

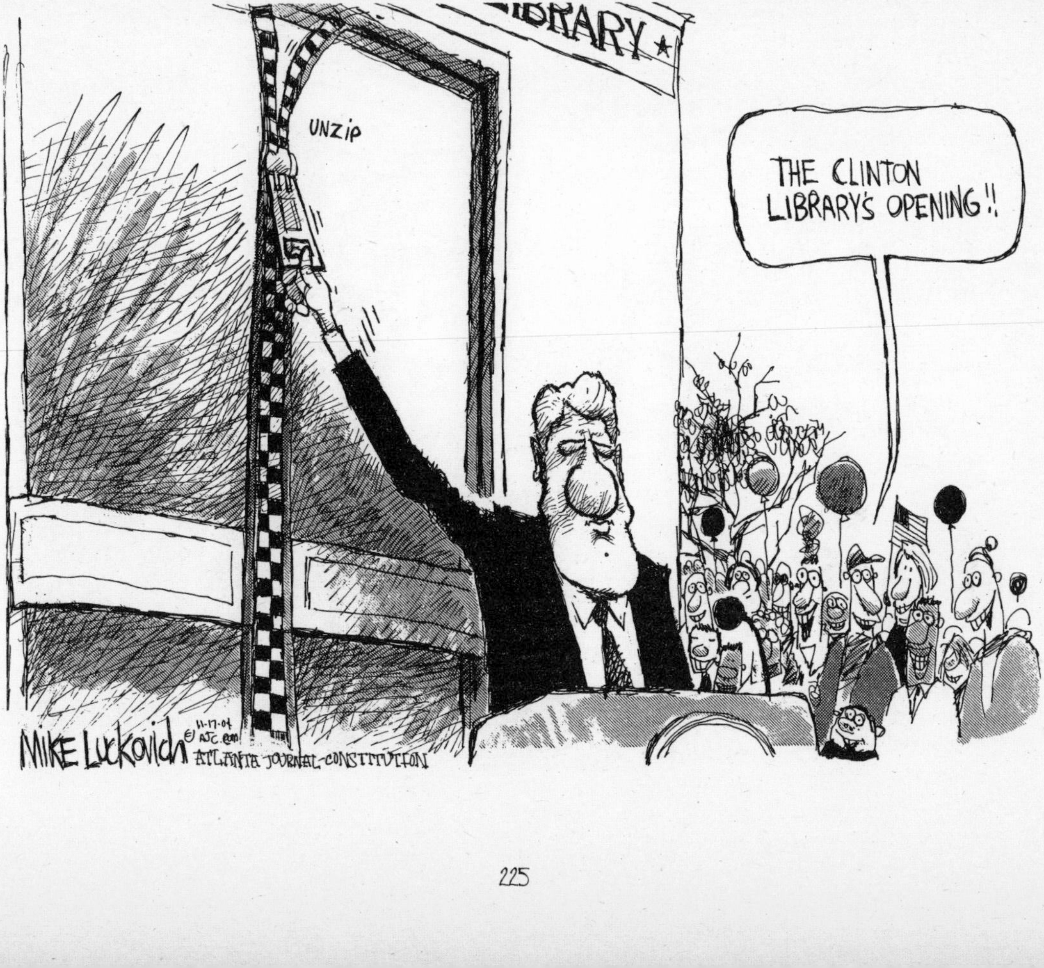
IBRARY
UNZIP
THE CLINTON LIBRARY'S OPENING!!
MIKE LUCKOVICH
11-17-04
AJC.com
ATLANTA JOURNAL-CONSTITUTION

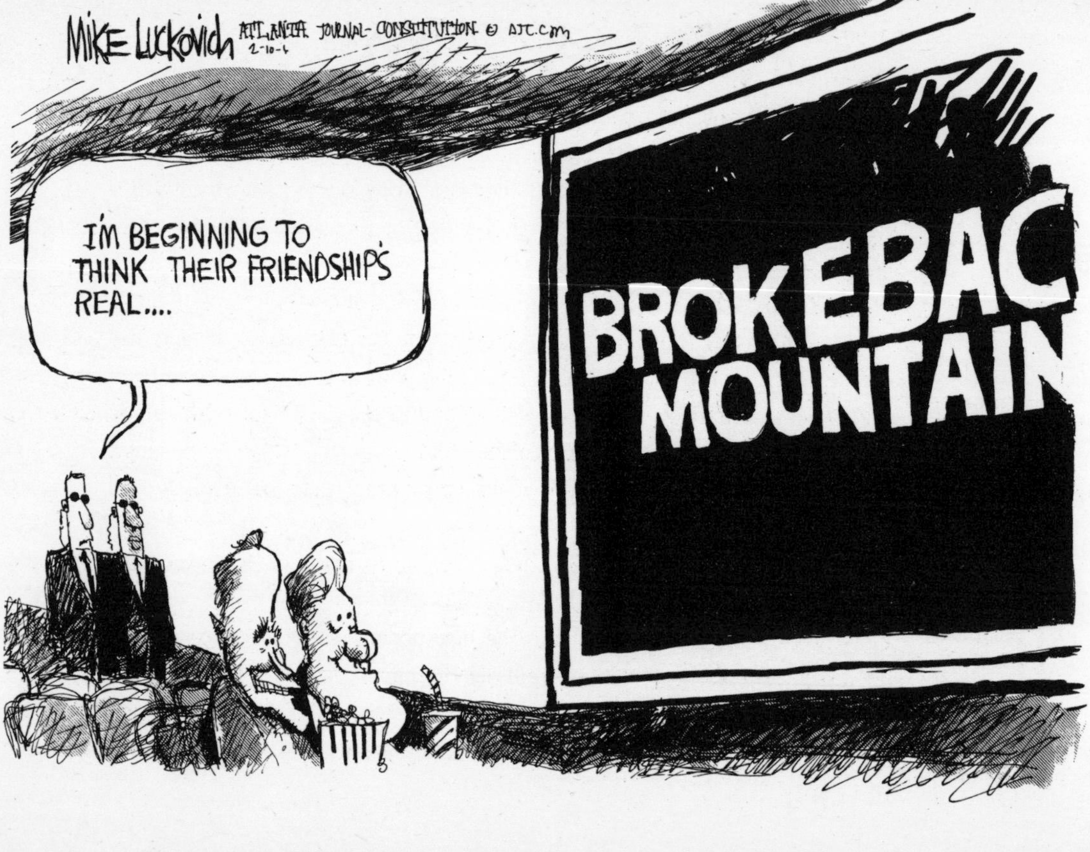
MIKE LUCKOVICH ATLANTA JOURNAL-CONSTITUTION © AJC.com 2-10-6
I'M BEGINNING TO THINK THEIR FRIENDSHIP'S REAL....
BROKEBAC
MOUNTAIN

Serious Stuff

Editorial cartoons aren't always funny. Sometimes the subject is so serious or tragic that using humor would be inappropriate. When the space shuttle *Challenger* blew up with an Israeli astronaut on board, I was watching Miles O'Brien's moving commentary on CNN. They kept showing the debris field in the sky where the shuttle broke apart. I drew the debris field as stars landing on the American flag. One was a Star of David to represent the Israeli.

Sometimes you draw a cartoon that you expect will generate a lot of controversy, but the next day when it runs, you hear absolutely nothing. That's a little disappointing. Then, there are other times, you do one that causes an explosion of criticism that leaves you scratching your head and wondering what happened.

In 1995, I did a cartoon on welfare reform. It showed a congressman holding an African-American baby by the shirt collar. It was meant to be sympathetic to the child, who would be an innocent victim if welfare reform didn't work. At the time, I didn't think it would. Fortunately, the great economy under President Clinton helped it succeed.

The day I came up with the idea, my editor, Cynthia Tucker, an African-American, looked at it and said she suspected that it might upset conservatives.

The next day when the cartoon ran, walking into the newspaper's editorial offices, I noticed the odd looks on the faces of my colleagues. One of them told me the paper was receiving hundreds of calls and faxes from readers, most of them African-American, who found the cartoon offensive. As the day progressed, Josea Williams, a local civil rights crusader, announced a protest march in front of the newspaper.

A local TV news station called me and asked to do a story about the growing controversy. I felt like I'd be able to explain what the cartoon was actually meant to convey, causing the brouhaha to evaporate.

The reporter interviewed me. He understood what I was trying to say with the cartoon. I was relieved. He told me the story would run that evening on the eleven o'clock news.

That night, my wife and I watched the season premiere of NBC's *Emergency*, waiting for the news. During commercials, the station would tease its upcoming newscast by showing my drawing as an announcer intoned, "Racist cartoon? Tune in at eleven."

I looked at my wife and said, "Uh-oh."

It led the newscast. The reporter basically spun the story as Mike Luckovich hits all types with his cartoons and today it was an African-American infant's turn. He reported that neither Mike nor the newspaper planned on apologizing. Well, I was annoyed. I knew the reporter understood what I was trying to say with the cartoon, and had chosen not to diffuse the controversy, but to fuel it.

The next day, someone called me from the newspaper, telling me to park in a different location and come in a side entrance, because they feared for my safety. The calls and faxes to the newspaper intensified. A pin I'd drawn on the infant's diaper was being called a devil's tail. Urban radio disk jockeys were describing the cartoon and further inflaming people. I was sick to my stomach. Finally, a reporter at another local station called and said he wanted to interview me. He said he'd seen the report the night before, which he described as a "hatchet job." He wanted to set the record straight. My editor and I each appeared on urban radio stations explaining the cartoon.

After that, the controversy dissipated, but not before someone had sued me, my editor, and newspaper for libel, which was quickly thrown out of court. The incident made me understand why people get angry with the media for distorting the facts.

My favorite cartoon from 2005 was a drawing I did when the two-thousandth American soldier had died in Iraq. I spent twelve hours at my kitchen table writing all two thousand names to form the word "WHY." My newspaper ran the cartoon full size (8.5 by 11 inches) on the editorial page. The next day, the paper ran a full page of letters, pro and con, on the cartoon. Thousands more commented on it on my blog at http://www.ajc.com.

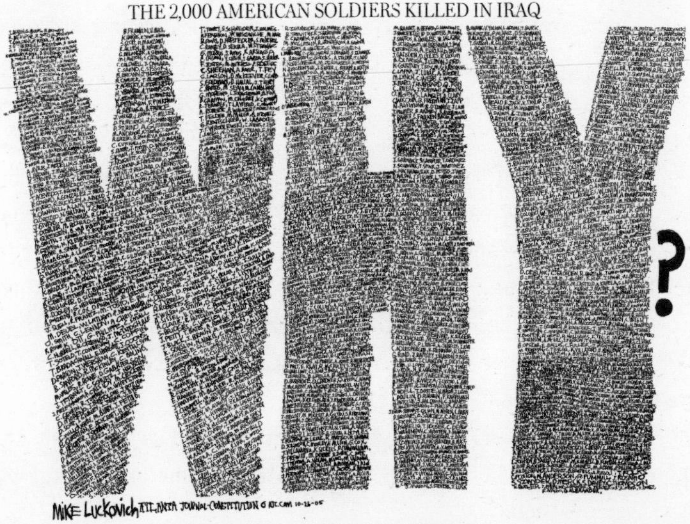
THE 2,000 AMERICAN SOLDIERS KILLED IN IRAQ
WHY?
MIKE LUCKOVICH ATLANTA JOURNAL-CONSTITUTION

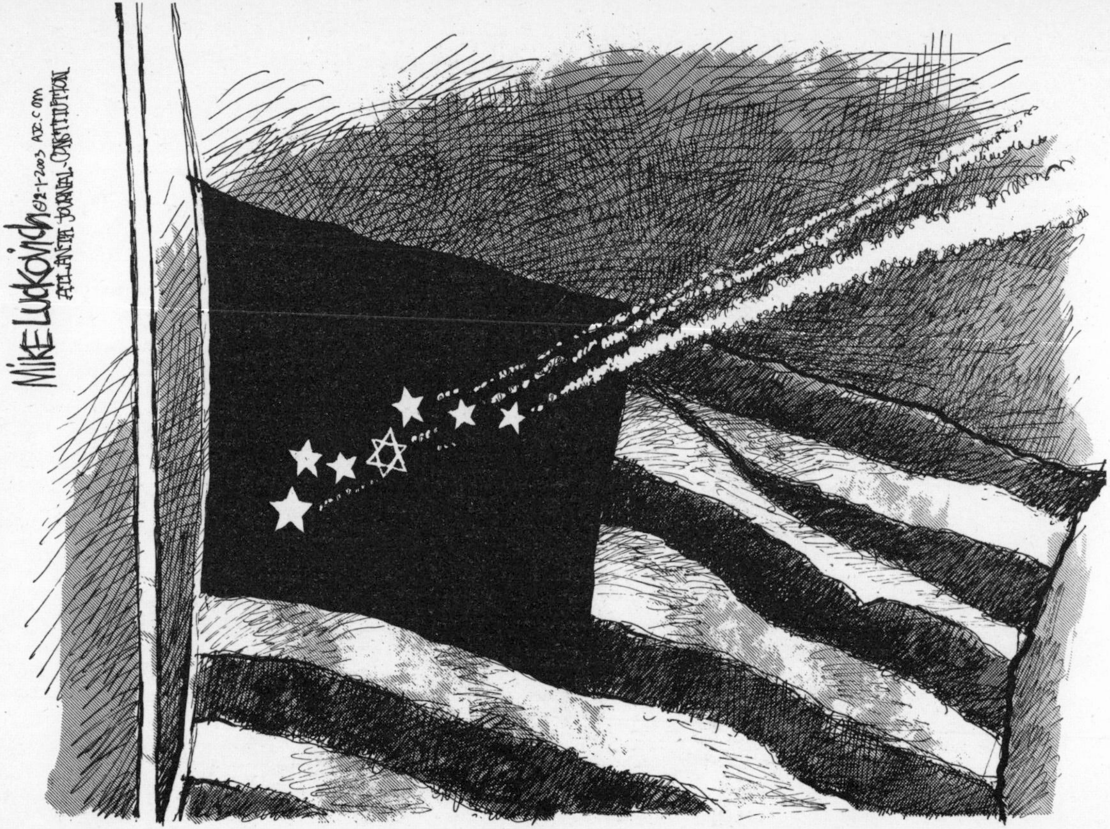
MIKE LUCKOVICH ©2-1-2003 AJC.COM
ATLANTA JOURNAL-CONSTITUTION

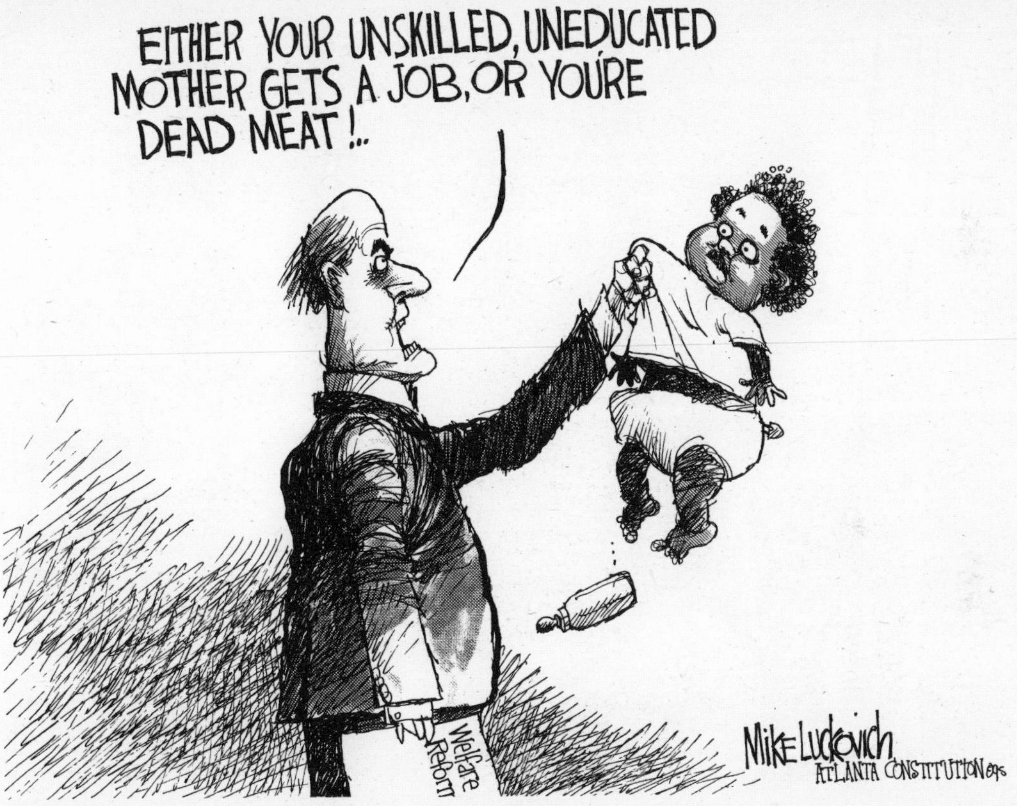
EITHER YOUR UNSKILLED, UNEDUCATED MOTHER GETS A JOB, OR YOU'RE DEAD MEAT!..
Welfare Reform
MIKE LUCKOVICH
ATLANTA CONSTITUTION

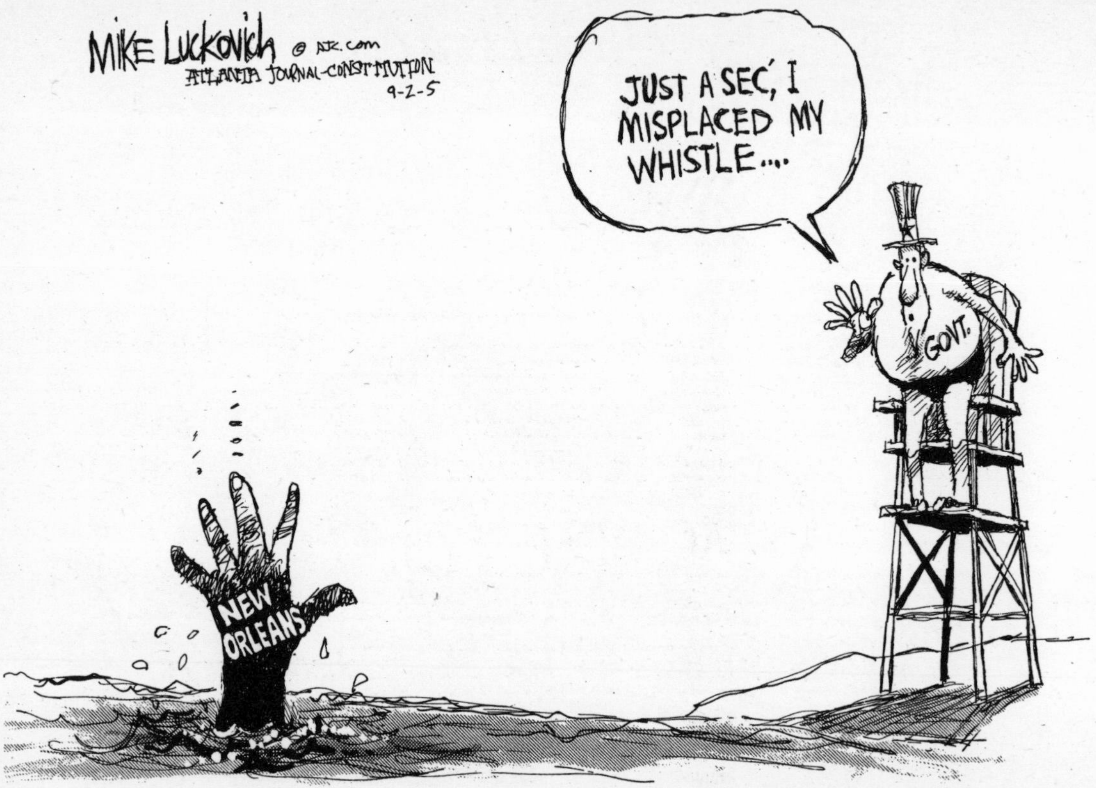
MIKE LUCKOVICH © AJC.com
ATLANTA JOURNAL-CONSTITUTION
9-2-5
JUST A SEC, I MISPLACED MY WHISTLE....
GOVT.
NEW ORLEANS

The Constitution

We the People of the United States, in Order to form a more perfect Union, establish Justice, insure domestic Tranquility, provide for the common Defence, promote the general Welfare, and secure the Blessings of Liberty to ourselves and our Posterity, do ordain and establish this CONSTITUTION for the United States of America.

Article. I.

(Except for Homos)

G.W.B.

MIKE LUCKOVICH 2-25-04
ATLANTA JOURNAL-CONSTITUTION © AJC.com

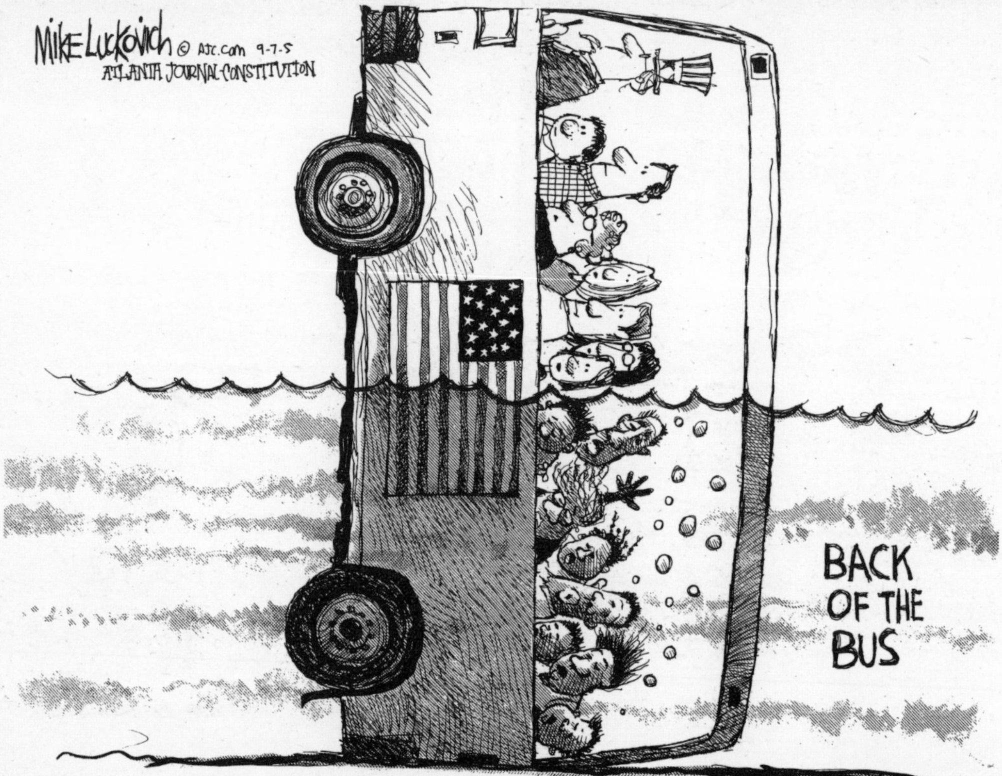
MIKE LUCKOVICH © AJC.com 9-7-5
ATLANTA JOURNAL-CONSTITUTION
BACK OF THE BUS

HELP US
MIKE LUCKOVICH ATLANTA JOURNAL-CONSTITUTION
© AJC.com 9-4-5
IRAQ
LA NATL. GUARD
MS NATL. GUARD

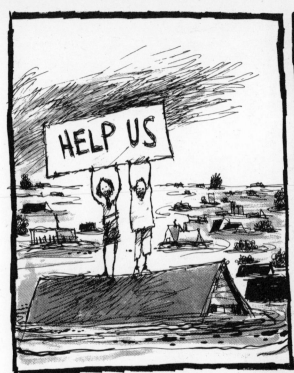

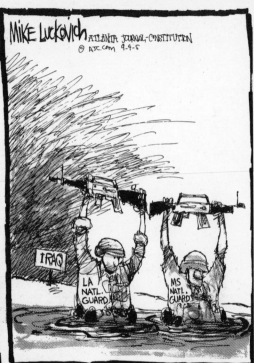

TRAPPED

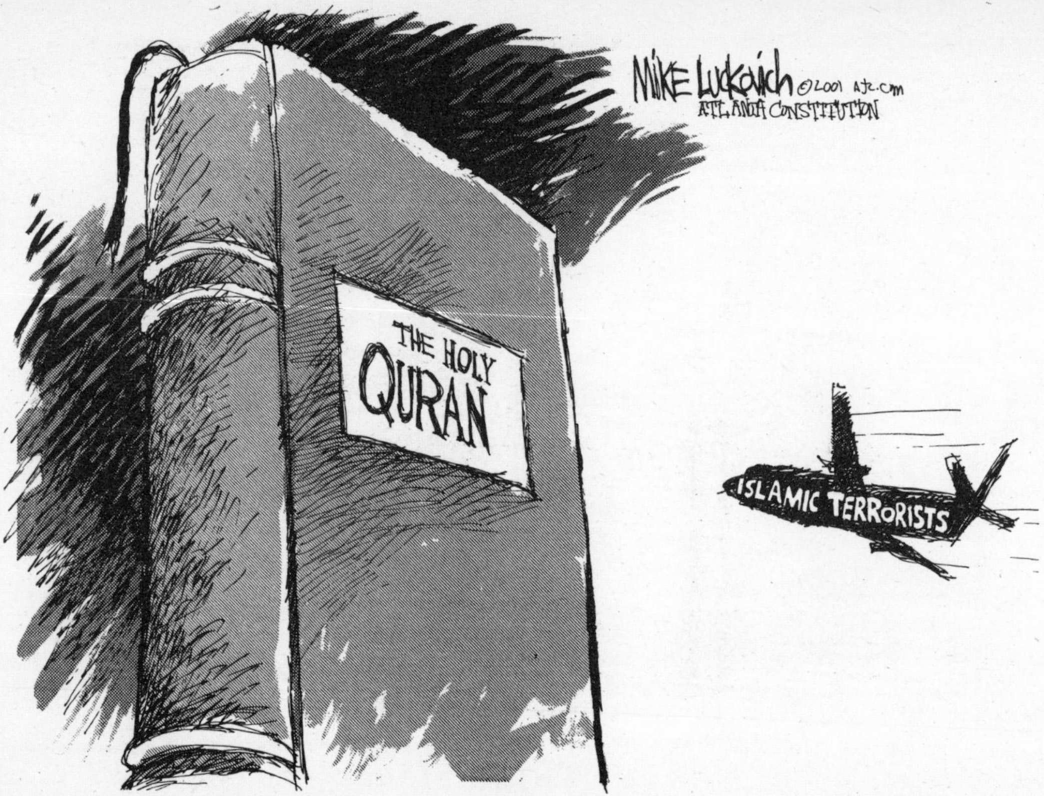

MIKE LUCKOVICH ©2001 AJC.COM
ATLANTA CONSTITUTION
THE HOLY QURAN
ISLAMIC TERRORISTS

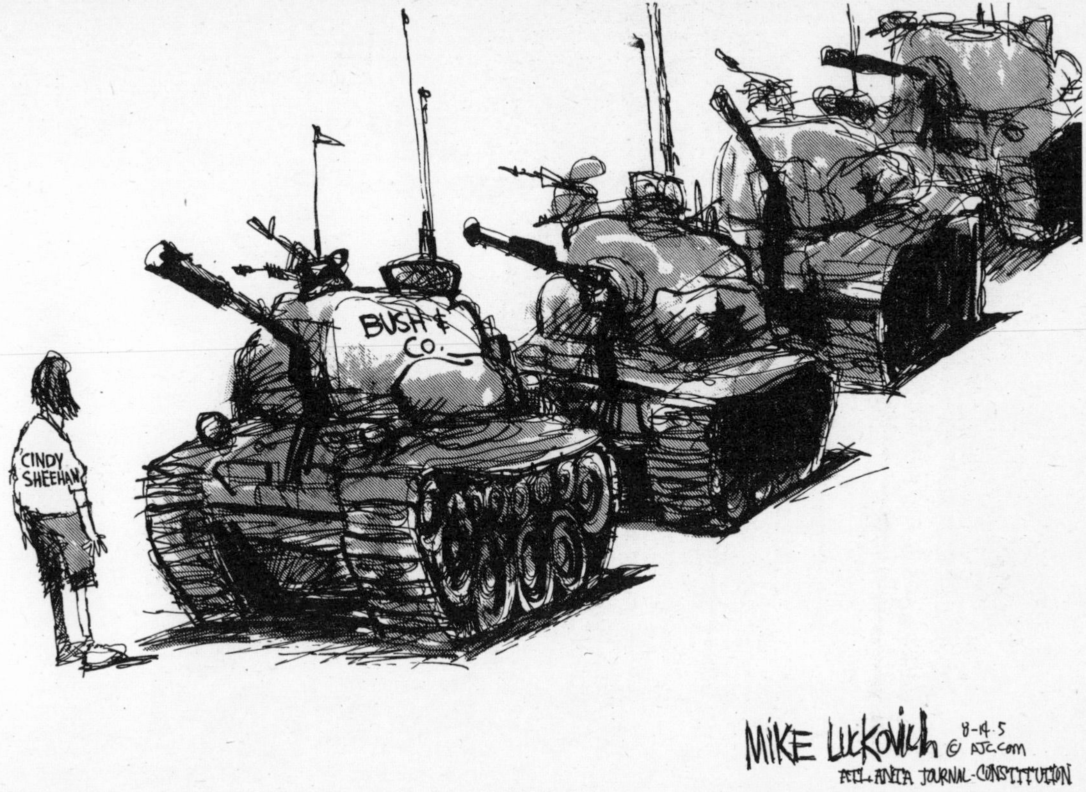
BUSH & CO.
CINDY SHEEHAN
MIKE LUCKOVICH 8-14-5 © AJC.com
ATLANTA JOURNAL-CONSTITUTION

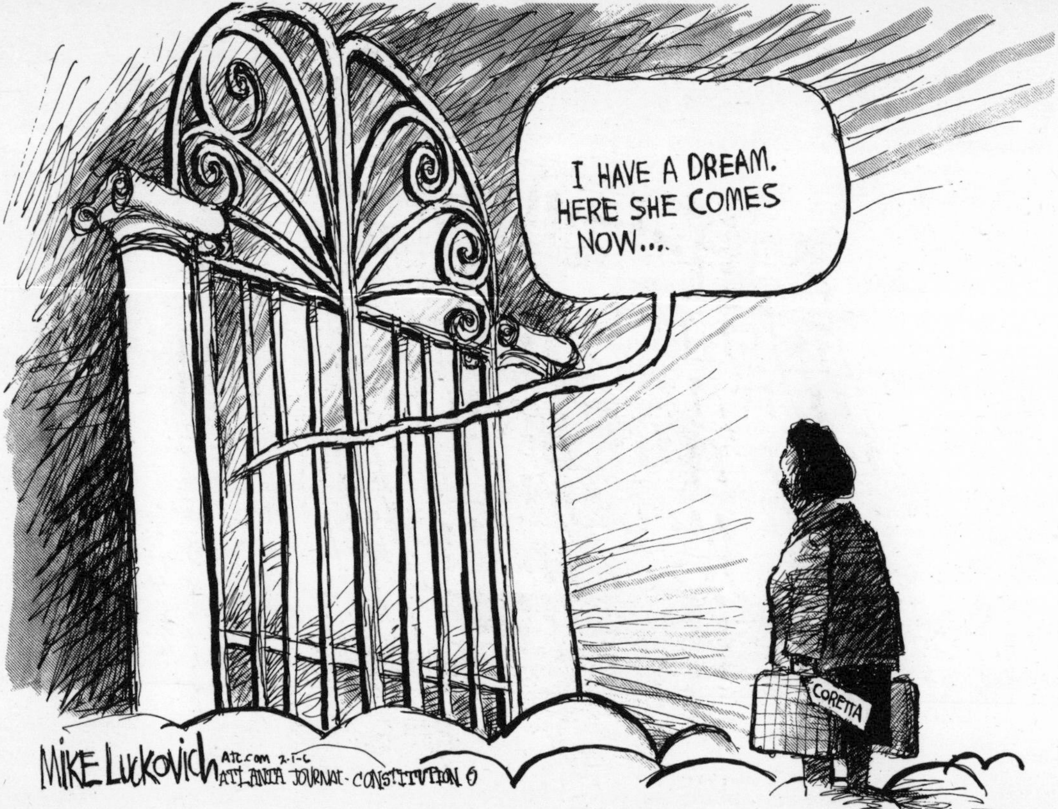
I HAVE A DREAM. HERE SHE COMES NOW....
CORETTA
MIKE LUCKOVICH
AJC.com 2-1-6
ATLANTA JOURNAL-CONSTITUTION

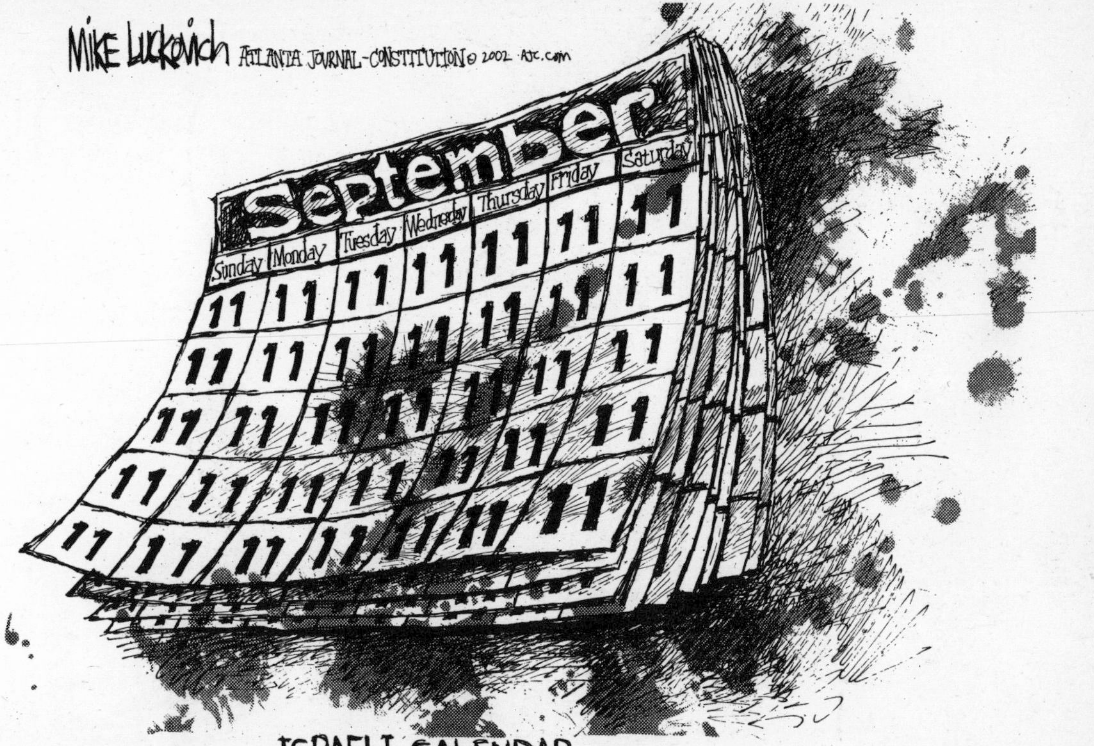
MIKE LUCKOVICH ATLANTA JOURNAL-CONSTITUTION © 2002 AJC.com
September
Sunday
Monday
Tuesday
Wednesday
Thursday
Friday
Saturday
11

ISRAELI CALENDAR

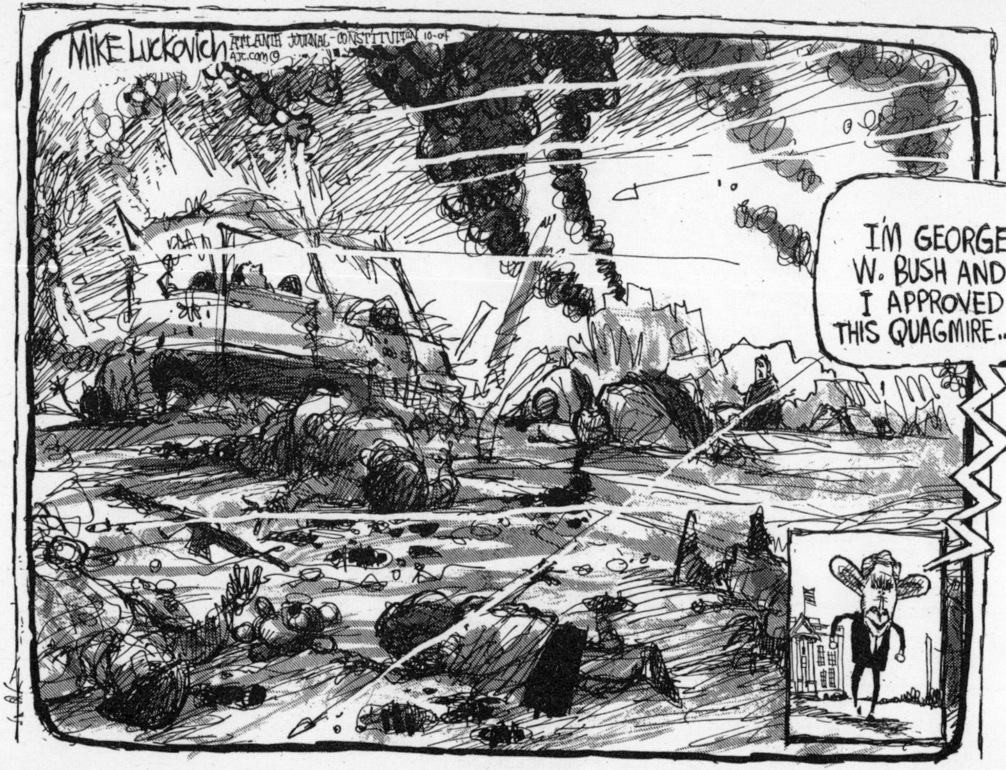
MIKE LUCKOVICH
ATLANTA JOURNAL-CONSTITUTION 10-04
AJC.COM ©
I'M GEORGE W. BUSH AND I APPROVED THIS QUAGMIRE....